SERIAL KILLERS

SERIAL KILLERS

A Psychological Perspective

Sarah K. Tracy

New Mexico Highlands University

cognella
SAN DIEGO

Bassim Hamadeh, CEO and Publisher
Angela Schultz, Senior Field Acquisitions Editor
Craig Lincoln, Senior Project Editor
Samantha Hansen, Production Editor
Juniper Perkins, Editorial Associate
Jess Estrella, Senior Graphic Designer
Laura Duncan, Licensing Specialist
Tiffany Mok, Senior Content Marketing Specialist
Natalie Piccotti, Director of Marketing
Kassie Graves, Senior Vice President, Editorial
Alia Bales, Director of Project Editorial & Production

Printed in the United States of America.

I would like to thank my three wonderful daughters, Arissa, Sierra, and Savannah, for their unwavering patience and unconditional love. I love you more than the world.

CONTENTS

CONTENTS

Web-Based Resources: Accessing QR Codes and Links

The author has selected some supporting web-based content for further engagement with the learning material that appears in this text, which can be accessed through QR codes or web links. These codes are intended for use by those who have purchased print copies of the book. You may scan them using a QR code reading app on your cell phone, which will take you to each website. You can also search for the link using a web browser search engine. Readers who have purchased a digital copy of the book can simply click on the hyperlinks beneath each QR code.

Cognella maintains no responsibility for the content nor availability of third-party links. However, Cognella makes every effort to keep its texts current. Broken links may be reported to studentreviews@cognella.com. Please include the book's title, author, and 7-digit SKU reference number (found below the barcode on the back cover of the book) in the body of your message.

Please check with your professor to confirm whether your class will access this content independently or collectively.

cognella®
SAN DIEGO

CHAPTER 1

DEFINING SERIAL KILLING

Scope and Characteristics

"You feel the last bit of breath leaving their body. You're looking into their eyes. A person in that situation is God!"

-Ted Bundy

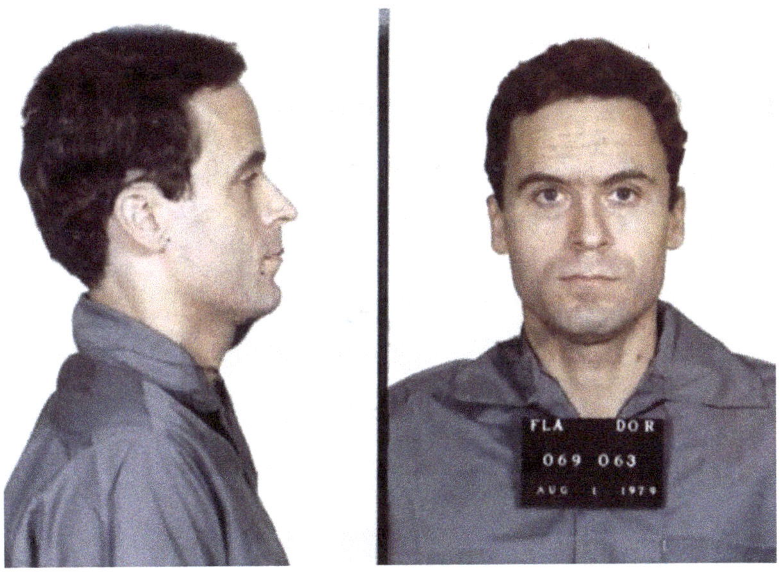

Figure 1.1 Ted Bundy Mugshot, 1979

Criminal actions and laws to combat them have been present since the dawn of humanity. Serial killing occupies a unique position, in part because it presents the potential for ongoing offenses until the perpetrator is apprehended and because the motives driving serial murder often differ from those that inspire other forms of criminal activity, including different types of homicide. Indeed, in the United States, there are currently believed to be 25–50 serial killers at large (Price, 2023). World estimates are unknown, likely due to varying prevalence and reporting rates. Additionally, sociocultural variations related to era have impacted the motives behind serial murder. The 1800s brought the industrial era, when people began to relocate to cities and socioeconomic classes became more divided (Bartels & Parsons, 2009). This resulted in a larger working class, or blue collar, population that was more vulnerable due to limited resources such as housing and education. Criminal activity was seen less as isolated incidents and increasingly related to deviant identities and fantasies (Bartels & Parsons, 2009). Cultural mores changed further in the 1900s with the creation of highways, computers, and forensic advancements. With it came progressions in our conceptualization of serial murder, resulting in the term 'lust murderer', coined by Reinhardt (1957). The addition of this sexual nomenclature, coupled with a majority of sexual serial killers being male, shifted our perception regarding their motives.

Samuel Little's primary motive was sexual sadism and he preyed on those who were most vulnerable. In fact, the Federal Bureau of Investigation (FBI) has dubbed Samuel Little the most prolific known serial killer in the United States, with 93 murders between 1970 and 2005; the FBI has been able to confirm 50 of the murders (United States Department of Justice, 2019). He strangled, raped, and killed women in Florida, Kentucky, Louisiana, Arkansas, Maryland, Mississippi, Ohio, California, and Georgia (Stephens, 2023). Fortunately, the FBI's Violent Criminal Apprehension Program (ViCAP) played a crucial role in linking Samuel Little to a series of unsolved murders across the country (FBI, 2018). After Little's 2012 arrest in California for drug charges, DNA evidence tied him to three cold case murders, and eventually countless more. This is just one of the cases that will be discussed at length in this book.

This chapter introduces the ways in which serial killing is a unique form of homicide as compared to other types of murder. It helps lay the foundation for common themes in serial killing. As such, historic prevalence and current incidence rates will be discussed. Foundational information regarding typologies or categories related to motive and phases that many serial killers go through before, during, and after each murder will also be discussed. Moreover, in-depth discussion of several recently apprehended serial killers will be explored. Thus, this chapter will focus on the nature of serial killing while subsequent chapters will concentrate on the psychological, social, physiological, and cultural influences on these perpetrators.

Learning Outcomes

After reading this chapter, students will be able to do the following:

1. Distinguish between the definitions of a serial killer, mass murderer, and active shooter.
2. Critically assess the reasons why the United States purportedly has the most serial killers.
3. Assess information about cases and infer reasons why some cases are still unsolved.

Definitions

Serial Killer, Mass Murderer, and Active Shooter

Figure 1.2 FBI Agent Robert Ressler, Who Coined the Term "Serial Killer"

The term **serial killer** did not emerge until the 1970s, when FBI agent Robert Ressler coined it at an international training session in Britain (Ressler & Shachtman, 1993). "Serial killers ... are obsessed with a fantasy, and they have what we must call non-fulfilled experiences that become part of the fantasy and push them toward the next killing. That's the real meaning behind the term *serial* killer" (Ressler & Shachtman, 1993, p. 33). At that time, the definition required a serial killer to have murdered four or more people in different locations, with cooling-off periods between each murder (Ressler & Shachtman, 1993). That original definition was revised in the late 1980s and again in the early 1990s to three or more murders in different locations with cooling-off periods (Douglas et al., 1992; Hickey, 1997; Ressler et al., 1988). Some have reduced the requirement to two or more murders (Morton et al., 2019). For the purposes of this book, the definition of a serial killer will require three or more murders by the same offender with emotional cooling-off periods between each murder.

Specifically, the impetus for serial killing is often a selfish desire for sexual gratification, power and control, and/or financial gain (Ramsland, 2006). They also want to be hands-on and close to their victim, often ending their lives through strangulation or stabbing. Both definition and motivation distinguish serial killing from mass murder and active shooters (Cohen, 2024), who most often use firearms and keep distance between themselves and the victims (Schechter, 2003).

Figure 1.3 Active Shooter Training

Mass murder occurs when a person kills three (or four by some accounts) or more people in a single incident and in the same location, not including the shooter (Cohen, 2024). An example of a **mass murderer** is an individual who drives a vehicle through a crowded street, killing everyone in their path. Conversely, an example of an **active shooter** would be a school shooter who enters the school and walks from room to room looking for victims (Cohen, 2024). Their motives are often personal and the result of being bullied or made an outcast by a specific group. While spree murder used to be distinguished from mass murder, it's now considered a subtype of the mass murder designation since the acts are not distinct enough to fulfill the need for a separate category (FBI, 2008). Further, mass murder and active shooting stem from the desire to harm and kill others; there is no secondary gain such as sexual gratification or money—rather, the act of murder itself is the primary goal (Cohen, 2024). They feel they have been wronged by life, perhaps due to their spouse leaving them or being fired from their job, and that catapults them over the threshold.

Armed Forces

In addition to mass murderers and active shooters, students often ask whether those who serve in the armed forces are serial killers. Discussion about gang violence or cult behavior has also been questioned in its correlation to serial killing. Since significantly more people have entered the armed forces as opposed to engaging in gang or cult murder, it is a more relevant topic in relation to serial killing. Therefore, do we consider people who have killed for their job serial killers? The short answer is no. It comes down to intent. Serial killers derive pleasure from killing others, including sexual pleasure, psychological thrill, or the desire to dominate others (Ramsland, 2006; Schechter, 2003). This is in stark contrast to those serving in the armed forces to protect and serve their country. There is no record of any serial killer murdering anyone in combat in the armed forces. This certainly does not mean it didn't happen, but there is no record of it, nor have any serial killers stated that they murdered anyone in the armed forces. However, there are examples of serial killers who were previously enlisted in the armed forces, though there is no way to correlate that experience with serial killing. Indeed, there is a higher percentage of serial killers who were enlisted in the military than the general U.S. population (Aamodt et al., 2023). A few examples include David Berkowitz, the Son of Sam killer; Gary Ridgway, the Green River Killer; and Dennis Rader, the Bind, Torture, Kill killer. This obviously does not mean that anyone who joins the armed forces will become a serial killer. The seeds for that kind of aberrant behavior are planted much earlier in life.

Table 1.1 Percentage of Serial Killers with Military Service

			United States			**United States & International**		
			Men	**Women**	**Total**	**Men**	**Women**	**Total**
Overall *N*			1,924	270	2,194	2,623	1,056	3,679
	No military		80.4%	99.6%	82.8%	79.3%	99.2%	82.5%
	Military		19.6%	0.4%	17.2%	20.7%	0.8%	17.5%
		Army	52.4%			61.0%		
		Navy	21.7%			17.9%		
		Air Force	7.9%			8.0%		

			United States			United States & International		
			Men	Women	Total	Men	Women	Total
		Marine Corps	17.7%			12.9%		
		Coast Guard	0.3%			0.2%		

Source: Michael G. Aamodt, Terence Leary, and Senthil Girimurugan, Selection from Radford/FGCU Annual Report on Serial Killer Statistics: 2023, p. 62. Copyright © 2023 by Radford University.

Discussion question: Given that there are more serial killers in the United States than in other countries, what are the possible reasons for the discrepancy?

Prevalence Rates Around the World

Varying Definitions' Impact on Recorded Rates

Changes in the definition of a serial killer and the number of murders required has resulted in inaccurate prevalence rates (Reid, 2017). Importantly, this lack of standard or agreed upon definition has limited the ability of the psychological community to construct an accurate etiology, or cause, of serial killers' thoughts and behaviors (Reid, 2017). Several countries around the world have a definition similar to the United States, yet a significantly lower number of reported serial killers in comparison. For example, laws in South Africa require a serial killer to murder only two victims, and research indicates there have been 117 documented serial killers in South Africa, versus 3,204 in the United States (Aamodt et al., 2023; Labuschange, 2021). Definitions and examples of serial killing in various countries around the world are examined in depth in Chapter 6.

Table 1.2 Yearly Average by Decade

Definition of Serial Killer		
Decade	**Two or more**	**Three or more**
1920–1929	17	14
1930–1939	17	14
1940–1949	13	10
1950–1959	20	14
1960–1969	39	28

Definition of Serial Killer		
Decade	**Two or more**	**Three or more**
1970–1979	114	85
1980–1989	173	122
1990–1999	157	105
2000–2009	98	64
2010–2019	53	31
2020–2021	14	10

Note. This table only contains U.S. serial killers that have been caught and identified. Numbers represent the number of separate serial killers who killed at least one person that year. The number of kills in the definition represents the total number of kills, not the number in a given year.

Source: Michael G. Aamodt, Terence Leary, and Senthil Girimurugan, Selection from Radford/FGCU Annual Report on Serial Killer Statistics: 2023, p. 20. Copyright © 2023 by Radford University.

U.S. Prevalence Rates

Given the above information, questions arise as to why there are so many more serial killers in the United States than any other country. First, there is no way to know whether that is fact or not, since there could be more serial killers than recorded, or the country may not document them or could be hesitant to share that information. One discrepancy in prevalence rates might be due to some countries having a different definition of serial killing than the United States. For example, some countries define serial killing to include two, three, or more murders (Aamodt et al., 2023). Further, infrastructure and socioeconomic differences influence the ability and rate at which law enforcement is able to track down and capture serial killers (World Population Review, 2024). Indeed, poverty predicts increases in murder rates, while inequality amplifies the social stress that makes violence more probable (Dolan, 2024). Globally, resources allocated to serial killer cases in some countries may be sparse, and access to technological advances, including DNA analysis, are often limited due to socioeconomic factors (Aamodt et al., 2023; Gibson, 2018; Jenkins, 1994). Similarly, sharing of information between countries may be more acceptable with some cultures versus others (i.e., England vs. North Korea). Indeed, record keeping of crimes may differ in each country and impede our knowledge of global data on serial murder (Gibson, 2018).

Table 1.3 Number of Serial Killers by Decade in Which Series Started

Decade	United States	Canada	Other countries	Total	% United States
1900	53	0	32	85	62.4
1910	62	0	33	95	65.3
1920	70	3	40	113	61.9
1930	67	0	34	101	66.3
1940	61	4	52	117	52.1
1950	93	1	50	144	64.6
1960	255	8	79	342	74.6
1970	673	20	175	868	77.5
1980	840	24	246	1,110	75.7
1990	729	18	441	1,188	61.4
2000	438	26	364	828	52.9
2010	215	20	189	424	50.7
2020	26	1	20	47	55.3

Source: Michael G. Aamodt, Terence Leary, and Senthil Girimurugan, Selection from Radford/FGCU Annual Report on Serial Killer Statistics: 2023, p. 14. Copyright © 2023 by Radford University.

World Prevalence Rates

Variances in the definition and recording of serial murder result in skewed statistics on serial murder around the world. Indeed, one study noted that 74% of serial killers were American (Jenkins, 1994), while another study of 1,000 serial killers around the globe found that "62.8% were American, followed by 7.2% from the U.K" (Gibson, 2018, p. ii). In fact, research has overwhelmingly demonstrated that there simply are more serial killers in the United States, despite its "newness" as a country (Gibson, 2018; Jenkins, 1994). Comparatively, World Population Review (2024) reports that, cumulatively, there have been 3,204 serial killers in the United States, 166 in England, 117 in South Africa, 106 in Canada, and 97 in Italy, to name the top five countries.

Table 1.4 Serial Killers by Country

Countries With at Least 10 Identified Serial Killers				
Country	**Number of serial killers**	**% of serial killers**	**Country's share of world population**	**Ratio**
United States	3,690	64.16	4.24%	15.12
England	182	3.16	0.68%	4.66
Russia	164	2.85	1.87%	1.52
Japan	138	2.40	1.62%	1.48
India	130	2.26	17.70%	0.13
South Africa	129	2.24	0.76%	2.95
Canada	125	2.17	0.48%	4.49
Germany	99	1.72	1.07%	1.60
Italy	95	1.65	0.78%	2.13
Australia	92	1.60	0.33%	4.89
France	89	1.55	0.84%	1.85
China	68	1.18	18.46%	0.06
Mexico	64	1.11	1.65%	0.67
Brazil	42	0.73	2.73%	0.27
Hungary	28	0.49	0.12%	3.93
Poland	28	0.49	0.49%	1.00
Spain	28	0.49	0.60%	0.81
Austria	24	0.42	0.12%	3.61
Colombia	24	0.42	0.65%	0.64
Netherlands	20	0.35	0.22%	1.58

Countries With at Least 10 Identified Serial Killers				
Country	**Number of serial killers**	**% of serial killers**	**Country's share of world population**	**Ratio**
Belgium	17	0.30	0.15%	1.99
Czech Republic	16	0.28	0.14%	2.03
Turkey	15	0.26	1.08%	0.24
Scotland	14	0.24	0.07%	3.59
Sweden	14	0.24	0.13%	1.88
Argentina	14	0.24	0.58%	0.42
Kenya	13	0.23	0.69%	0.33
Thailand	13	0.23	0.90%	0.25
Iran	13	0.23	1.08%	0.21
Nigeria	13	0.23	2.64%	0.09
Ukraine	12	0.21	0.56%	0.37

Note. Caution should be taken in reviewing this table, as the number of serial killers by country is a function of the number of actual killers, the number caught, and the number reported by police or the media. Serial killers operating in multiple countries are not included in the counts.

Source: Michael G. Aamodt, Terence Leary, and Senthil Girimurugan, Selection from Radford/FGCU Annual Report on Serial Killer Statistics: 2023, pp. 23-24. Copyright © 2023 by Radford University.

Serial Killer Typology

In the literature, serial killers have traditionally been organized by type of killer to aid in profiling efforts (Douglas et al., 2006). The study of organized versus disorganized offenders informs investigators about the likely planning and predictability of an offender's actions. These types are used to distinguish motive, which helps police understand the killer more clearly and leads to higher arrest rates. Do they plan? Stalk? Or do they kill at random? Is their end goal sexual sadism or are they fueled by anger and insecurity? Within these categories are additional identifiers that provide valuable information not only about the killer's modus operandi, but also their intent. These are more specific and include visionary, mission-oriented, hedonistic, and control-oriented killers (Ramsland, 2006). As you venture through this book, think about how you would categorize each killer based on your understanding of the categories below.

Organized vs. Disorganized

While some serial killers may vary the way in which they approach murder, many of the acts are indicative of their personality, which provides insights into their psyche (Canter et al., 2004). Specifically, *organized* serial killers can put on the mask of normalcy. They tend to plan their murders, are of average intelligence, and can balance a perceived "normal" life with a stable job and family. This façade is countered with their use of restraints on victims, having the forethought and premeditation to bring a weapon, and removing evidence from the scene to evade capture (Canter et al., 2004; LaBrode, 2007). They are the epitome of Jekyll and Hyde and are able to compartmentalize each persona. Moreover, there is often a clear catalyst that spurs their perceived need to kill, such as divorce or financial ruin (Canter et al., 2004). Additionally, they often take items or body parts as trophies, hiding them in their home and revisiting them to relive their kills (Miller, 2014).

In contrast, *disorganized* serial killers choose victims who are closer in proximity to the killers' residence, indicating the need to know the lay of the land and kill within their comfort zone (Canter et al., 2004). They choose victims more randomly or on the spur of the moment, indicating almost no planning, have lower than average intelligence levels, are often loners with few social ties (LaBrode, 2007), leave evidence at the crime scene (Canter et al., 2004), and "may confront, assault, kill, and leave the body all in the same location" (Douglas et al., 2006, p. 9). They lack the ability to think abstractly and use sophisticated planning strategies, and instead are more childlike in their approach, attacking their victims with brute force rather than verbal prowess (Miller, 2014). These serial killers lack social decorum, making deviant behaviors seem more appropriate in their minds.

Table 1.5 Variables From the Missen Corpus Reflecting Organized or Disorganized Crime Scenes

Organized	**Disorganized**
Variable %	**Variable %**
Victim alive during sex acts (91%)	Vaginal rape (74%)
Body positioned (75%)	Overkill (70%)
Murder weapon missing (67%)	Multiple sex acts (66%)
Multiple crime scenes (61%)	Beaten (61%)
Body concealed (58%)	Body left in isolated spot (54%)
Torture (53%)	Belongings scattered (47%)
Restraints (40%)	Tease cuts (38%)
Body covered post-mortem (37%)	Bludgeoned (38%)

Organized	**Disorganized**
Variable %	**Variable %**
Ligature strangulation (34%)	Clothing scattered (36%)
Firearm used (23%)	Object penetration (35%)
Tampered with evidence (21%)	Improvised murder weapon (31%)
Gagging (16%)	Manual strangulation (27%)
Bite marks (5%)	Violence directed at genitalia (23%) Weapon left in victim (19%) Facial disfigurement (19%) Throat cut (19%) Trail of clothing to murder scene (13%) Ransacking (11%) Genital mutilation (10%) Body parts missing (10%) Thoracic mutilation (9%) Burns on victim (8%) Abdominal mutilation (8%) Innards extracted (6%) Decapitation (5%) Dismemberment (3%)

Note. Frequency across the sample of 100 cases indicated in parentheses.

Source: David Canter et al., Selection from "The Organized/Disorganized Typology of Serial Murder: Myth or Model?," Psychology, Public Policy, and Law, vol. 10, no. 3, pp. 22-23. Copyright © 2004 by American Psychological Association.

Visionary

These killers are motivated by a vision, which is rooted in delusions, and believe they must kill to keep themselves or others safe (Poovarasan & Jain, 2023). They may hear voices that tell them to kill (Schechter, 2003). These beliefs are not based in reality and are often the result of psychosis (Simon, 2015). An example of a visionary serial killer was David Berkowitz, who stated that his neighbor's dog spoke to him through his bark, telling him to kill people.

Mission-Oriented

Mission-oriented serial killers are coined so because of their delusional beliefs that they have been sent by a higher power to complete a mission to rid the earth of the undesirables (Poovarasan & Jain, 2023; Schechter, 2003). Examples of the victims this type of killer chooses include women, the homeless, sex workers, and other marginalized groups (Simon, 2015). Peter Sutcliffe is an example of this type of killer. In fact, he stated that he murdered women to "clean up the streets."

Hedonistic

Aligned with sexual sadism as mentioned above, lust serial killers feel that their urges are uncontrollable and that they must kill to achieve orgasm. They seek pleasure and enjoyment while avoiding pain and discomfort. Ultimately, their goal is to sexually assault an unwilling victim. Jeffrey Dahmer is a prime example, as he was motivated by sexual gratification and had an obsessive desire to create a living sex slave.

Control-Oriented

As you might guess by the name of this type of killer, they are motivated by control. They seek power and dominance over others (Schechter, 2003). When these killers sexually assault their victims, it's not due to hedonism, but control, as sexual gratification is a secondary gain (Simon, 2015). They enjoy the process of stalking, luring, and dominating their victims. They are organized and revise their techniques to ensure a greater likelihood of snaring a victim. This is exactly what Ted Bundy did; he tried various tactics to isolate his victims, such as stating he needed help moving a boat and then explaining that it was close to his vehicle to ensure he was able to push the victim into his vehicle and drive away (Williams, 2020).

Phases

Serial killers tend to follow predictable patterns or phases (Lampley, 2020). Specifically, they typically progress through distinct phases, including the aura phase (emotional disturbance and withdrawal), trolling phase (searching for a victim), wooing phase (luring the victim), capture phase (isolating the victim), murder phase (committing the act), totem phase (keeping souvenirs or reliving the crime), and finally, the depression phase (experiencing emptiness post-crime; Lampley, 2020; Malizia, 2017).

Aura

In the aura phase, fantasy is all-consuming. The fantasy of the acts they envision have excited them for years. The excitement has built to a point where there is no return; they have crossed the line and now are focused on finding a victim (Malizia, 2017). This leads them to the trolling phase. The more organized serial killer is going to troll and stalk his victims. He will want to learn everything he can about them, especially the days and times they are home alone. He is choosing victims based on the ease with which he can capture and murder them (Malizia, 2017). Dennis Rader explained how he spent a vast amount of time trolling his victims to learn more about their daily patterns.

Seduction

Next, the seduction phase is where they pour on the charm and swagger, though that behavior is more indicative of organized killers, while disorganized ones tend to use a blitz attack to quickly subdue the victim (Schechter, 2003). Ted Bundy is a prime example of a serial killer who wooed victims by feigning injury (a broken arm in a cast), preying on the niceties that females are socialized to possess. Other killers, such as Dennis Nilsen, enticed victims by offering sex and alcohol. John Wayne Gacy lured teenage boys to his house with promises of summer employment. After they have identified the victim, they focus on capture and securing them in a location where they can't escape. The capture phase is when the killer finally has the victim all to himself (Lampley, 2020; Malizia, 2017). He may have solicited the company of a sex worker, then driven to a secluded location, where he then takes off his mask and becomes the real killer within. Now he is able to do what he has wanted to all along, in the murder phase. His fantasy is now reality and he couldn't be more thrilled. Once he has lived out his fantasy and his victim is no longer alive, he enters the depersonalization phase where he plays with the body (Malizia, 2017). He may engage in necrophilia or mutilation.

Totem

Once he is finished with his perverse actions, he enters the totem phase, where the serial killer seeks to preserve the memory of the murder, often by collecting souvenirs or trophies from the victim or the crime scene. These items can include personal belongings, body parts, photographs, or even written accounts. The purpose is to help the killer relive the emotional high and psychological satisfaction achieved from the murder. This phase allows the killer to maintain a sense of control, power, and excitement long after the act itself. The trophy serves as a physical representation of dominance and achievement, and for many serial killers, it becomes an essential part of sustaining their fantasy life between killings.

Depression

Lastly, the depression phase is when the emotional "high" of the murder wears off (Malizia, 2017). In this stage, they may experience intense feelings of emptiness, disappointment, or emotional numbness (Lampley, 2020). The act that they anticipated and fantasized about for all too long fails to provide lasting fulfillment. This can lead to frustration, self-loathing, or a deepening sense of alienation. However, rather than deterring them from killing again, this emotional downturn often acts as a catalyst for the cycle to start again (Ramsland, 2006). To escape the depressive feelings and recapture the psychological thrill, the killer may soon begin planning their next crime, starting the phases over again with renewed intensity.

History of Serial Killing

Serial killing has always been a part of humankind. Richard von Krafft-Ebing's *Psychopathia Sexualis* (1886/1999) first linked sadistic lust to homicide, replacing moral or religious explanations with medicalized ones. Twentieth-century criminologists elaborated on motivational categories, while the FBI created the "organized/disorganized" dichotomy as a policing tool. In the 2000s, media interest exploded (e.g., 270 serial killer films were released in the 2000s versus 23 in the 1990s), bringing greater awareness of the prevalence of serial murder (James & Proulx, 2014).

Historically, it was easier to get away with murder due to lack of DNA evidence and medical technology. Further, the world population was much lower and people were isolated in rural towns. In fact, some serial killers hid their horrific crimes by pursuing careers as doctors or law enforcement officers, leveraging those positions of authority to conceal their actions and demonstrate a perceived intellectual superiority over their victims. What we do know for sure is that serial killers have been in existence forever, long before the examples below, and there will be countless more in the future. These cases, and more current ones, provide us with insights into the ways in which serial killers think, act, and hide evidence to ensure their ability to continue to live their fantasies at the expense of innocent people.

H. H. Holmes

Figure 1.4 H. H. Holmes

For example, H. H. Holmes was a medical doctor who lured travelers who needed lodging at the 1893 World's Fair in Chicago, Illinois (Schechter, 2003). Under the guise of a hospitable doctor and boarder, H. H. Holmes was able to torture and kill 27 people (Holmes touted 133 victims) in his aptly dubbed murder castle, rife with hidden doors, extensive tunnels, and sinister torture chambers (Brown et al., 2015; Schechter, 2003). Born in New Hampshire in 1861, Holmes was a highly intelligent and quirky child. With religiously dogmatic and emotionally distant parents, he experienced emotional and physical abuse at home. School didn't offer respite from abuse; he was regularly bullied by schoolmates for being smart and "odd" (Brown et al., 2015; Schechter, 2003). In fact, one instance of bullying is said to be the catalyst for his interest in anatomy (Brown et al., 2015). He was pulled into a doctor's office by peers and forced to touch a skeleton. After this incident, he began to run experiments on animals to learn more about how their bodies worked (Brown et al., 2015). Clearly unable to legally perform these experiments on humans, he forged checks and engaged in other criminal activities to afford to build his murder castle. With his medical degree in hand and welcoming lodging for travelers, he lured unsuspecting boarders into secret rooms where he experimented on them with gas, poison, and torture devices. He was eventually caught when he murdered a colleague and his entire family and was subsequently turned in by another colleague; this resulted in his arrest. Officers were shocked at the elaborate maze of tunnels and evidence of torture they discovered in Holmes' castle. After being tried and convicted, Holmes was hanged for his crimes in 1896 and his castle was burned to the ground.

Jack the Ripper

Jack the Ripper is often thought of as the "first" serial killer. His killing rampage occurred in England in the late 1800s. His nickname was formed from the manner in which he murdered sex workers. He cut their bodies from the groin to their neck, slit their throats, and cut other parts of their bodies (Ramsland, 2006). He also likely chose victims who were disenfranchised and less likely to be reported missing, allowing him to continue killing. Though he was never caught, the case is renowned partially because he would taunt police with letters (Schechter, 2003). Law enforcement eventually published the letters in a bid to catch the killer. This led to documentation of serial killing in a way that had never existed prior, hence the infamy of the case (Schechter, 2003). In a surprising twist, a scholar recently stated that he has evidence pointing to the real face behind Jack the Ripper. A shawl of one of the victims was up for auction and purchased by a man who had it tested for DNA evidence, which linked the shawl to a man named Aaron Kosminski. Kosminski was a Polish barber and one of the original suspects in the case (Edwards, 2014). Though unconfirmed by additional scholars, this is the closest we've come to possibly identifying this notorious killer.

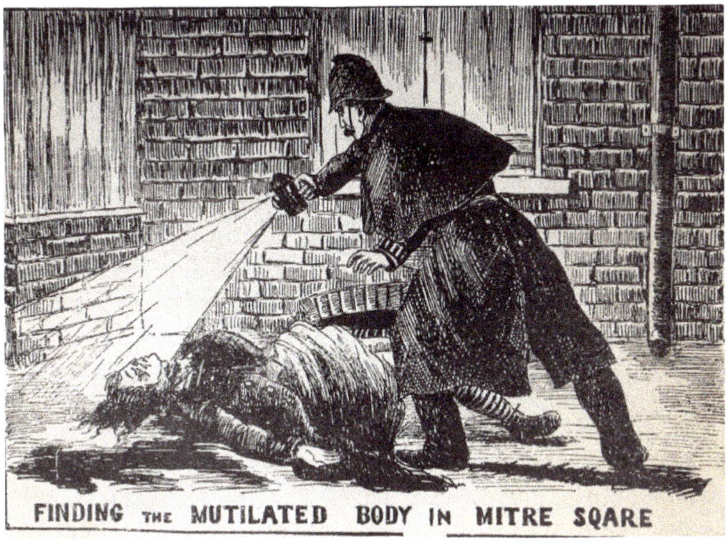

Figure 1.5 Police Sketches of "Jack the Ripper"

Recently Apprehended Serial Killers

While there are still numerous serial killers who remain at large, solid police work and community assistance led to the arrest and conviction of a few serial killers who evaded capture for years. They continued to enjoy terrorizing victims, their families, and communities until they were finally caught and convicted. Psychopaths use people for their own gratification; they lack empathy. The only thing they are remorseful about is getting caught.

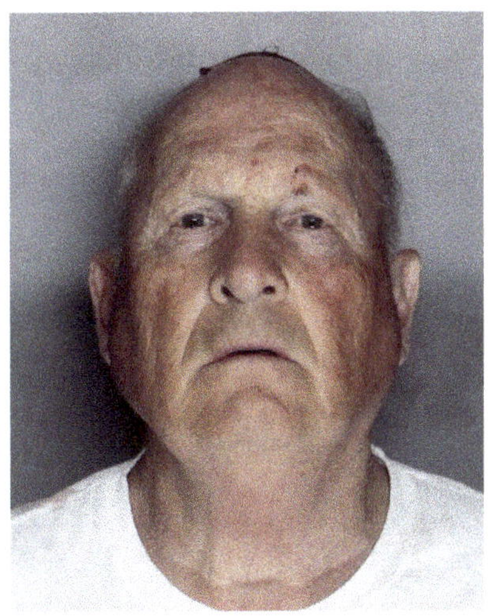

Figure 1.6 Joseph DeAngelo Mugshot, 2018

Golden State Killer

One example is Joseph DeAngelo, dubbed the Golden State Killer (O'Hara, 2020). DeAngelo was a former police officer in California, who used his authority to "protect and serve" as a cover to murder at least 13 people (and rape countless more) in the 1970s and 1980s (Racher, 2023; Rossmo, 2026). Born in New York in 1945, DeAngelo had a father who was strict, militant, and often absent, leaving DeAngelo plenty of time to stir up trouble. As a teenager, he engaged in petty crime and abused animals (Rossmo, 2026). In his 20s, he was in the Vietnam War, where he worked as a carpenter (O'Hara, 2020). He later married, had three children, and took up employment in law enforcement. In this role of power and authority, he planned and committed his crimes, which began in 1976 with the rape and robbery of a young woman (O'Hara, 2020).

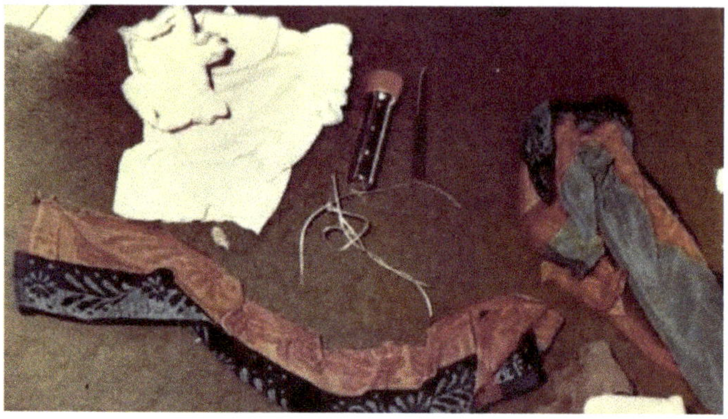

Figure 1.7 Joseph DeAngelo Crime Scene Photo from the FBI

As an organized killer, he made sure to leave no trace. Moreover, his crimes escalated from rape to murder. Over the next 10 years, DeAngelo fulfilled his fantasies of torture and murder, until he was caught in 2018 due to DNA evidence from the ancestry service *23andMe* (Browne & Scheck, 2024; Martin et al., 2020; O'Hara, 2020). DNA technology wasn't advanced enough to be used as an effective tool in forensic cases prior to the 1980s. In fact, the first case in which it was utilized to convict a murderer didn't occur until 1987 (O'Hara, 2020). As a police officer, DeAngelo might have realized that this new technology would make it more difficult to avoid apprehension. That fact, coupled with his aging body, which would have made it more difficult to subdue his victims, likely resulted in the end of his killing phase, since the case went cold and he stopped killing (as far as we know). With his DNA in the national database and a curious family member who submitted her DNA to an ancestry company, authorities discovered familial connections and were finally able to home in on the potential Golden State Killer (Rossmo, 2026). Indeed, technological advances will inevitably lead to the resolution of a greater number of unsolved cases, as will be discussed in Chapter 9. Finally arrested and sentenced to 13 life sentences, DeAngelo sits in prison, a feeble old man in his late 70s.

Figure 1.8 Rex Heuermann Mugshot, 2023

Long Island Serial Killer

Another case that was recently solved is the Long Island Serial Killer/Gilgo Beach Killer. These crimes puzzled law enforcement for years. In 2010, the bodies of four women were found along Gilgo Beach in Long Island, New York (Martin et al., 2020). Police were searching for a missing woman who called 911 to report that someone was trying to harm her. Though they didn't find her, their search led to the discovery of other bodies and a distinct pattern: All four women were petite escorts who had been murdered, dismembered, and placed in burlap sacks in the thick brush by Gilgo Beach on Long Island (Jonsson, 2011; Martin et al., 2020). The suspect even had the audacity to use a victim's phone to contact and taunt her family (Jonsson, 2011; Newman & Schweber, 2023). Using burner phones to cover his tracks ironically provided police with information about his whereabouts, as the phones' signals were connected to the victims' disposal sites.

With a suspect on their radar due to a victim's roommate providing information about his appearance and vehicle, police collected DNA on discarded pizza crust and matched hair on the victims to the killer and his family members. DNA analysis determined the women were murdered by the same person, leading to the arrest of the sexually sadistic serial killer (Jonsson, 2011). On July 13, 2023, a Long Island architect named Rex Heuermann, age 60, was arrested and charged with three of the murders (Whiteside, 2026). As a child, he was described as a loner who was frequently bullied by peers, which may have resulted in a sense of anger at the world and women who rejected him as a teen (Mercuri, 2025). He grew up to be a tall, overweight adult who people described as an "ogre." Despite this, he married, had a daughter, and focused on his career. However, his violent tendencies were confirmed when police searched his house and found a vault, ropes, and handcuff keys in his basement "kill-room" (Whiteside, 2026). In 2024, he was charged with two more murders when police collected information from his computer where he described his crimes in detail (Whiteside, 2026). He organized a comprehensive list of "to-do" tasks to complete before, during, and after each murder. Heuermann, in April 2026, confessed to murdering eight women, verifying that he is the Long Island Serial Killer. Due to his legal acknowledgement of the murders, the case will not go to trial. This change in plea was apparently due to his desire to save his family from additional emotional harm surrounding the case.

Figure 1.9 Gilgo Beach map of Victim Locations

Discussion question: How are serial killers able to get away with committing these crimes?

Summary

Serial killing is a distinct crime. The motive is most often the expression of a long-lived fantasy where control and power reign supreme, though the motives behind these atrocities vary. Further, it is a global phenomenon and has always existed. To assist in profiling and capturing serial killers, typologies have been created to aid in understanding their personality, lifestyle, and motive. Understanding the phases many serial killers experience also helps us understand their psychological states. Historical cases demonstrate the static nature of serial killing and how little it has changed, though these cases have also provided information that has assisted in the arrest of serial killers who escaped capture for years. With this foundational information, the next chapters will focus on psychological aspects of their being, including familial attachment issues, personality disorders, head trauma, cultural influences, modus operandi, and thoughts about the future of serial killing.

Keywords

Active shooter

Mass murderer

Serial killer

Chapter Review Questions

1. How does the definition of a serial killer differ from that of a mass murder or active shooter?
2. Who are the first documented serial killers in the world and in the United States?
3. Which serial killers have recently been caught?

References

Aamodt, M. G., Leary, T., & Girimurugan, S. (2023). *Radford/FGCU annual report on serial killer statistics*. Radford University.

Bartels, R., & Parsons, C. (2009). The social construction of a serial killer. *Feminism & Psychology, 19*(2), 267-280.

Brown, J., Hickey, E., & Harris, B. (2015). H. H. Holmes: One of America's first recorded serial murderers. *Forensic Scholars Today, 1*(2), 1–6.

Browne, T., & Scheck, B. (2024). Regulating forensic investigative genetic genealogy: The case for judicial oversight and bipartisan model legislation passed in Maryland. *Judges' Journal, 63*(2), 4–9.

Canter, D. V., Alison, L. J., Alison, E., & Wentink, N. (2004). The organized/disorganized typology of serial murder: Myth or model? *Psychology, Public Policy, and Law, 10*(3), 293–320.

Cohen, J. B. (2024). How to define mass shootings: Policy implications. *Congressional Research Service*. https://www.congress.gov/crs-product/R48276

Dolan, E. (2024, January 13). *The combination of poverty and inequality predict homicide rates in the United States. PsyPost*. https://www.psypost.org/the-combination-of-poverty-and-inequality-predict-homicide-rates-in-the-united-states/

Douglas, J. E., Burgess, A., & Ressler, R. K. (1992). *Crime classification manual.* Lexington Books.

Douglas, J. E., Burgess, A. W., Burgess, A. G., & Ressler, R. K. (2006). *Crime classification manual: A standard system for investigating and classifying violent crimes (2nd ed.).* Jossey-Bass.

Edwards, R. (2014). *Naming Jack the Ripper: New crime scene evidence, a stunning forensic breakthrough, the killer revealed.* Pan.

Federal Bureau of Investigation. (2008). *Serial murder: Multidisciplinary perspectives for investigators* [Report]. National Center for the Analysis of Violent Crime. https://www.fbi.gov/stats-services/publications/serial-murder

Federal Bureau of Investigation. (2018, November 27). Convicted killer linked to 90 murders: FBI's Violent Criminal Apprehension Program connects cases to prolific serial killer. https://www.fbi.gov/news/stories/vicap-links-murders-to-prolific-serial-killer-112718

Gibson, D. C. (2018). *Serial killers around the world: The global dimensions of serial murder.* Bentham Books.

Hickey, E. W. (1997). *Serial murderers and their victims (2nd ed).* Wadsworth Publishing Company.

James, J., & Proulx, J. (2014). A psychological and development profile of sexual murderers: A systematic review. *Aggression and Violent Behavior, 19*(5), 592–607.https://doi.org/10.1016/j.avb.2014.08.003

Jenkins, P. (1994). *Using murder: The social construction of serial homicide*. Routledge.

Jonsson, P. (2011, April 15). Long Island serial killer: Portrait of a sunning criminal slowly emerges. *Christian Science Monitor.*

Krafft-Ebing, R. von. (1999). *Psychopathia sexualis: The case histories* (B. King, Ed.). Creation Books. (Original work published 1886).

LaBrode, R. T. (2007). Etiology of the psychopathic serial killer: An analysis of antisocial personality disorder, psychopathy, and serial killer personality and crime scene characteristics. *Brief Treatment and Crisis Intervention, 7,* 151–160.

Labuschange, G. (2021). An overview of serial murder and its investigation in South Africa. In H. C. Chan & S. Adjorlolo (Eds.), *Crime, mental health and the criminal justice system in Africa: A psycho-criminological perspective* (pp. 121–148). Macmillan.

Lampley, S. (2020, August 25). *The psychological phases of serial killers. Psychology Today*. https://www.psychologytoday.com/us/blog/captivating-crimes/202008/the-psychological-phases-serial-killers

Malizia, N. (2017). Serial killer: The mechanisms from imagination to the murder phases. *Sociology Mind, 7,* 44-59.

Martin, E., Schwarting, D. E., & Chase, R. J. (2020). Serial killer connections through cold cases. *National Institute of Justice Journal,* 282. https://nij.ojp.gov/topics/articles/serial-killer-connections-through-cold-cases

Mercuri, M. (2025, April 1). Where is Rex Heuermann now? The latest on the Long Island serial killer's trial. *Forbes.* https://www.forbes.com/sites/monicamercuri/2025/04/01/where-is-rex-heuermann-now-the-latest-on-the-long-island-serial-killers-trial/

Miller, L. (2014). Serial killers: I. Subtypes, patterns, and motives. *Aggression and Violent Behavior, 19*(1), 1-11.

Morton, R. J., Tillman, J. M., Gaines, S. J. (2019). *Serial murder: Pathways for investigations.* Federal Bureau of Investigation.

Newman, A., & Schweber, N. (2023, July 15). *Suspect in Gilgo Beach killings led a life of chaos and control. The New York Times.* https://www.nytimes.com/2023/07/15/nyregion/rex-heuermann-gilgo-beach-killings.html

O'Hara, J. F. (2020). 23, me, and the police: The fourth amendment implications of familial DNA searching. *Civil Rights Law Journal, 30*(2), 177-204.

Price, C. (2023). How many serial killers are on the loose today? *World Atlas*. https://www.worldatlas.com/crime/how-many-serial-killers-are-on-the-loose-today.html

Poovarasan, P., & Jain, M. (2023). The role of forensic psychology in profiling serial killers. *Medico-Legal Update, 23*(Special Issue), 3468. https://doi.org/10.37506/mlu.v23i5.3468

Racher, J. (2023). *Serial killers identified by their handwriting: A look at 10 of the worst.* Dorrance Publishing Co.

Ramsland, K. (2006). *Inside the minds of serial killers: Why they kill*. Praeger.

Reid, S. (2017). Compulsive criminal homicide: A new nosology for serial murder. *Aggression and Violent Behavior, 34,* 290–301.

Reinhardt, J. M. (1957). *Sex perversions and sex crimes*. Charles C Thomas.

Ressler, R. K., Burgess, A. W., & Douglas, J. E. (1988). *Sexual homicide: Patterns and motives.* Lexington Books.

Ressler, R. K., & Shachtman, T. (1993). *My twenty years tracking serial killers for the FBI: Whoever fights monsters.* St. Martin's Paperbacks.

Rossmo, D. K. (2026). Behavioral profiling in the golden state killer investigation: A comparative analysis. *Homicide Studies, 30*(1), 25-38.

Schechter, H. (2003). *The serial killer files: The who, what, where, how, and why of the world's most terrifying murders.* Ballantine Books.

Simon, G. (2015). The traits and the thrill of serial killers. *Internal Security, 7*(2), 33–42.

Stephens, H. M. (2023). Samuel Little: A brief summary and analysis of America's most prolific serial killer. *The Mid-Southern Journal of Criminal Justice, 22*(4), 1–15.

United States Department of Justice, Federal Bureau of Investigation. (2019, October). FBI confirms Samuel Little is most prolific serial killer in U.S. history. Retrieved May 8, 2024, from https://www.fbi.gov/news/press-releases/fbi-confirms-samuel-little-is-most-prolific-serial-killer-in-us-history

Whiteside, S. (2026, April 8). A timeline of the Gilgo Beach killings, suspect. *NewsNation*. https://www.newsnationnow.com/crime/gilgo-beach-killings/timeline-rex-heuermann-gilgo-beach/

Williams, D. J. (2020). Is serial sexual homicide a compulsion, deviant leisure, or both? Revisiting the case of Ted Bundy. *Leisure Sciences, 42*(2), 205-223.

World Population Review. (2024). *Countries with the most serial killers 2024.* Retrieved August 5, 2024, from https://worldpopulationreview.com/country-rankings/countries-with-the-most-serial-killers

Image Credits

Fig. 1.1: Florida Department of Corrections, https://commons.wikimedia.org/wiki/File:TedBundy1979MugshotFull.png, 1979.

Fig. 1.2: Federal Bureau of Investigation, https://commons.wikimedia.org/wiki/File:Robert_Ressler_2.png, 1986.

Fig. 1.3: U.S. Customs and Border Protection, https://commons.wikimedia.org/wiki/File:Pilots_participate_in_an_Active_Shooter_Scenario_at_NATC_(20232395246).jpg, 2015.

Fig. 1.4: Source: https://commons.wikimedia.org/wiki/File:H._H._Holmes.jpg.

Fig. 1.5: The Illustrated Police News, https://commons.wikimedia.org/wiki/File:Illustrated_Police_News_-_Jack_the_Ripper_2.png, 1888.

Fig. 1.6: Sacramento Sheriff, https://commons.wikimedia.org/wiki/File:Joseph_DeAngelo_mugshot.jpg, 2018.

Fig. 1.7: Federal Bureau of Investigation, https://www.bbc.com/news/world-us-canada-53226327, 2020.

Fig. 1.8: Suffolk County Sheriff's Office, https://commons.wikimedia.org/wiki/File:230714155519-rex-heuermann-booking-photo-giglo-beach-investigation.jpg, 2023.

Fig. 1.9: Copyright © 2021 by Atiru (CC BY-SA 4.0) at https://commons.wikimedia.org/wiki/File:SCPD_Gilgo_Death_Investigation.jpg.

CHAPTER 2

BIOPSYCHOSOCIAL DEVELOPMENT OF SERIAL KILLERS

"When I was a little kid, I was just like anybody else."

-Jeffrey Dahmer

We don't choose our family of origin. Some of us win the proverbial lottery, and are born into a loving and emotionally stable home. Others are born into a family rife with physical, emotional, and/or sexual violence, substance abuse, and parents who are struggling with depression and anxiety. These are obvious extremes, and often there is a combination of all of these events to differing degrees throughout someone's childhood. When we think of serial killers' childhoods, our default belief is that their homes are filled with neglect and abuse, and that's most often correct. Being raised in an abusive home commonly results in traits like lack of empathy, grandiosity, and manipulation, as they are often connected to childhood trauma and violent fantasies (Kalat, 2022). In a desperate bid to escape their abusive parents and find some solace in their life when they are also rejected by peers, many serial killers develop a secret inner fantasy world. This provides a buffer against the harshness of the real world that is hostile. There are a few cases where, based on our current knowledge, a serial killer's upbringing was fairly normal. However, it seems as

Figure 2.1 Jeffrey Dahmer, High School Senior Yearbook, 1978

though one must have a genetic predisposition, head trauma, and experiences of childhood abuse, to name a few factors, to become a serial killer.

Ultimately, there are numerous causes, or etiologies, of serial killer behavior. **Etiology** is defined as "the cause of a disease or abnormal condition" (Merriam-Webster, n.d.). Thus, this chapter will review the most common influences, including nature and social factors, in psychological development that exacerbate antisocial thinking and behavior (Viding et al., 2005). Each section will include a case example or two connecting facts of the case to the killer's psychological development.

Learning Outcomes

After reading this chapter, students will be able to do the following:

1. Explain how developmental disorders modify behavior.
2. Understand the impact of abuse on children's behavior.
3. Critically assess psychological development's effect on serial killers.

Sociocultural Factors

We do not live in a vacuum. Our family, friends, and community influence the ways in which we think and interact with the world around us. They provide us with information about behaviors that are socially appropriate, and those that are deemed inappropriate (Raine, 2013). There are unique cultural norms characteristic of urban versus rural settings, poor versus affluent neighborhoods, geographical location, and so on (Miller, 2014). Research indicates a correlation between warmer climates and higher crime rates, suggesting that increased outdoor activity and reduced clothing might influence the prevalence of criminal activity (Miller, 2014). To account for these factors with regard to the psychological development of serial killers, Hickey (1997) developed the Trauma and Control Model. This model comprises not only biological factors, such as prenatal and childhood exposure to alcohol and tobacco, and brain trauma (Arndt et al., 2004), but also psychosocial factors, including abuse and divorce, that culminate and result in a higher propensity to commit crime (Miller, 2014).

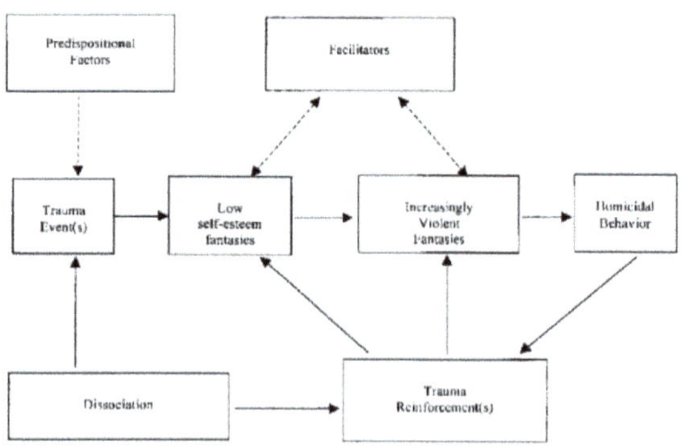

Figure 2.2 Hickey's Trauma and Control Model, 1997

Specifically, serial killers acquire an understanding of sociocultural norms from their family and community of origin; these may include aggression, degradation of women, and pornography (Miller, 2014). While not always the case, generally speaking, these communities tend to be of lower socioeconomic status, where incidents of crime are commonplace. Thus, the stress and trauma of living in a destitute and violent community accumulates. If the individual has a predisposition toward feelings of mistrust and defensiveness, that results in amplified reactions to slights in order to maintain emotional homeostasis (Ramsland, 2006). The mask of certainty and confidence serves to conceal their true feelings of self-doubt and inadequacy (Arndt et al., 2004). Though spurious, this allows them to feel better about themselves and their ability to survive in the chaotic world, reinforcing and strengthening maladaptive behaviors.

Psychobiological Influences

Our mother's nutrition, hygiene, alcohol or drug use, and mental health affect our psychological development in utero (Kalat, 2022; Reid et al., 2019). In fact, prenatal exposure to tobacco, specifically the mother smoking cigarettes, is a significant environmental factor that increases the risk of antisocial behavior (Kolla & Bortolato, 2020; Raine, 2002). The more cigarettes a pregnant mother smokes, the higher the likelihood her child will display violent behaviors (Raine, 2002). Furthermore, when a child is raised in a lower income community where clean water and proper infrastructure is subpar, there is an increased likelihood that the child will have higher blood lead levels (Willmont & Jones, 2022). Environmental toxins, such as lead, have been linked to antisocial behavior (Raine, 2002; Willmont & Jones, 2022). Elevated blood lead levels coupled with child abuse have been found to influence the propensity toward criminal activity as an adult (Willmont & Jones, 2022).

Moreover, paternal mental health issues can also disrupt family dynamics and the stability of the household. One study found that one third of sexual serial killers were raised with drug-addicted fathers (Reid et al., 2019). Further, studies have discovered specific associations between exposure to abuse during childhood, PTSD symptoms, and psychotic disorders (Powers et al., 2016). For example, the Adverse Childhood Experiences (ACE) Study by Felitti et al. (1998) examined the relationship between childhood adversity and long-term health outcomes, identifying a cumulative association between childhood experiences of interpersonal violence, parental drug abuse, and parental mental illness with an increased risk of physical and mental health conditions, including cardiovascular disease, depression, and substance abuse. Essentially, genetics and environmental variations influence our life. Furthermore, developmental disorders affect our personality and relationships as well. There are also incidences where accidents result in brain trauma, or even intentional "accidents," such as physical abuse. Further, social learning and attachments influence our understanding of relationships with others (Bandura, 1977; Bowlby, 1978). Not only does our world shape us, but we exert influence on it as well.

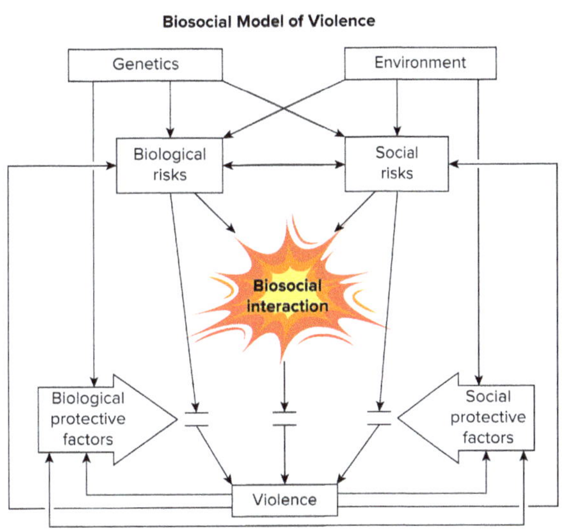

Figure 2.3 Raine's Heuristic Biosocial Model of Violence, 2002

Developmental Disorders

Developmental disorders may contribute to a serial killer's atypical behavior. In fact, research has shown that these disorders are more prevalent in serial killers than the general population (Allely et al., 2014). An example of a neurodevelopmental disorder that is more common in serial killers than the general population is **autism spectrum disorder** (ASD; Allely et al., 2014; Reid, 2017). Children with ASD lack theory of mind, which is the ability to think about and attempt to perceive a situation from another person's point of view (American Psychiatric Association [APA], 2022). In other words, they have difficulty "putting themselves in someone else's shoes." Coupled with that is the inner world they create through fantasy. Fantasy is a driving force behind serial killing, resulting in intrusive thoughts and cognitive distortions (Malizia, 2017).

Jeffrey Dahmer

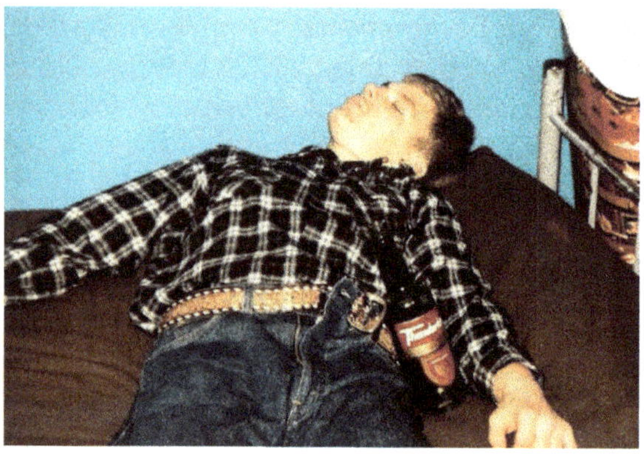

Figure 2.4 Jeffrey Dahmer Passed Out After a Night of Drinking While in Germany in the Army in 1979

This was the case for Jeffrey Dahmer. Though he was never diagnosed with ASD, he displayed many of the symptoms, including difficulty forming meaningful relationships, reduced or absent theory of mind, and narrowed interests (APA, 2022). Instead of playing video games with friends like other young boys, Jeffrey was fixated on death and had an interest in learning about the insides of animals (Schechter, 2003). His interests eventually transitioned from animals to men, where he longed to find connection and companionship. Inept at relationships, he killed men so they couldn't leave him (Ramsland, 2006). Desperate to create his own sex slave, he drilled a hole and poured acid into the brain of one of his victims, eager to incapacitate him yet keep him alive. Empathy and conscience were completely absent while his fantasies were abundant. Therefore, serial killers may be more likely to have or be diagnosed with ASD, but these factors often combine with difficult life experiences, like childhood trauma, making it difficult to discern nature from nurture.

Arthur Shawcross

Another developmental disorder speculated to be involved in antisocial behaviors, including serial killing, is **Jacob's syndrome** (XYY; Reid, 2017). A rare disorder only affecting 0.001% of the population, though more common in offenders, it's marked by behavioral problems, lack of empathy, impulsivity, and learning disabilities (National Organization for Rare Disorders [NORD], 2012). It only affects males, who tend to be taller than average and have bad acne (NORD, 2012; Reid, 2017). The most well-known serial killer diagnosed with Jacob's syndrome is Arthur Shawcross (Reid, 2017; Schechter, 2003). In addition to enduring numerous incidents of sexual abuse at the hands of family members, Shawcross felt compelled to start fires, and rape and murder children and women (Schechter, 2003).

His ability to manage his emotions was null. Any perceived annoyance propelled him to violence. For example, after saving a young boy from a mud hole, Shawcross planned to let him go until he felt bothered by the child's insistence on following him. He impulsively killed the boy and raped him post-mortem (Real Stories, 2016). The same sentiment was expressed in an interview with Shawcross, where he noted that a homeless elderly woman who was living with him started stealing from him; lacking empathy for her situation, he choked her to death. When asked by the interviewer if that justified killing her, he replied that it did to him (Real Stories, 2016). This lack of understanding and ability to control one's emotions and actions has not only been linked to neurodevelopmental and chromosomal disorders, but also to genes.

Figure 2.5 Arthur Shawcross, Sullivan Correctional Facility, 2002

Warrior Gene

The **warrior gene**, more aptly defined as monoamine oxidase A (MAOA), has been implicated in violent behavior. It's actually not a gene, but an enzyme that is responsible for the breakdown of the neurotransmitters norepinephrine, dopamine, and serotonin (Subramanian, 2020; Tiihonen et al., 2015). Specifically, the low-MAOA genotype has been shown to increase impulsive and emotionally charged antisocial behaviors, especially with regard to childhood maltreatment, often the result of hypersensitivity to interpersonal insults and criticism (Kolla & Bortolato, 2020; Raine, 2013). As it is genetically determined, its expression is evident at a young age (Allely et al., 2014).

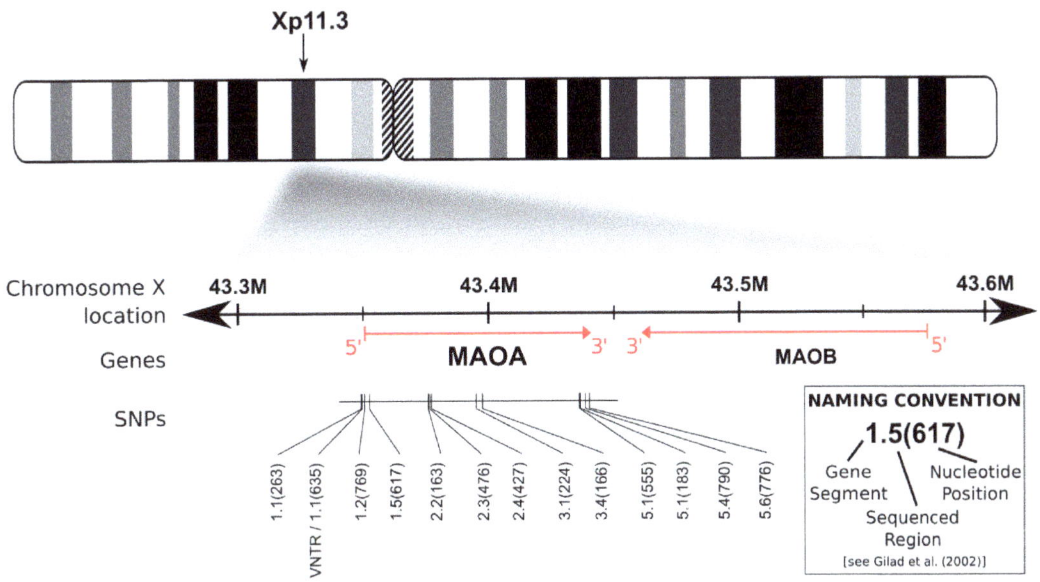

Figure 2.6 Warrior Gene Ideogram

Further, a study on violent offenders discovered that the presence of low levels of MAOA was associated with impulsivity, reactive aggression, and more frequent and severe criminal activity (i.e., serial killing; Heide & Solomon, 2006; Kolla & Bortolato, 2020; Tiihonen et al., 2015). Interestingly, this finding held constant regardless of gender and the presence of childhood abuse. Additionally, evidence points to disorganized serial killers being more likely to have the low-MAOA genotype, which results in their inability to control their temper and compartmentalize their "normal" life and "serial killer" persona (Reid, 2017). Disorganized serial killers are more likely than organized ones to choose victims based on opportunity rather than stalking or planning (Schechter, 2003). Indeed, disorganized perpetrators are more likely to have antisocial tendencies, which limit their impulse control, especially in situations where they are emotionally charged (Raine, 2013).

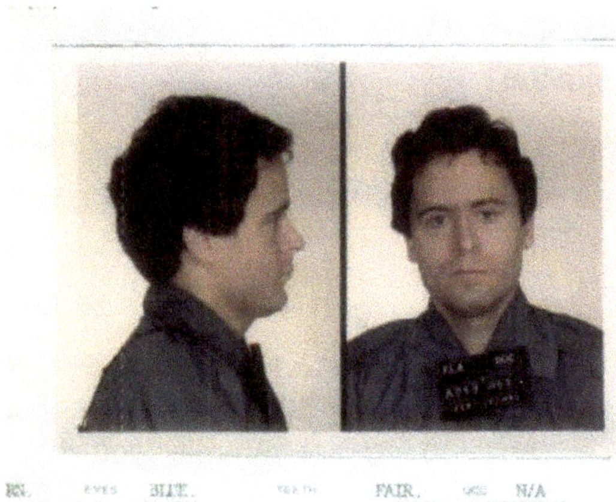

Figure 2.7 Ted Bundy Mugshot, 1980

Ted Bundy

While there is minimal scientific evidence of low-MAOA in serial killers due to ethical constraints and their unwillingness to provide blood samples, one high-profile case has confirmed this connection. Categorized as an organized serial killer due to his intellect, planning, and control, Theodore (Ted) Bundy is one of the most notorious serial killers. Blood samples indicated that he had low-MAOA, validating his propensity toward aggression (Hernandez et al., 2015). Born in 1946, Bundy was raised by his grandparents, but was told they were his actual parents (Piccotti & Kettler, 2023). In fact, his sister, as he knew her, was his mother (Rosewood & Lo, 2017). Due to having a child out of wedlock, the family wanted to keep the "mistake" a secret. Upon discovering this falsehood, Bundy was distraught and learned that the world was not honest or safe. Shortly after, he began displaying signs of antisocial behavior and psychopathy through increased interest in knives and peeping into neighbor's windows (Rosewood & Lo, 2017).

Figure 2.8 Ted Bundy, Florida State Penitentiary, 1978

In college, Bundy met and fell in love with an attractive brunette. Despite his desire to continue the relationship, she broke it off and it devastated him. It was yet another message that the world was cruel and harsh. Stalking his victims on the campus where he was a law student, he stalked women with long brown hair like his ex-girlfriend. The fact that his victims all had long, brown, straight hair points to his need for revenge and retribution against women. For example, one victim he selected was waiting in the rain for a bus to her next class when he offered her a ride to campus (KIRO 7 News, 2018). She was initially reluctant, but Bundy poured on the charm and made her feel safe; he would also pretend to be injured with a fake cast on his arm to lure unsuspecting women into his car. Shortly after agreeing to the ride, she noticed he was not driving the right way. After telling her to take her hat off, thus revealing her new short haircut, he flipped from friendly to hostile, yelling at her for taking the ride. He blamed her for getting in the car rather than himself for stalking and desiring to kill her. So distraught was he by the fact that her appearance no longer matched his fantasy, he let her go. Afraid for her life, she didn't tell anyone about the incident until Bundy was caught (KIRO 7 News, 2018).

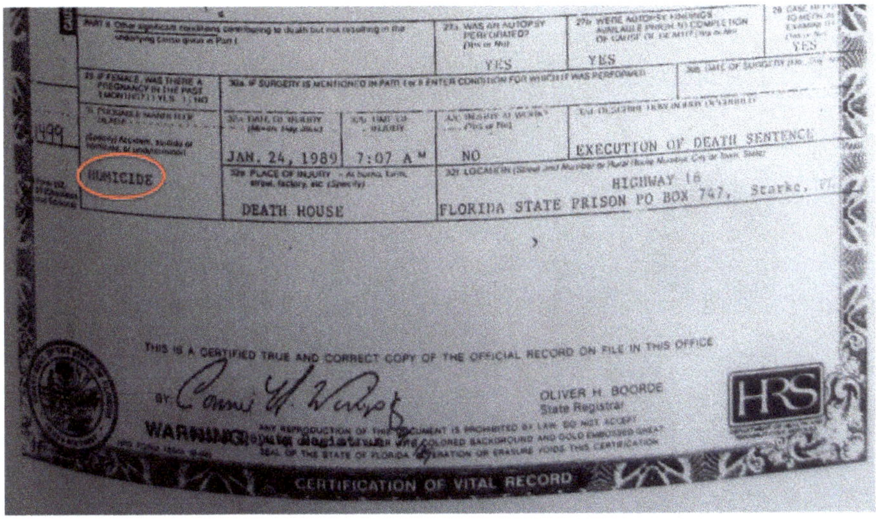
YES
YES
HOMICIDE
JAN. 24, 1989
7:07 A M
NO
EXECUTION OF DEATH SENTENCE
DEATH HOUSE
HIGHWAY 16
FLORIDA STATE PRISON PO BOX 747, Starke,
THIS IS A CERTIFIED TRUE AND CORRECT COPY OF THE OFFICIAL RECORD ON FILE IN THIS OFFICE
OLIVER H. BOORDE
State Registrar
WARNING
HRS
CERTIFICATION OF VITAL RECORD

Figure 2.9 Partial View of Ted Bundy's Death Certificate, 1989

Further, Bundy needed his victims to be anonymous. If he knew you, you were safe from his murderous rage. Working at a crisis hotline, he befriended a woman named Ann Rule (Rule, 1980). She was also a crime author, ironically. Not once did she think the person she worked with at the crisis center at 1:00 a.m. was a serial killer. Often, they would be the only two on a shift. He would tell her to be careful walking to her car and seemed to genuinely care about her (Rule, 1980). Bundy even had a girlfriend for years and helped raise her daughter (ABC News, 2020). Neither the girlfriend nor her daughter suspected they were living with a psychopath, though she noticed his demeanor change over time as he became distant and aloof, a change that coincided with his progression from fantasizing about murder to committing it (ABC News, 2020). He would beat, strangle, and rape his victims, then return to the bodies for additional sexual gratification (Rosewood & Lo, 2017). He was finally convicted of murdering 30 women after representing himself in court, and died by electric chair in 1989 (Ramsland, 2006). While Bundy was born with a genetic predisposition toward aggressive behavior, other serial killers become psychopathic due to accidents and abuse that resulted in head trauma.

Figure 2.10 Ted Bundy's Volkswagen Beetle

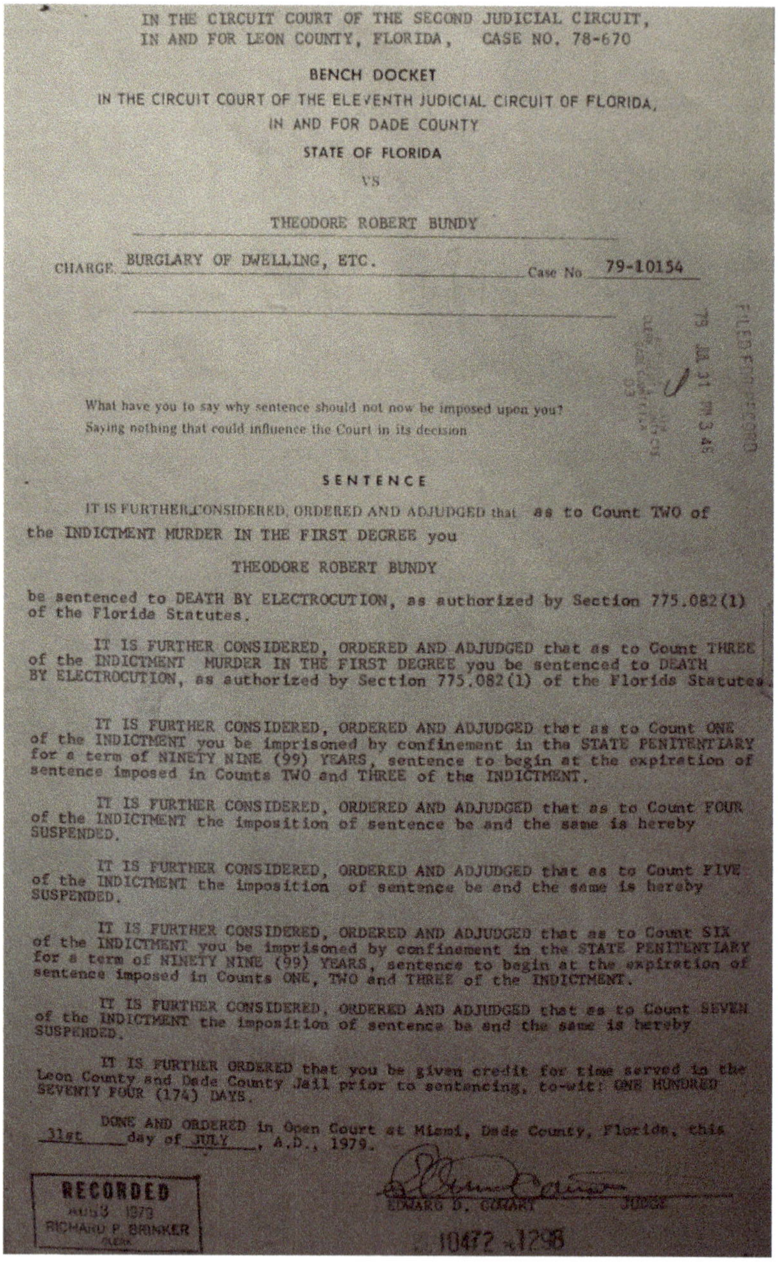

IN THE CIRCUIT COURT OF THE SECOND JUDICIAL CIRCUIT,
IN AND FOR LEON COUNTY, FLORIDA, CASE NO. 78-670

BENCH DOCKET

IN THE CIRCUIT COURT OF THE ELEVENTH JUDICIAL CIRCUIT OF FLORIDA,
IN AND FOR DADE COUNTY

STATE OF FLORIDA

VS

THEODORE ROBERT BUNDY

CHARGE BURGLARY OF DWELLING, ETC. Case No 79-10154

FILED FOR RECORD 79 JUL 31 PM 3 45

What have you to say why sentence should not now be imposed upon you?
Saying nothing that could influence the Court in its decision

SENTENCE

IT IS FURTHER CONSIDERED, ORDERED AND ADJUDGED that as to Count TWO of the INDICTMENT MURDER IN THE FIRST DEGREE you

THEODORE ROBERT BUNDY

be sentenced to DEATH BY ELECTROCUTION, as authorized by Section 775.082(1) of the Florida Statutes.

IT IS FURTHER CONSIDERED, ORDERED AND ADJUDGED that as to Count THREE of the INDICTMENT MURDER IN THE FIRST DEGREE you be sentenced to DEATH BY ELECTROCUTION, as authorized by Section 775.082(1) of the Florida Statutes.

IT IS FURTHER CONSIDERED, ORDERED AND ADJUDGED that as to Count ONE of the INDICTMENT you be imprisoned by confinement in the STATE PENITENTIARY for a term of NINETY NINE (99) YEARS, sentence to begin at the expiration of sentence imposed in Counts TWO and THREE of the INDICTMENT.

IT IS FURTHER CONSIDERED, ORDERED AND ADJUDGED that as to Count FOUR of the INDICTMENT the imposition of sentence be and the same is hereby SUSPENDED.

IT IS FURTHER CONSIDERED, ORDERED AND ADJUDGED that as to Count FIVE of the INDICTMENT the imposition of sentence be and the same is hereby SUSPENDED.

IT IS FURTHER CONSIDERED, ORDERED AND ADJUDGED that as to Count SIX of the INDICTMENT you be imprisoned by confinement in the STATE PENITENTIARY for a term of NINETY NINE (99) YEARS, sentence to begin at the expiration of sentence imposed in Counts ONE, TWO and THREE of the INDICTMENT.

IT IS FURTHER CONSIDERED, ORDERED AND ADJUDGED that as to Count SEVEN of the INDICTMENT the imposition of sentence be and the same is hereby SUSPENDED.

IT IS FURTHER ORDERED that you be given credit for time served in the Leon County and Dade County Jail prior to sentencing, to-wit: ONE HUNDRED SEVENTY FOUR (174) DAYS.

DONE AND ORDERED in Open Court at Miami, Dade County, Florida, this 31st day of JULY, A.D., 1979.

RECORDED
AUG 3 1979
RICHARD P. BRINKER
CLERK

EDWARD D. COWART JUDGE

10472 1298

Figure 2.11 Ted Bundy's Sentencing Document

Traumatic Brain Injury

Traumatic brain injury (TBI) occurs when there is injury to the brain from an external force (Williams et al., 2018). Historically, TBI has primarily been studied in war veterans (United States Department of Veterans Affairs [USDVA], 2024). Head injury, depending on the area of the brain that is injured, can result in marked changes in personality, including emotional instability, lack of impulse control, depression, impairment to executive functioning, and suicidal ideation (Allely et al., 2014; Williams et al., 2018). Studies have noted that roughly one-fourth of all serial killers experienced head trauma, most commonly during childhood (Allely et al., 2014). Examples of head injuries that could result in TBI include being hit in the head by a fist or other hard object, or smashing your head against the side of a vehicle during a crash (USDVA, 2024). Furthermore, children who are rambunctious and aggressive are more likely to end up with a TBI (Williams et al., 2018).

Phineas Gage

A historical case that illustrates the impact of brain trauma on personality is Phineas Gage. A railroad construction foreman in Vermont in the mid-1800s, Gage was affable and competent (Filho, 2020; Lapinski, 2022). He was popular in his community, until an explosion resulted in an iron rod being thrust through his left eye, entering the frontal lobe of his brain (Filho, 2020). Though he lived through the ordeal with his cognitive processes and motor functioning returning to normal, his personality changed dramatically (Filho, 2020; Lapinski, 2022). Gage became irritable, impatient, and aggressive, which led to being fired from the railroad. This incident was one of the first to reveal the specific functions of different regions of our brain, especially the frontal cortex.

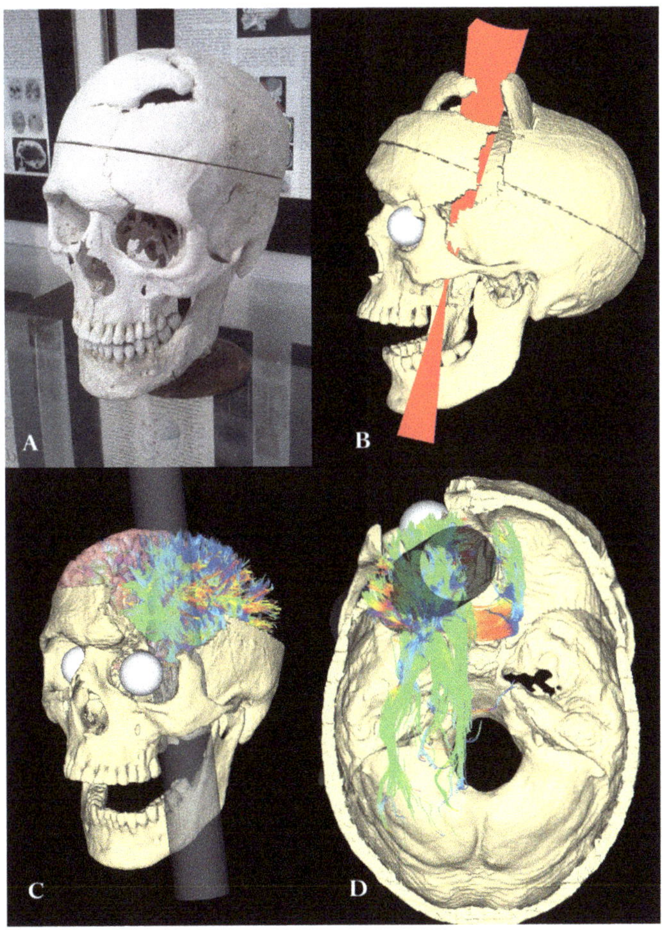

Figure 2.12 Depiction of Iron Rod Through Phineas Gage's Skull, 2012

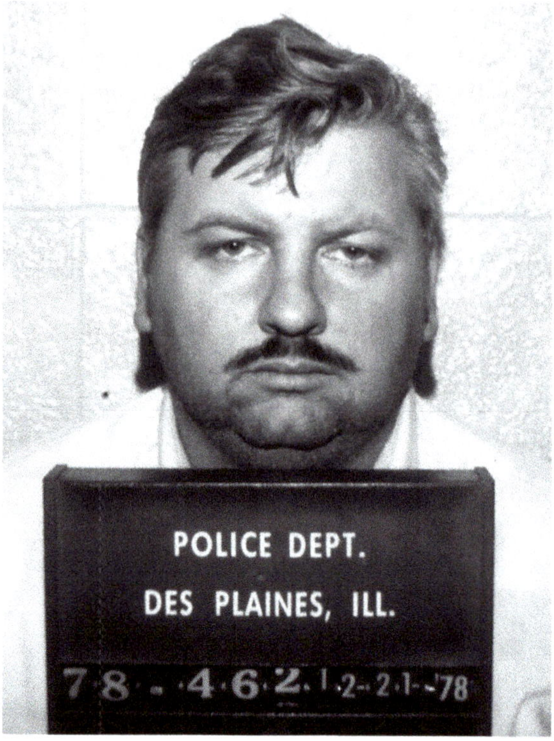

Figure 2.13 John Wayne Gacy Mugshot, 1987

Serial Killers With Head Trauma

Numerous serial killers experienced head trauma as children. For example, Fred West was in a motorcycle accident, which led to a skull fracture when he was only 17 years old (Ramsland, 2006). He was mild mannered prior to the accident, yet a few years afterwards his aggressive behavior toward women began at first with groping, and eventually escalated to murder. While that isolated incident led to, at least in part, West's violent behavior, John Gacy experienced more than his fair share of head trauma. As a child, he was hit in the head by a swing, resulting in a blood clot in his brain (Schechter, 2003). Despite his injury, his father continued to call him a sissy and beat him, causing more brain trauma. Gacy became a calculated killer, luring victims to his home before bludgeoning them to death and raping them (Schechter, 2003). In order to conceal evidence, he buried the 33 boys and men in the crawl space under his house.

Another example of the influence of head trauma on aggressive behavior is the case of Richard Ramirez. Ramirez experienced numerous head injuries, including a dresser falling on his head and being knocked unconscious by a swing, both before he was six years old (Biography.com, 2023). In addition to experiencing severe neglect as a child, he was introduced to violence by a cousin who engaged in criminal activity and even shot his wife right in front of Ramirez. He ended up murdering 14 victims before being caught in 1985.

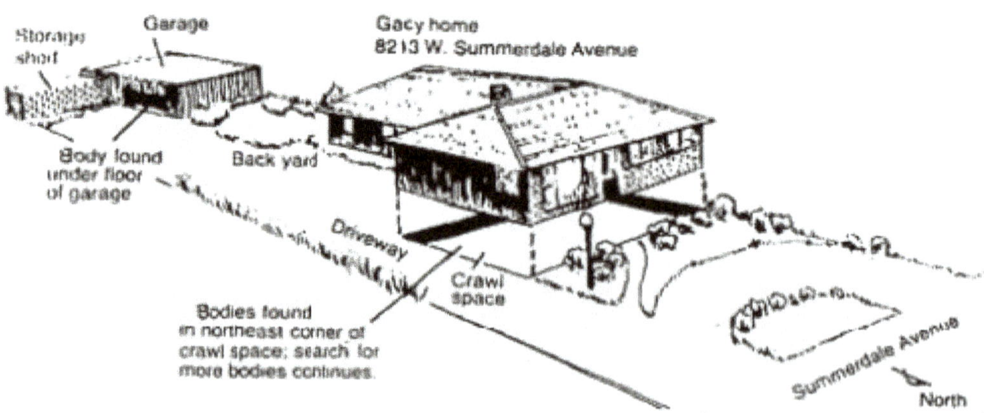

Figure 2.14 Drawing Depicting Gacy's House and Victim Burial Locations, 1978

Discussion question: How do our relationships from childhood, including family, friends, peers, and teachers, inform our notions of "healthy" relationships?

Child Abuse

Per the Radford University's continued documentation of serial killers (Aamodt et al., 2023), as of 2023, 73.2% of serial killers reported experiencing child abuse. While facing abuse as a child doesn't mean you will become a serial killer, a majority of serial killers experienced sexual, physical, and/or psychological abuse as children (Marono et al., 2020). Indeed, serial killers are at least three times as likely to have suffered from childhood abuse and neglect than non-offenders (Allely et al., 2014). Uninvolved parents do little to engage with their children (Kalat, 2022). When they do, it may be contentious in nature, through physical, psychological, and/or sexual abuse. Therefore, serial killers often experienced inadequate mirroring or validation from caregivers, leaving them with a profound sense of inadequacy that they defended against through a façade of grandiosity and other maladaptive behaviors (Kalat, 2022; Knight, 2006).

Figure 2.15 John Gacy Dressed as a Clown, 1978

Furthermore, early exposure to abuse and violence can normalize aggressive behavior, which can be the catalyst for acting on their murderous fantasies (Malizia, 2017; Marono et al., 2020). Subsequently, serial killers' violent behavior may be the result of early abuse and unmet emotional needs, framing murder as a twisted means of asserting power to counteract deep feelings of helplessness. Abuse in general, and especially sexual abuse, often informs a serial killer's modus operandi; they incorporate some form of sexual cruelty on their victims while they are still alive or postmortem, depending on their fantasy (Marono et al., 2020). Severe rejection by family and peers leads a child to create a fantasy life in their head as a way to dissociate. Thus, understanding serial killers requires examining how early trauma and unmet psychological needs contribute to their behaviors.

Sexual Abuse

A little over a fourth of all known serial killers reported experiencing childhood sexual abuse (26.4%; Aamodt et al., 2023). A family member or family friend is most often the perpetrator (Daley & Gutovitz, 2026). The abuse results in low self-esteem, trust issues, and increased violent behavior as an adult, compared to children who didn't experience sexual abuse (Allely et al., 2014; Daley & Gutovitz, 2026). Moreover, serial killers who were sexually abused as a child were more likely to engage in sexual sadism and kill for power to obtain complete control over their victims (Marono et al., 2020). In fact, characteristics common to sexually motivated serial killers include manipulative tendencies, a history of cruelty or violence beginning in childhood, and escalation of violent acts over time (Knight, 2006). This is no surprise given their experience of sexual assault as a child. Their view of sexual relationships and physical gratification is skewed. They believe they must have certain conditions, such as complete power, in order to achieve sexual satisfaction. Furthermore, serial killers who were sexually abused as children are more likely to partake in "mutilation, torture, and binding the victim" (Marono et al., 2020, p. 134). This could be due to their unconscious need to displace their rage and guilt on the victim (Marono et al., 2020). Indeed, research noted that women who were sexually abused as children were more likely to express antisocial personality traits (Kolla & Bortolato, 2020). However, not all survivors of childhood sexual abuse who end up as serial killers engage in sexual acts with their victims.

Juana Barraza

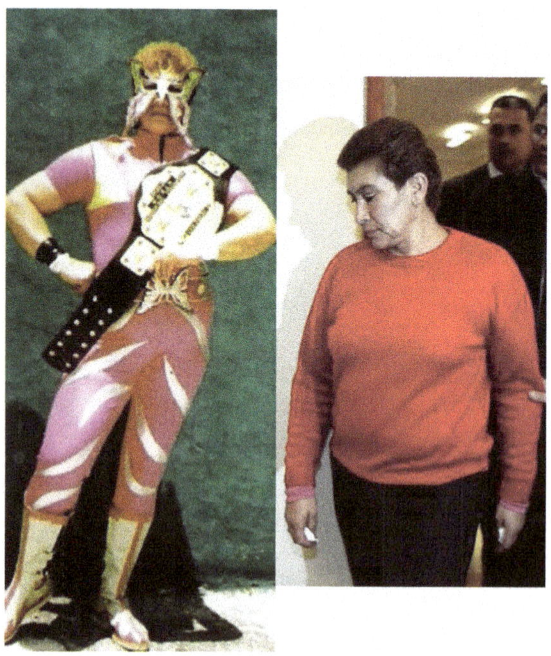

Figure 2.16 Juana Barraza as a Wrestler and After Her Arrest

For example, Juana Barraza's childhood was rife with neglect and sexual abuse. Born and raised in poverty in Mexico City, Juana was pimped by her mother, an alcoholic prostitute, who sold her for sex for only three beers (Cervantes, 2017; Tefler, 2021). The man then continued to rape Barraza for five years, resulting in two pregnancies when she was 13 and 16 years old, both of which ended in miscarriage (Cervantes, 2017). With an absent father, there was no one to save her from her abusers. Finally, free from her rapist's grasp as an adult, she worked as a professional wrestler who went by the moniker the Silent Lady, where she gained the strength and skill she eventually used to strangle an alleged 49 (she was convicted of 16) elderly victims between 2002 and 2006 (Tefler, 2021). She gained access to their homes by pretending to be a nurse or housekeeper who was there to assist them, then stole their possessions and sold them to pay for rent and food. They all lived alone, and were between 60 and 84, so were easy prey. Barraza admitted that she hated older women since they reminded her of her mother (Cervantes, 2017; Tefler, 2021). A result of the abuse and neglect during her childhood, Juana was never nurtured or taught basic life skills, leading to her descent into a life of violent crime. In addition to sexual abuse, serial killers often experienced psychological and physical abuse as children, as they tend to go hand in hand.

Video of Juana Barraza's case:

QR Code 2.1

Physical Abuse

The most common type of abuse reported by serial killers was physical (48.9%; Aamodt et al., 2023). Experiencing physical abuse during childhood, especially when coupled with a genetic predisposition toward violent behavior (Raine, 2002), often leads to behavioral problems, such as hostile attributional bias and positive feelings toward aggression and antagonistic responses (Marono et al., 2020). Hostile attributional bias occurs when a person assumes the behavior of others is hostile in nature when it has nothing to do with them, or is benign or ambiguous (Lee et al., 2020). Parents who exhibit hostile attributional bias assume the child is being disobedient even when the child is not (Lee et al., 2020). This, in turn, influences the child's behavior. If the child has a natural inclination toward being defiant, he might continue or increase these behaviors since they are expected of him by his caregiver anyway. It's also a form of social modeling where the child learns, albeit incorrectly, how to interact with others (Bandura, 1977; Bowlby, 1978). These experiences are carried with the child into adulthood, resulting in their physical abuse of others and the assumption that the world is malevolent and dangerous.

In fact, this could be why so many serial killers physically harm or kill animals and bully their peers. Serial killers who have experienced physical abuse as children tend to torture and use very violent methods of killing, often continuing the vicious acts (e.g., mutilation), even after the victim has died (Marono et al., 2020). Trauma from physical abuse can also lead to fire setting, which is a childhood trait that many serial killers have in common; this will be discussed in depth in Chapter 3.

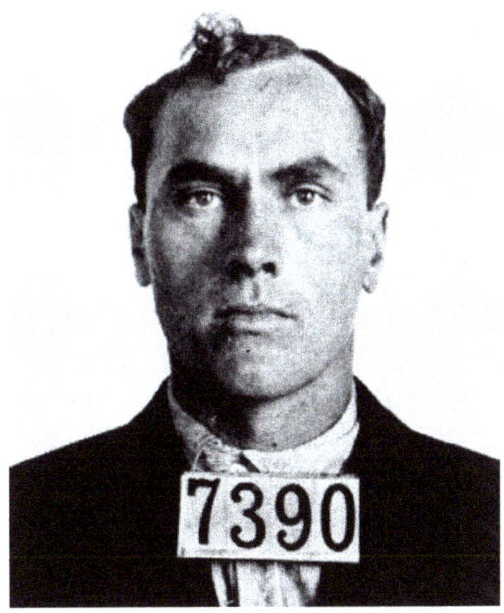

Figure 2.17 Carl Panzram Mugshot, 1915

Carl Panzram

When all you've known is abuse and neglect, not only do you continue to expect it, but it incites a feeling of anger toward others and the world. One such serial killer who never experienced anything but pain and suffering at the hands of those who were supposed to care for him was Carl Panzram. Born in 1891 in Minnesota, his childhood was fairly normal for a family in the late 1800s until his father left when he was seven. Panzram was left to his own devices and was arrested for being drunk at age eight (Ramsland, 2006). When he was then sent to a reform school, the abuse and neglect only continued, leading to his lack of faith in humankind. In fact, he stated, "I was so full of hate that there was no room in me for such feelings as love, pity, kindness or honor or decency. My only regret is that I wasn't born dead or not at all" (Criminal Minds, n.d.). Hatred for those who he saw as "less than" was also part of his modus operandi (Blanco, n.d.). Most of his victims were also homeless. He didn't discriminate based on age, gender, or ethnicity, raping and killing anyone. Using aliases and moving from state to state via the railroad, he was able to evade capture for years (Blanco, n.d.). In and out of jail for offenses ranging from robbery to assault, he became accustomed to being seen as a derelict. Panzram killed a total of 22 victims (Blanco, n.d.), and was eventually hanged in 1930.

Psychological Abuse

There are a plethora of serial killer cases where childhood neglect, which is physical *and* psychological abuse, is a central factor in their impetus for maladaptive behavior. Specifically, psychological abuse is prevalent in the backgrounds of almost half of serial killers (48.7%; Aamodt et al., 2023). One viewpoint on the importance of the home environment is object relations theory, which emphasizes the impact of early relationships, especially between mother and child, on psychological development (Knight, 2006). Abuse and trauma at the hands of a parent, coupled with the message that women are tainted, is a recipe for future manipulative, cruel, and sexually violent behavior (Knight, 2006). Without love and validation from at least one parent or guardian (National Scientific Council on the Developing Child, 2023), children with a genetic predisposition for murderous behavior are more likely to become serial killers due to their need for power that stems from childhood feelings of helplessness and hopelessness. These feelings can result from a lack of parental affection, neglect in the form of being left alone for lengthy periods of time at inappropriate ages, and lack of proper education and recreational activities, both of which aid in socialization skills. When abuse and neglect occur in these forms, children have difficulty cognitively assessing situations, which can result in "aggressive thought patterns—for example, encoding errors, hostile attributional biases, accessing of aggressive responses, and positive evaluations of aggression" (Marono et al., 2020, p. 128). In essence, the perfect (or imperfect) storm is created by the genetic markers for killing in addition to unmet psychological needs as a child, resulting in adults who are pathological and narcissistic (Knight, 2006; Marono et al., 2020).

Ed Kemper

A prime example of this type of psychopath is Edmund (Ed) Kemper. As a child, his mother constantly berated him and locked him in the basement for days as punishment for typical child behavior (Kosman, 2023). Unfortunately, they lived with his grandparents and his grandmother encouraged the abuse. Mirroring the manipulation, Kemper would play a game with his sister where they were in a gas chamber or electric chair pretending to die (Kosman, 2023). Perhaps this is what he really wanted—to finally escape the abuse. It's an extreme response, albeit to an extreme situation. He took his anger out further by first dismembering his sister's dolls and then moving on to animals when that no longer satiated him.

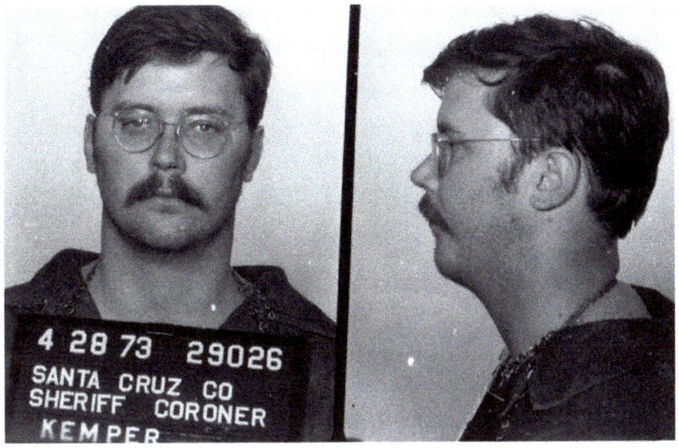

Figure 2.18 Ed Kemper Mugshot, 1973

The lack of nurturing and loving parental figures resulted in his inability to form relationships, especially with the opposite sex. He felt inept. To compensate for that feeling, he fantasized about murdering his female teacher and having sex with her. Kemper even told a friend that before he could kiss his teacher he would have to kill her first (Ramsland, 2006). Sick and tired of the ongoing abuse, Kemper shot and killed his grandmother when he was 15 years old (Kosman, 2023; Ramsland, 2006). He then shot his grandfather only to save him from seeing his dead wife. Kemper was arrested and convicted of those murders, but since he was 15 years old at the time of those murders, his record was wiped clean when he turned 18 and he was freed. This didn't stop him from stalking and murdering more innocent victims. After killing one girl and seven female co-eds at the university where his mother worked, he finally silenced his true target when he killed his mother, subsequently removing her larynx and obliterating it in the garbage disposal (Ramsland, 2006). Then, in highly unusual behavior for a serial killer, he drove away and called police, confessing to the murders. In 1973, he received eight life sentences and will never be free again.

Figure 2.19 Clarnell Kemper, Ed's Mother

Table 2.1 Percentage of Serial Killers Abused as Children

Type of abuse	***N***	**% abused**
No abuse reported	232	26.76
Any abuse reported	635	73.24
Psychological abuse	422	48.67

Type of abuse	***N***	**% abused**
Physical abuse	424	48.90
Sexual abuse	229	26.41
Date of birth	***N***	**% abused**
1900–1919	15	66.67
1920–1939	71	74.65
1940–1959	354	71.19
1960–1979	345	76.52
1980–2010	38	78.95

Source: Michael G. Aamodt, Terence Leary, and Senthil Girimurugan, Selection from Radford/FGCU Annual Report on Serial Killer Statistics: 2023, p. 55. Copyright © 2023 by Radford University.

Summary

Human development is a combination of genetics and environment. The childhood of a serial killer must encompass a myriad of unfortunate genetic components plus environmental stressors. Sociocultural influences, such as socioeconomic status and exposure to environmental toxins can have a lasting impact on an individual's brain and behavior. Injury to the brain due to falls and physical abuse negatively impact a child's cognitive faculties. Furthermore, many of the serial killers described in this chapter endured physical, psychological, and/or sexual abuse by the very people who were supposed to nurture them. This undoubtedly destroyed their trust in humankind, disintegrating any shred of empathy they had. Add to that a biological predisposition toward anger and aggression, and the result is evidenced in some of the cases detailed above.

Keywords

Autism spectrum disorder (ASD)

Etiology

Jacob's syndrome

Traumatic brain injury (TBI)

Warrior gene

Chapter Review Questions

1. What are some of the negative experiences most serial killers endured as children?
2. How does the warrior gene affect behavior?
3. What are the three main types of abuse discussed in this chapter, and how do they affect the behavior of serial killers?

References

Aamodt, M. G., Leary, T., & Girimurugan, S. (2023). *Radford/FGCU annual report on serial killer statistics*. Radford University.

ABC News. (2020, January 31). *Ted Bundy: The monster among us*. (Season 42, Episode 18) [Television series episode]. In *20/20*. American Broadcasting Company.

Allely, C. S., Minnis, H., Thompson, L., Wilson, P., & Gillberg, C. (2014). Neurodevelopmental and psychosocial risk factors in serial killers and mass murderers. *Aggression and Violent Behavior, 19*, 288–301.

American Psychiatric Association. (2022). *Diagnostic and statistical manual of mental disorders (5th ed., text revision)*. https://doi.org/10.1176/appi.books.9780890425787

Arndt, W. B., Heitpas, T., & Kim, J. (2004). Critical characteristics of male serial murderers. *American Journal of Criminal Justice, 29*(1), 117–131.

Bandura, A. (1977). *Social learning theory*. Prentice-Hall.

Biography.com. (2023). Richard Ramirez. https://www.biography.com/crime/richard-ramirez

Blanco, J. (n.d.). Carl Panzram. Murderpedia. Retrieved August, 28, 2024, from https://murderpedia.org/male.P/p/panzram-carl.htm

Bowlby, J. (1978). Attachment theory and its therapeutic implications. *Adolescent Psychiatry, 6*, 5–33.

Cervantes, S. V. (2017). *The little old lady killer: The sensationalized crimes of Mexico's first female serial killer*. New York University Press.

Carl Panzram. (n.d.). Criminal Minds Wiki. https://criminalminds.fandom.com/wiki/Carl_Panzram"

Daley, S. F., & Gutovitz, S. (2026). *Child sexual abuse*. StatsPearls Publishing. https://www.ncbi.nlm.nih.gov/books/NBK470563/

Felitti, V. J., Anda, R. F., Nordenberg, D., Williamson, D. F., Spitz, A. M., Edwards, V., Koss, M. P., & Marks, J. S. (1998). Relationship of childhood abuse and household dysfunction to many of the leading causes of death in adults: The adverse childhood experiences study. *American Journal of Preventative Medicine, 14*(4), 245–258.

Filho, R. V. T. (2020). Phineas Gage's great legacy. *Dementia and Neuropsychology, 14*(4), 419–421.

Hernandez, J., Highsmith, J., Madrigal, S., & Mercado, M. (2015). Nature (MAOA) and nurture in a criminal. *UC Merced Undergraduate Research Journal*, *8*(1). http://dx.doi.org/10.5070/M481029475 Retrieved from https://escholarship.org/uc/item/5w51b7bg

Heide, K. M., & Solomon, E. P. (2006). Biology, childhood trauma, and murder: Rethinking justice. *International Journal of Law & Psychiatry, 29*(3), 220–233.

Hickey, E. W. (1997). *Serial murderers and their victims*. Wadsworth.

Kalat, J. W. (2022). *Introduction to psychology (12th ed.)*. Cengage.

KIRO 7 News. (2018, February 15). *For the first time, woman tells story of surviving Ted Bundy in 1972* [Video]. YouTube. https://www.youtube.com/watch?v=nDUr4mNHPIU

Knight, Z. G. (2006). Sexually motivated serial killers and the psychology of aggression and "evil" within a contemporary psychoanalytic perspective. *Journal of Sexual Aggression, 13*(1), 21–25.

Kolla, N. J., & Bortolato, M. (2020). The role of monoamine oxidase A in the neurobiology of aggressive, antisocial, and violent behavior: A tale of mice and men. *Progress in Neurobiology, 194*, 101875.

Kosman, P. (2023). Staring into the abyss: The origins of serial killer behavior. *Journal of the Utah Academy of Sciences, Arts & Letters, 100*, 333–351.

Lapinski, S. (2022, August 12). *Who was Phineas Gage?* Harvard Countway Library. https://asklib.hms.harvard.edu/faq/153359

Lee, S., Chang, H., Ip, K. I., & Olson, S. L. (2020). Early socialization of hostile attributional bias: The roles of parental attributions, parental discipline, and child attributes. *Social Development, 28*(3), 549–563.

Malizia, N. (2017). Serial murder: The mechanisms from imagination to the murder phases. *Sociology Mind, 7*, 44–59.

Marono, A. J., Reid, S., Yaksic, E., & Keatley, D. A. (2020). A behaviour sequence analysis of serial killer's lives: From childhood abuse to methods of murder. *Psychiatry, Psychology, and Law, 27*(1), 126–137.

Merriam-Webster. (n.d.). Etiology. In *Merriam-Webster.com dictionary*. Retrieved December 16, 2024, from https://www.merriam-webster.com/dictionary/etiology

Miller, L. (2014). Serial killers: I. Subtypes, patterns, and motives. *Aggression and Violent Behavior, 19*(1), 1-11.

National Organization for Rare Disorders. (2012). XXY Syndrome. https://rarediseases.org/rare-diseases/xyy-syndrome/

National Scientific Council on the Developing Child. (2023). *Place matters: The environment we create shapes the foundations of healthy development: Working paper No. 16*. Harvard University. Retrieved November 14, 2024, from https://developingchild.harvard.edu/resources/working-paper/place-matters-the-environment-we-create-shapes-the-foundations-of-healthy-development/

Piccotti, T., & Kettler, S. (2023). Inside Ted Bundy's troubled and disturbing childhood.

Biography. https://www.biography.com/crime/ted-bundy-childhood

Powers, A., Fani, N., Cross, D., Ressler, K. J., & Bradley, B. (2016). Childhood trauma, PTSD, and psychosis: Findings from a highly traumatized, minority sample. *Child Abuse & Neglect, 58*, 111–118.

Raine, A. (2002). Biosocial studies of antisocial and violent behavior in children and adults: A review. *Journal of Abnormal Child Psychology, 30*(4), 311–26.

Raine, A. (2013). *The anatomy of violence: Biological roots of crime*. Vintage.

Ramsland, K. (2006). *Inside the minds of serial killers: Why they kill*. Praeger.

Real Stories. (2016, May 5). *Interview with a serial killer (true crime documentary)* [Video]. YouTube. https://www.youtube.com/watch?v=NQNwjEkszvg

Reid, S. (2017). Developmental pathways to serial homicide: A critical review of the biological literature. *Aggression and Violent Behavior, 35*, 52–61.

Reid, S., Katan, A., Ellithy, A., Stua, R. D., & Denisov, E. V. (2019). The perfect storm: Mapping the life trajectories of serial killers. *International Journal of Offender Therapy and Comparative Criminology, 63*(9), 1621–1662.

Rosewood, J., & Lo, R. (2017). *The big book of serial killers: An encyclopedia of serial killers*. CreateSpace Publishing.

Rule, A. (1980). *The stranger beside me*. Norton.

Schechter, H. (2003). *The serial killer files: The who, what, where, how, and why of the world's most terrifying murders*. Ballantine Books.

Subramanian, A. (2020, July 21). Born to kill? The story of 'serial killer' genes. *Berkeley Scientific Journal*. https://bsj.studentorg.berkeley.edu/born-to-kill-the-story-of-serial-killer-genes/

Tefler, T. (2021). *Juana Barraza: The woman who was killing Mexico's elderly women*. CrimeReads.

Tiihonen, J., Rautiainen, M. R., Ollila, H. M., Repo-Tiihonen, E., Virkkunen, M., Palotie, A., Peitilainen, O., Kristiansson, K., Joukamaa, M., Lauerma, H., Saarela, J., Tyni, S., Vartiainen, H., Paananen, J., Goldman, D., & Paunio, T. (2015). Genetic background of extreme violent behavior. *Molecular Psychiatry, 20*, 786–792.

United States Department of Veterans Affairs. (2024). Effects of TBI. https://www.mentalhealth.va.gov/tbi/index.asp

Viding, E., Blair, R. J. R., Moffitt, T. E., Plomin, R. (2005). Evidence for substantial genetic risk for psychopathy in 7-year-olds. *Journal of Child Psychology and Psychiatry, 46*(6), 592-597.

Willmot, P., & Jones, L. (Eds). (2022). *Childhood maltreatment and its links to offending*. Routledge.

Williams, W. H., Chitsabesan, P., Fazel, S., McMillan, T., Highes, N., Parsonage, M., & Tonks, J. (2018). Traumatic brain injury: A potential cause of violent crime? *Lancet Psychiatry, 5*(10), 836–844.

Image Credits

Fig. 2.1: Revere Senior High School, https://commons.wikimedia.org/wiki/File:Jeffrey_Dahmer_HS_Yearbook.jpg, 1978.

Fig. 2.2: Bruce A. Arrigo and Catherine E. Purcell, "Explaining Paraphilias and Lust Murder: Toward an Integrated Model," International Journal of Offender Therapy and Comparative Criminology, vol. 45, no. 1. Copyright © 1997 by SAGE Publications.

Fig. 2.3: Adapted from Adrian Raine, "Biosocial Studies of Antisocial and Violent Behavior in Children and Adults: A Review," Journal of Abnormal Child Psychology, vol. 30, no. 2, p. 312. Copyright © 2002 by Springer Nature.

Fig. 2.3a: Copyright © 2020 Depositphotos/studioworkstock.

Fig. 2.4: David Rodriguez/U.S. Army, https://commons.wikimedia.org/wiki/File:Jeffrey_L._Dahmer_during_his_army_deployment_to_Baumholder,_West_Germany_in_1979.jpg, 1979.

Fig. 2.5: Source: https://commons.wikimedia.org/wiki/File:Arthur_Shawcross_et_al_(cropped).jpeg.

Fig. 2.6: Copyright © 2012 by Gringer (CC BY-SA 4.0) at https://commons.wikimedia.org/wiki/File:MAOA_Gene_with_ChrX_Ideogram.svg.

Fig. 2.7: Florida Department of Corrections, https://commons.wikimedia.org/wiki/File:TedBundy1980MughsotFull.jpg, 1980.

Fig. 2.8: Florida Memory Project, https://commons.wikimedia.org/wiki/File:TedBundyprisonFlorida.jpg, 1978.

Fig. 2.9: State of Florida, https://commons.wikimedia.org/wiki/File:Ted_Bundy,_lower_half_of_death_certificate.JPG, 1989.

Fig. 2.10: Copyright © 2010 by DCTWINKIE5500 (CC BY-SA 2.0) at https://commons.wikimedia.org/wiki/File:Ted_Bundy_Volkswagen.jpg.

Fig. 2.11: Copyright © 2008 by dbking (CC BY 2.0) at https://commons.wikimedia.org/wiki/File:Ted_Bundy_Sentencing_Document.jpg.

Fig. 2.12: John Darrell Van Horn et al., "Mapping Connectivity Damage in the Case of Phineas Gage," PLoS ONE, vol. 7, no. 5, p. 3. Copyright © 2012 by John Darrell Van Horn et al. (CC BY 4.0) at https://doi.org/10.1371/journal.pone.0037454.

Fig. 2.13: Des Plaines Police Department, https://commons.wikimedia.org/wiki/File:John_Wayne_Gacy_1978_mugshot.jpg, 1978.

Fig. 2.14: Tribune Graphic Artist, https://commons.wikimedia.org/wiki/File:John_Gacy_Home_Diagram_Kokomo_Tribune_December_28_1978.jpg, 1978.

Fig. 2.15: Martin Zielinski, https://commons.wikimedia.org/wiki/File:John_Gacy_Pogo_December_1976_Martin_Zielinski.jpg, 1978.

Fig. 2.16: Shana Lewis, https://commons.wikimedia.org/wiki/File:Juana_Barraza_as_a_wrestler_(left)_and_after_her_arrest_(right).jpg, 2017.

Fig. 2.17: Oregon State Penitentiary, https://commons.wikimedia.org/wiki/File:Carl_Panzram.jpg, 1915.

Fig. 2.18: Santa Cruz County Sheriff's Office, https://commons.wikimedia.org/wiki/File:Edmund_Kemper_(mug_shot_-_1973).jpg, 1973.

Fig. 2.19: Copyright © 1970 by Hamzacetins (CC BY-SA 4.0) at https://commons.wikimedia.org/wiki/File:Clarnell_Elizabeth_Strandberg.jpg.

CHAPTER 3

PSYCHOPATHOLOGY OF SERIAL KILLERS

Clinical Profiles and Diagnostic Considerations

"I would like to be transferred to a hospital on the east coast so I am closer to the government and further from the UFOs."

-Richard Chase

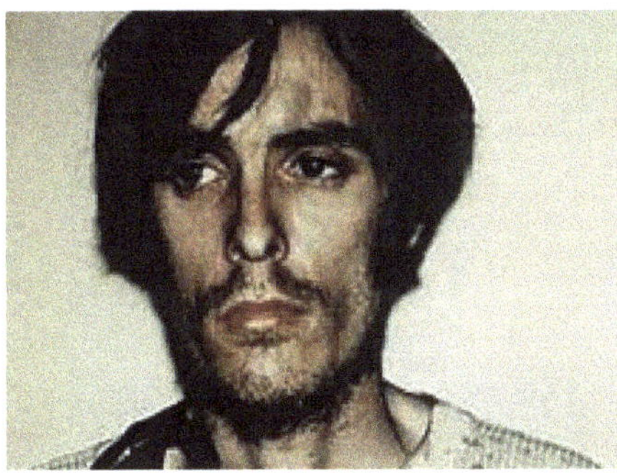

Figure 3.1 Richard Chase Mugshot, 1978

This chapter will review the American Psychiatric Association's (APA) *Diagnostic and Statistical Manual of Mental Disorders, 5th Edition Text Revision* (*DSM-5-TR*, 2022) diagnostic criteria for the most common mental disorders diagnosed in serial killers, including conduct disorder, antisocial personality disorder, narcissistic personality disorder, borderline personality disorder, schizophrenia, bipolar disorder, and sexual sadism. The diagnostic criteria will be applied to serial killers' behaviors. To meet the criteria for a mental health disorder, the severity of symptoms must be distressing and interfere with the person's ability to operate in society. In other words, the individual is unable to function in school or retain steady employment. Additionally, maintaining healthy boundaries and relationships proves very difficult. "The disturbance in behavior causes clinically significant impairment in social, academic, or occupational functioning" (APA, 2022, p. 5).

It is important to note that any proper psychological evaluation must include a battery of tests administered, scored, and interpreted by a licensed counselor or psychologist. The assessments should include a clinical interview; a personality questionnaire, such as the Structured Clinical Interview for *DSM-5®* Personality Disorders (SCID-5-PD; First et al., 2015) or the Minnesota Multiphasic Personality Inventory–3 (MMPI-3; Ben-Porath & Tellegen, 2020); an intelligence assessment, such as the Wechsler Adult Intelligence Scale–IV (WAIS-IV; Wechsler, 2008); and collateral interviews or observational reports from parents and teachers for children under age 18. Discussing the results with the individual and noting their verbal and nonverbal responses provides even more information about their personality.

Further, comorbidity exists, which means individuals may be diagnosed with more than one mental disorder. Therefore, they are not necessarily mutually exclusive. Additionally, it is possible to meet the requirements for a few of the diagnostic criteria, but not the full disorder. Personality traits including psychopathy, Machiavellianism, and sociopathy, in addition to the mental disorders noted above, will be explored and connected to the behavior of serial killers. To specify, personality traits comprise emotional expression, behaviors, and cognitions.

Learning Outcomes

After reading this chapter, students will be able to do the following:

1. Comprehend the diagnostic criteria for mental disorders most often diagnosed in serial killers.
2. Understand how the mental disorder manifests in the serial killer's behavior.
3. Use the information about mental disorders and apply it to serial killers other than the ones described in this chapter.

Conduct Disorder

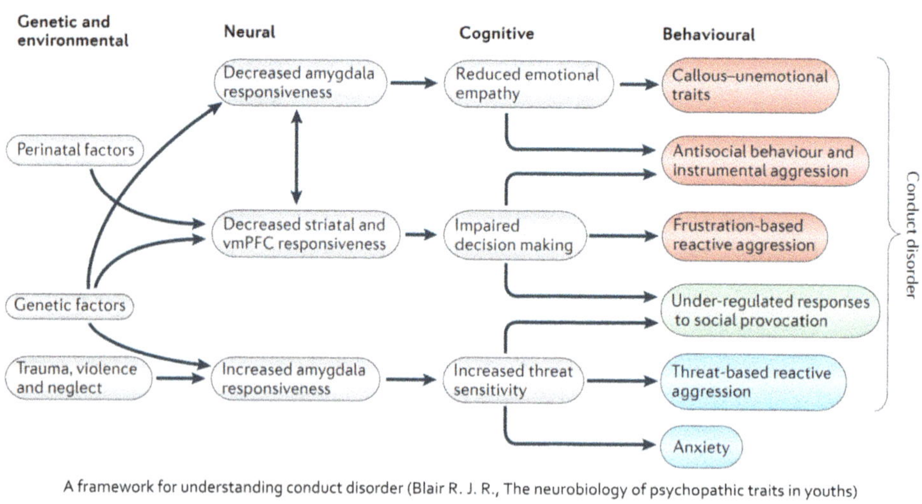

Figure 3.2 Conduct Disorder Framework

Children diagnosed with **conduct disorder (CD)** lack empathy, thrill seek, are impulsive, and display shallow emotions (APA, 2022). In fact, research revealed that callous-unemotional traits in children, which are central to psychopathy, are highly heritable (Viding et al., 2005). In other words, the apple doesn't fall far from the tree. Though it won't be explained in depth, it's important to note that children with CD are not merely defiant and combative, as you would see in children diagnosed with **oppositional defiant disorder (ODD)**. CD is a significant increase in the severity of ODD behavior (APA, 2022). Running away from home, sexually assaulting, and breaking and entering are typical behaviors of children diagnosed with CD (APA, 2022). They lack the capacity to contemplate how their actions affect others; they simply don't care (Garcia-Baamonde et al., 2022). Children with these diagnostic traits will use people to get what they want. They can easily manipulate a peer who has a weak sense of self and con them into taking part in their crimes. When push comes to shove, they will happily rat out their accomplice to avoid responsibility for their actions. Indeed, the more severe the symptoms at a younger age, the direr the prognosis (APA, 2022). These behaviors often manifest as the characteristic serial killer triad—bed-wetting, fire setting, and animal abuse (Ramsland, 2006; Schechter, 2003).

Conduct Disorder Diagnostic Criteria

A conduct disorder diagnosis requires the child to meet specific criteria related to the behaviors noted below within the past 12 months (APA, 2022).

"Conduct disorder involves severe behaviors that violate the rights of others or societal norms. Behaviors may involve aggression towards others, animals, and/or destruction of property all of which could result in legal consequences....

Symptoms of conduct disorder include varying patterns of:

- Aggression to people and animals (bullies, intimidates others, initiates fights, use of weapons, cruelty to others, cruelty to animals, stolen while confronting a victim, raped others).
- Destruction of property (deliberate fire setting, vandalization).
- Deceitfulness or theft (broken into properties, manipulates others, stolen).
- Serious violations of rules (runs away from home, truant from school, stays out at night)." (Luna, 2024, para. 14)

Figure 3.3 Mary's brazen note, misspelled with childish handwriting, is indicative of inadequate education coupled with sociopathic tendencies. She lacked the ability to fully appreciate the magnitude of her actions. At only 11 years old, she was a child, yet that doesn't excuse her evil deeds.

Mary Bell

Born in England in 1957 to a felonious father and prostitute mother, Bell was neither nurtured nor loved (Sereny, 1998). Her childhood was riddled with sexual, emotional, and physical abuse. Her mother openly tried to pawn her off on others or kill her. In fact, her mother brought "johns" to their home and allowed them to engage in sexual acts with Bell when she was only five years old (Sereny, 1998). Therefore, it's no surprise that when left to her own devices in the working-class town of Scotswood, she would wander the streets, skip school, and find devious ways to occupy her 11-year-old mind. Teaming up with a school friend, the girls killed two young boys who were only four and three years old (Ramsland, 2006). They lured each boy into an alley and hit them on the head with a concrete block (Ramsland, 2006). Bell even had the audacity to carve an M into the three year old's chest. She revealed herself as she grinned while watching the funeral of one of the boys. Officers noticed and homed in on her as a suspect, even though outwardly she seemed like a sweet little girl. Arrested in 1968 when she was 11 years old, Bell was eventually convicted of both murders (yes, she is not officially a serial killer by U.S. definition, as she did not commit three, but may have if not caught) and spent only 12 years in prison due to her juvenile status (Sereny, 1998). Judge and jury both felt that her ability to distinguish right from wrong was underdeveloped due to her age, and she was convicted of manslaughter rather than murder (*The Guardian*, 1968). Once released in 1980 at age 23, she changed her name and had a daughter of her own. As far as we know, her criminal activity was confined to her childhood.

Antisocial Personality Disorder

Often, but not always, the diagnosis of CD is converted to **antisocial personality disorder (ASPD)** when a child turns 18, due to diagnostic criteria (APA, 2022). Therefore, you will notice similarities between CD and ASPD. Just as children and adolescents with CD display aggressive and violent behavior, so do adults who have been diagnosed with ASPD (Kolla & Bortoleto, 2020). For example, individuals with ASPD simply have no regard for the rights of others (APA, 2022). They do not become upset at events or scenes that would be distressing for most people, such as witnessing a terrible car crash (Reid et al., 2019). Specifically, males have higher prevalence rates of ASPD than females—between 3 and 7 times (Kolla & Bortolato, 2020). Moreover, this lack of respect is also shown for institutions; they will break the law whenever it suits them (Jewel & Raypole, 2024; Morana et al., 2006). They will lie, cheat, and steal to improve their lives, all at the expense of others.

Figure 3.4 Signs of Antisocial Personality Disorder

Individuals often receive a diagnosis of ASPD following the conviction of a crime. Rarely will they seek treatment prior to being forced to do so. In fact, they don't believe there is anything wrong with them and instead blame others for their downfall (Morana et al., 2006). Therefore, it is surprising when someone who fits this profile eludes detection for extended periods, as serial killers do. However, people often dismiss "red flags," such as stealing, since the individual with ASPD uses manipulation and gaslighting to validate their actions. In order to convince others of their innocence, they use charm and jargon to appear blameless (APA, 2022).

Psychopathy

While not formal mental disorders listed in the *DSM-5-TR* (APA, 2022), psychopathic traits are directly tied to serial killers' maladaptive and deceitful behaviors. Psychopathy includes personality traits and behaviors associated with violence (Pieperhoff et al., 2025). Incepted in 1941 to describe dangerous yet charming clients, the term psychopathy was used to distinguish these individuals and aid in treatment to mitigate their negative impact on society (Kay & Arrow, 2022). Psychopaths exhibit criminal behavior, such as preying on or using others for their benefit and demonstrating severe antagonism (Pieperhoff et al., 2025). They are capable of feigning concern for others for personal gain (Bhambhani et al., 2021).

One of the most common ways to measure psychopathic traits in individuals is with the Psychopathy Checklist–Revised (Hare et al., 1990). Questions aim to assess psychopathic traits such as low frustration tolerance, pathological lying, a short temper, drug or alcohol use, and failure to take responsibility for own actions, along with others (Hare et al., 1990). Psychopaths' inordinate levels of anger and impatience lead them to engage in behaviors that are socially unacceptable, including physical fights, and these acts result in a preponderance of brushes with the law (Jewel & Raypole, 2024; Myers et al., 2009). In fact, this is the case for many of the serial killers discussed in this book. Their rap sheets are long, though there are always anomalies who can commit crimes without detection or who refrain from criminal activity until they reach a threshold, and then there is no going back. Many of these traits align with antisocial personality disorder, as noted above.

Sociopathy

Though sociopathy is similar in symptomology to psychopathy, including comparable behaviors and thought patterns, it is distinct in several ways. Psychopathy is thought to be more genetically determined than sociopathy, which is more so the result of childhood abuse. A sociopath's personality traits are even more closely affiliated with antisocial personality disorder than psychopathic traits. In fact, ASPD used to be called sociopathy. Indeed, a person who is a sociopath disregards rules, manipulates others, is impulsive, aggressive, and lacks empathy (Bhambhani et al., 2021). These behaviors result in unstable and/or abusive relationships, loss of jobs due to inability to conform to schedules as needed by society, and anger outbursts. Unlike psychopaths, sociopaths are unable to mask their aggression and lack of empathy. Furthermore, sociopathy usually stems from childhood trauma (Bhambhani et al., 2021). Many sociopaths were raised in violent homes where they were forced to care for themselves at a young age (Jewel & Raypole, 2024). Their tumultuous childhood results in a negative trajectory toward violence and emotional lability, leading them to objectify and depersonalize their victims for their personal gain.

Antisocial Personality Disorder Symptoms

Antisocial Personality Disorder, Diagnostic Criteria, F60.2[1]

A. A pervasive pattern of disregard for and violation of the rights of others, occurring since age 15 years, as indicated by three (or more) of the following:
   1. Failure to conform to social norms with respect to lawful behaviors, as indicated by repeatedly performing acts that are grounds for arrest.
   2. Deceitfulness, as indicated by repeated lying, use of aliases, or conning others for personal profit or pleasure.
   3. Impulsivity or failure to plan ahead.
   4. Irritability and aggressiveness, as indicated by repeated physical fights or assaults.
   5. Reckless disregard for safety of self or others.
   6. Consistent irresponsibility, as indicated by repeated failure to sustain consistent work behavior or honor financial obligations.
   7. Lack of remorse, as indicated by being indifferent to or rationalizing having hurt, mistreated, or stolen from another.

B. The individual is at least age 18 years.

C. There is evidence of conduct disorder with onset before age 15 years.

D. The occurrence of antisocial behavior is not exclusively during the course of schizophrenia or bipolar disorder.

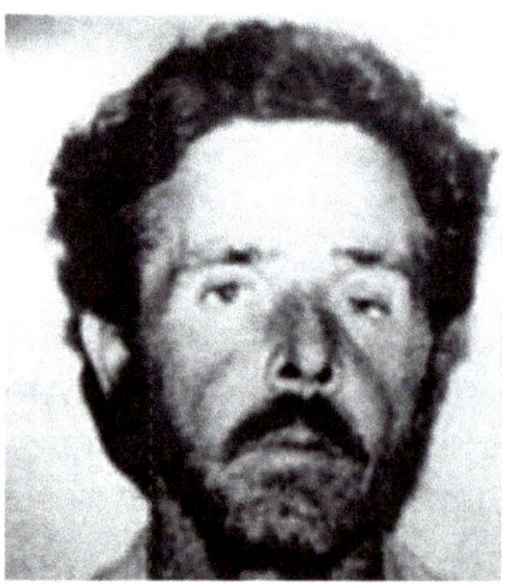

Figure 3.5 Henry Lee Lucas Mugshot, 1983

Henry Lee Lucas

Not only can parental mental illness, stress, and trauma genetically predispose a child to hostility, but that coupled with abuse at the hands of those very parents results in a child that is angry at the world. Such was the case for Henry Lee Lucas, who was born in 1936 in Virginia. He explained that his mother dressed him like a girl and treated him like a dog, beating and neglecting him (Raine, 2013; Reid et al., 2019). The abuse was predominantly perpetuated by his mother. Lucas's mother berated her husband and believed her son's only purpose was as a workhorse to do her bidding while she had sex with other men for money in front of both of them (Reid et al., 2019). His legs amputated following an accident, Lucas's father was a wheelchair-bound alcoholic with little will to live. Lucas lacked supervision and attention to nutrition or education during his childhood. In fact, he would go through neighbors' trash cans for sustenance (Raine, 2013). This level of severe neglect may have been responsible for his low average IQ of 89 (Gudjonsson, 1999).

Between the stench of trash and the lack of proper hygiene, Lucas was bullied relentlessly by peers. Between his brother accidentally stabbing him in the face and a teacher also inadvertently slapping him, Lucas became blind in his left eye (Raine, 2013). His childhood set the

1. Reprinted with permission from the Diagnostic and Statistical Manual of Mental Disorders, Fifth Edition, Text Revision

stage for the rest of his life, during which he consistently lacked regard for others, failed to plan, and was irresponsible. That attitude toward life, coupled with low self-esteem and inappropriate sexual fantasies, led Lucas to seek the company of dead animals and sex workers (Biography.com, 2021). When that didn't fill the void caused by his belligerent mother, he murdered her. Using manipulation and superficial charm to convince a parole board of his reformation, he was paroled, only to kill two more women, a male lover, and his landlord (Raine, 2013). When authorities questioned him about the missing landlord in 1983, they were able to arrest him due to a warrant for unlawful possession of a firearm (Gudjonsson, 1999). Once incarcerated and without a care in the world, Lucas confessed and inflated the number of victims he reportedly killed when interrogated by police. He had already gotten caught, so he might as well embellish a little ... or a lot. Lying wasn't difficult for him, especially when it afforded him notoriety. Lucas was convicted of murdering 11 people, not the 600-plus he claimed (Gudjonsson, 1999). His life ended of natural causes in prison in 2001.

Discussion question: Is it possible for children with CD to learn and utilize appropriate behaviors to reduce the likelihood of being diagnosed with ASPD once they turn 18?

Narcissistic Personality Disorder

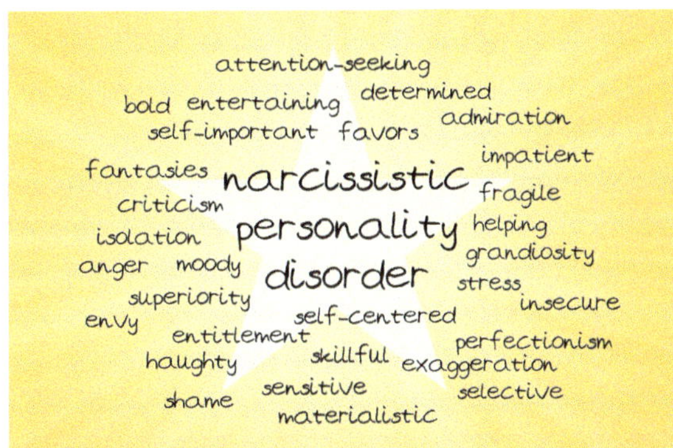

Figure 3.6 Narcissistic Personality Disorder Traits

Looking into the mirror to make sure his outfit was just right before leaving his apartment for our counseling appointment is exactly how I imagine one former client behaving prior to any outing. He noted that he wanted to look nice for our sessions and commented on my office décor, which consisted of the old bricks at a university counseling center. The superficial charm was over the top. The real kicker was his fantasy of becoming an emergency room doctor who rushed into the patient's room and saved the day. This overinflated sense of importance is a hallmark of **narcissistic personality disorder** (**NPD**; APA, 2022). He wanted to play God, just like Dennis Rader. People with this diagnosis use others as pawns, as objects only wanted to do their bidding. They lack real connections with others and will only associate with others of their perceived high status. Further, they brag about minor accomplishments (APA, 2022). When they perceive that they are undervalued or not appreciated for being remarkable, they become angry and hostile. Ironically, underneath the veneer of superiority is an insecure individual who feels the need to overcompensate for their inadequacies; this is why they react so strongly to an insult or affront (APA, 2022).

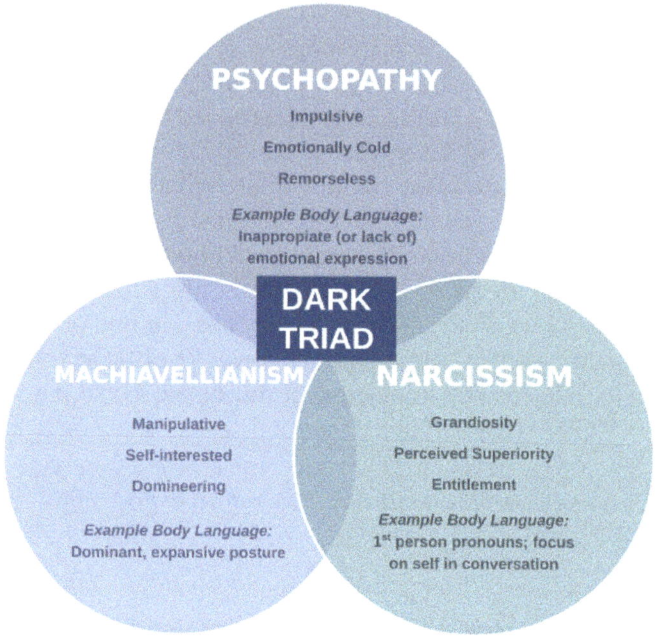

Figure 3.7 The Dark Triad—Psychopathy, Narcissism, and Machiavellianism

Machiavellianism

While many Machiavellianism traits overlap with narcissism and psychopathy, there are some distinctions. "Machiavellianism and psychopathy both consist of callousness, manipulation, arrogance, and distrust. However, while psychopathy also includes aspects of rashness, impersistence, and impulsivity, Machiavellianism includes aspects of order, achievement orientation, and competence" (Kay & Arrow, 2022, p. 7). Thus, Machiavellianism has many traits in common with narcissistic personality disorder. Certainly, a serial killer could be diagnosed with all of the above. Indeed, the overlapping traits include cunning and manipulation to achieve a goal (Kay & Arrow, 2022). The term derived from a diplomat named Niccolo Machiavelli, who lived in the late 1400s and early 1500s and was tasked with advising the rulers in Italy. His approach lacked compassion and scruples (Kay & Arrow, 2022). What it did include was meticulousness and conscientiousness, which is what made him an effective strategist.

Narcissistic Personality Disorder

Narcissistic Personality Disorder, Diagnostic Criteria, F60.81[2]

A pervasive pattern of grandiosity (in fantasy or behavior), need for admiration, and lack of empathy, beginning by early adulthood and present in a variety of contexts, as indicated by five (or more) of the following:

1. Has a grandiose sense of self-importance (e.g., exaggerates achievements and tal-

2. Reprinted with permission from the Diagnostic and Statistical Manual of Mental Disorders, Fifth Edition, Text Revision (Copyright © 2022). American Psychiatric Association. All Rights Reserved.

ents, expects to be recognized as superior without commensurate achievements).

2. Is preoccupied with fantasies of unlimited success, power, brilliance, beauty, or ideal love.
3. Believes that he or she is "special" and unique and can only be understood by, or should associate with, other special or high-status people (or institutions).
4. Requires excessive admiration.
5. Has a sense of entitlement (i.e., unreasonable expectations of especially favorable treatment or automatic compliance with his or her expectations).
6. Is interpersonally exploitative (i.e., takes advantage of others to achieve his or her own ends).
7. Lacks empathy: is unwilling to recognize or identify with the feelings and needs of others.
8. Is often envious of others or believes that others are envious of him or her.
9. Shows arrogant, haughty behaviors or attitudes.

Dennis Rader

Figure 3.8 Dennis Rader Yearbook Picture, 1963

All it takes is one minute of watching Dennis Rader's court confession (see QR code below), in which he coldheartedly provides details of his crimes, to see he's a narcissist. The glib and arrogant manner in which he recounts his actions is shocking. He has zero regard for the life of anyone but himself. Outwardly, a family man raising two children in Wichita, Kansas, he seemed like a pillar of the community. He had steady employment, was a Boy Scout leader, head of his church's congregation, and, all too ironically, was part of the neighborhood watch, placing him in the category of an organized and "successful psychopath" (Gao & Raine, 2010; Ramsland, 2006). His ability to feign the lifestyle of an admirable man to his family, coworkers, and neighbors, while tying, strangling, and masturbating over the dead body of his latest victim, is appalling. In fact, his first victims were neighbors who he and his children waved to as they rode their bikes down the street (Ramsland, 2006). Rader's target was the mother, but after breaking in to kill her, other family members returned to the house, so he made sure there were no witnesses and murdered the entire family. Moreover, working as an employee for a security system company provided him with the perfect cover, which he used to choose his next "project," as he called them (Ramsland, 2016). After actualizing his fantasy during his first murders, his appetite grew stronger and drove him to stalk, strangle, and masturbate over the bodies of 10 innocent people in total.

Figure 3.9 Picture BTK Mailed to Police to Taunt Them

Demonstrating additional narcissistic traits, Rader taunted police with letters, giving himself his own nickname—Bind, Torture, Kill (BTK). Within these letters were several drawings, presumably of victims that he bound and gagged (see Figure 3.9). The significance of these images is that they show the victims bound in barns, which gave law enforcement clues about the location of some of the murders. Police used the pictures to solicit the assistance of the public in locating additional victims. His narcissistic anger was blatantly evident in these communications with police. In fact, Rader told them that they hadn't given him enough air time in the media (Ramsland, 2016). The letters to the media ceased in 1979 and he assumedly stopped killing in 1991. Perhaps he shifted his focus to his wife and two young children. Then, in 2005, a journalist revived the case with an article noting years of silence from BTK. Rader's ego couldn't stand the thought of just letting it go, so he wrote a note to the police and included a computer disk that was eventually traced back to him through his church (Ramsland, 2006). His need for acknowledgement led to his demise. Arrested and convicted of serial murder in 2005, he was sentenced to 10 consecutive life terms (Ramsland, 2016).

Video of Dennis Rader's court confession:

QR Code 3.1

Find out more about Dennis Rader and his impact on his family in his daughter's book.

QR Code 3.2

Discussion question: What can we learn about serial killers from their correspondence with police or the media?

Borderline Personality Disorder

While men are more often diagnosed with ASPD and NPD, women are more commonly diagnosed with **borderline personality disorder (BPD)**. As with all personality disorders, BPD is pervasive and long-standing (APA, 2022). Usually due to a lack of parental figures and adequate attachments in childhood, individuals with BPD have difficulty maintaining stable relationships (APA, 2022). Their actions are often impulsive and unexpected. To add insult to injury, traumatic events exacerbate the deep feelings of abandonment. As their family member or friend, you feel like you're on an emotional roller coaster. One minute your connection and communications are stable and cordial, and the next minute something you said triggered them. They feel unjustly slighted and are livid. This is because they view the world as unsafe and they unconsciously feel like they must be on the defense to maintain homeostasis. In bids to keep people from leaving, individuals with BPD will often attempt suicide (APA, 2022). It is conceivable that they have sincere intent to die, but often these attempts are bids for validation so those around them will not leave. Unsurprisingly, research has shown numerous common traits between BPD and psychopathy (Ramsland, 2016).

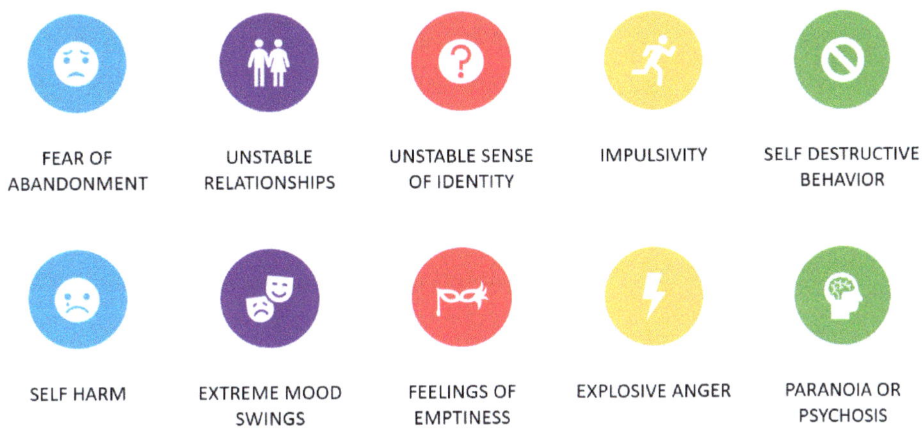

Figure 3.10 Signs of Borderline Personality Disorder

Borderline Personality Disorder Diagnostic Criteria

Borderline personality disorder affects how you feel about yourself, relate to others and behave.

Symptoms may include:

- A strong fear of abandonment. This includes going to extreme measures so you're not separated or rejected, even if these fears are made up.
- A pattern of unstable, intense relationships, such as believing someone is perfect one moment and then suddenly believing the person doesn't care enough or is cruel.
- Quick changes in how you see yourself. This includes shifting goals and values, as well as seeing yourself as bad or as if you don't exist.
- Periods of stress-related paranoia and loss of contact with reality. These periods can last from a few minutes to a few hours.

- Impulsive and risky behavior, such as gambling, dangerous driving, unsafe sex, spending sprees, binge eating, drug misuse, or sabotaging success by suddenly quitting a good job or ending a positive relationship.
- Threats of suicide or self-injury, often in response to fears of separation or rejection.
- Wide mood swings that last from a few hours to a few days. These mood swings can include periods of being very happy, irritable or anxious, or feeling shame.
- Ongoing feelings of emptiness.
- Inappropriate, strong anger, such as losing your temper often, being sarcastic or bitter, or physically fighting.

(Mayo Clinic Staff, 2024, para. 5)

Aileen Wuornos

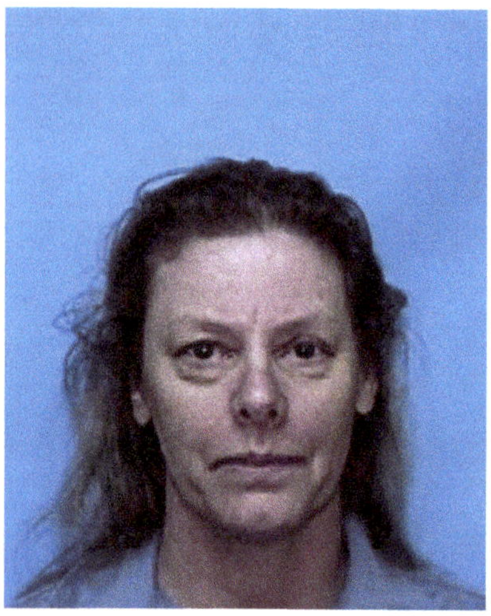

Figure 3.11 Aileen Wuornos, 2002

A well-known serial killer diagnosed with BPD is Aileen Wuornos, whose childhood was rampant with neglect (Ramsland, 2006). Born in 1956 in Michigan, she was abandoned by her mother and her father committed suicide in prison. He had been convicted of rape and kidnapping (Ramsland, 2006). Sent to her grandparents, she was soon raped by her grandfather's friend when she was only 14 years old (Arrigo & Griffin, 2004; Ramsland, 2006). Wuornos was blamed for the incident and was kicked out of their house. Wuornos likely felt angry, unwanted, and alone. She attempted suicide multiple times just like several of her family members, though they were "successful" in their attempts (Arrigo & Griffin, 2004). The sexual and emotional abuse she endured as a child resulted in her inability to maintain stable emotions. Lacking secure attachments to caregivers during her formative years, she missed out on learning the fundamental dynamics of both friendships and romantic relationships. This led her to "love to hate and hate to love" people.

Lacking skills or education, she sold her body to survive. Wuornos had difficulty sustaining stable relationships and accepted love when it was given. She met a woman in a bar while drinking away her loneliness, and they were in a relationship for several years (Ramsland, 2006). During this time, they stole to make ends meet. As a sex worker in Florida, she realized a way to make even more money—kill and rob the "john." Once she killed her first victim, there was no stopping her from murdering six more. This afforded her and her girlfriend the life they had always dreamed of, until her girlfriend became increasingly suspicious of Wuornos's activities and left the relationship, only returning to wear a wiretap to solidify a confession for police (Ramsland, 2006). Police had seen Wuornos in the vehicle of her latest victim. Throughout her incarceration and prior to her execution, Wuornos flip-flopped about her motive to kill (Arrigo & Griffin, 2004). She said the men raped her and so she killed them in self-defense. She later recanted her story and admitted to killing them for financial gain. Life had been cruel and uncaring toward Wuornos, and she would enact the same fate onto the men who solicited her for sex. After being found guilty of serial killing, she was executed via lethal injection in 2002 (Arrigo & Griffin, 2004).

Schizophrenia

While BPD seems to be largely due to nature, research has discovered that **schizophrenia** is passed down through genetics (APA, 2022). Symptoms usually emerge in the early to mid 20s for males and late 20s for females (APA, 2022). The final region of the brain to form is the frontal lobe, which is responsible for emotional regulation and executive functioning, hence the initial presentation of symptoms at this formative time (Raine, 2013). It is this very area where a lack of proper development results in symptoms of schizophrenia. Diagnosis can prove difficult at times, given the flat affect and inappropriate social responses that are hallmarks of several mental disorders, including schizophrenia, ASPD, and autism spectrum disorder (Morana et al., 2006).

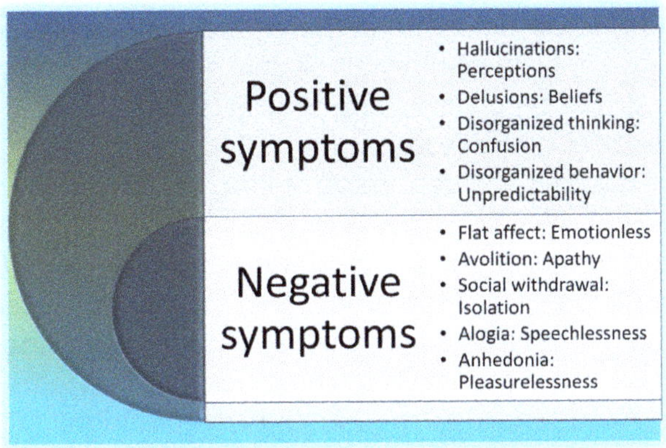

Figure 3.12 Positive and Negative Symptoms of Schizophrenia

Importantly, while people with schizophrenia are more likely to be victims of violence, research has established a strong relationship between murder and schizophrenia. One study discovered that people diagnosed with schizophrenia are six to ten times (for males) and eight to ten times (for females) more likely to be violent and homicidal (Richard-Devantoy et al., 2009). Another study found that males diagnosed with schizophrenia were three times more likely to kill than males without the diagnosis; similarly, females diagnosed with schizophrenia were 22 times more likely to be homicidal (Raine, 2013). Clearly, having schizophrenia may exacerbate violent tendencies, as was the case for Richard Chase.

Schizophrenia

Schizophrenia, Diagnostic Criteria, F20.9[3]

A. Two (or more) of the following, each present for a significant portion of time during a 1-month period (or less if successfully treated). At least one of these must be (1), (2), or (3):
   1. Delusions.

3. Reprinted with permission from the Diagnostic and Statistical Manual of Mental Disorders, Fifth Edition, Text Revision (Copyright © 2022). American Psychiatric Association. All Rights Reserved.

2. Hallucinations.
3. Disorganized speech (e.g., frequent derailment or incoherence).
4. Grossly disorganized or catatonic behavior.
5. Negative symptoms (i.e., diminished emotional expression or avolition).

B. For a significant portion of the time since the onset of the disturbance, level of functioning in one or more major areas, such as work, interpersonal relations, or self-care, is markedly below the level achieved prior to the onset (or when the onset is in childhood or adolescence, there is failure to achieve expected level of interpersonal, academic, or occupational functioning).
C. Continuous signs of the disturbance persist for at least 6 months. This 6-month period must include at least 1 month of symptoms (or less if successfully treated) that meet Criterion A (i.e., active-phase symptoms) and may include periods of prodromal or residual symptoms. During these prodromal or residual periods, the signs of the disturbance may be manifested by only negative symptoms or by two or more symptoms listed in Criterion A present in an attenuated form (e.g., odd beliefs, unusual perceptual experiences).
D. Schizoaffective disorder and depressive or bipolar disorder with psychotic features have been ruled out because either 1) no major depressive or manic episodes have occurred concurrently with the active-phase symptoms, or 2) if mood episodes have occurred during active-phase symptoms, they have been present for a minority of the total duration of the active and residual periods of the illness.
E. The disturbance is not attributable to the physiological effects of a substance (e.g., a drug of abuse, a medication) or another medical condition.
F. If there is a history of autism spectrum disorder or a communication disorder of childhood onset, the additional diagnosis of schizophrenia is made only if prominent delusions or hallucinations, in addition to the other required symptoms of schizophrenia, are also present for at least 1 month (or less if successfully treated).

Specify if:

The following course specifiers are only to be used after a 1-year duration of the disorder and if they are not in contradiction to the diagnostic course criteria.

First episode, currently in acute episode: First manifestation of the disorder meeting the defining diagnostic symptom and time criteria. An acute episode is a time period in which the symptom criteria are fulfilled.

First episode, currently in partial remission: Partial remission is a period of time during which an improvement after a previous episode is maintained and in which the defining criteria of the disorder are only partially fulfilled.

First episode, currently in full remission: Full remission is a period of time after a previous episode during which no disorder-specific symptoms are present.

Multiple episodes, currently in acute episode: Multiple episodes may be determined after a minimum of two episodes (i.e., after a first episode, a remission and a minimum of one relapse).

Multiple episodes, currently in partial remission

Multiple episodes, currently in full remission

Continuous: Symptoms fulfilling the diagnostic symptom criteria of the disorder are remaining for the majority of the illness course, with subthreshold symptom periods being very brief relative to the overall course.

Unspecified

Specify if:

With catatonia (refer to the criteria for catatonia associated with another mental disorder, p. 135, for definition).

Coding note: Use additional code F06.1 catatonia associated with schizophrenia to indicate the presence of the comorbid catatonia.

Specify current severity:

Severity is rated by a quantitative assessment of the primary symptoms of psychosis, including delusions, hallucinations, disorganized speech, abnormal psychomotor behavior, and negative symptoms. Each of these symptoms may be rated for its current severity (most severe in the last 7 days) on a 5-point scale ranging from 0 (not present) to 4 (present and severe). (See Clinician-Rated Dimensions of Psychosis Symptom Severity in the chapter "Assessment Measures.")

Note: Diagnosis of schizophrenia can be made without using this severity specifier.

Richard Chase

Richard Chase was born in 1950 in Santa Clara, California, to an abusive father (Fouche et al., 2015). He started drinking alcohol in his teens, and began reporting delusions in his early 20s (Ramsland, 2006). Classmates remember him as being odd and often smelling bad (Fouche et al., 2015). Institutionalized numerous times due to his bizarre behavior, he was eventually diagnosed with paranoid schizophrenia (Ramsland, 2006). In fact, Chase told investigators that the Nazis were after him because of the Star of David that was etched into his forehead; there was no Star of David on his forehead or anywhere else on his body (Federal Bureau of Investigation [FBI], 1979). Further, Chase felt there was a connection between the Nazis and unidentified flying objects (UFOs). He believed that messages from UFOs told him to kill and drink blood. Additional paranoid ideation resulted in his concern about being poisoned by UFOs. He felt that he had to drink blood and inject the blood of animals and humans to evade detection by extraterrestrial beings (Fouche et al., 2015).

An excerpt from a document Richard wrote to Congress in 1979 from San Quentin jail illustrates his unusual thoughts (FBI, 1979)[4]:

> They have found it is possible to discourage people trying to help me with the UFO death ray. In sur I need to see Federal Government Agents so that this racket fall into legal hands, before I am systematically executed or held for life by bribes from them. The DA's referred more than one to a UFO death ray and even threatened one of my Doctors if he did not restate his presumption that I was insane. Another of my Doctors who had stated that I was under the Law not aware of right from wrong because of physical damage from what he apparently knew was true by introspection only. The same attitude was given to all the psychiatric and physical diagnoses. Their was apparent a great doubt to my charac-

4. Richard Chase/Federal Bureau of Investigation, Selection from "Letter to Congress," U.S. Department of Justice, 1979.

ter because I had practiced cannibalism as I knew they had done to women of my race in Sacramento. The officers who first controlled me at Sacto. and made the first million dollars from the nazi underground in sacto were [...] and Sgt. [...]. I can go into more detail and explanation if you will please send the necessary officials and documents so that I may be moved to a Federally controlled situation and prove that all facts and statements contained herein are true. A trial without the Sacramento following gathered at the trial who are the cause of the problems involved, especially Sacto. media. A federal court is suggested because of their coverage is abnormal, unnecessary and phony from the 'stance of their being a family dedicated and directly related by media to the happenstance and coverup of the UFO interruption. The case is enormous circulation in the papers, even sold in US and Canada; if possible these people will give up to a pressure that is to large and tell the truth behind the story of indoctrination of me, and its relationship to all circumstances involved. A list of suppressed material and documentary systems is enclosed and is available to me through a Federal Court.

THANK YOU
RICHARD CHASE

After killing and drinking the blood of countless animals and six human victims, Richard was finally apprehended and tried for murder in 1979. The last four victims, a family, the killing of which would be considered mass murder separate from the other two people he killed on separate occasions, resulted in his capture when he fled their home in their car. After his conviction, he only lasted two years in prison before committing suicide by overdosing on antidepressants (Fouche et al., 2015).

Figure 3.13 Happy and Sad Masks

Bipolar Disorder

Comprising mania (bipolar I disorder) or hypomania (bipolar II disorder) and major depressive symptoms, **bipolar disorder** is characterized by phases of intense energy, grandiosity, and lack of need for sleep, offset by feelings of worthlessness, anhedonia, and sadness (APA, 2022). Anger can be expressed in both phases (mania and depression). While therapy and medication can help reduce symptom severity, the caveat is that people tend to enjoy the manic/hypomanic phases, so medication compliance becomes an issue. They feel amazing and are extremely productive, needing less sleep than usual (APA, 2022). There are also baseline periods where the individual feels neither manic/hypomanic nor depressed. A serial killer diagnosed with bipolar disorder is most likely going to kill during the manic/hypomanic phase; he won't have the energy or mental faculties to do so during depressive phases, though he certainly could stalk during baseline phases. The fantasies are likely developing during the major depressive episodes when the serial killer thinks about how much the world has wronged them. Given the more extreme emotional, cognitive, and behavioral symptoms expression inherent in a bipolar I disorder diagnosis, as opposed to the milder symptoms of bipolar II disorder, only the diagnostic criteria for bipolar I disorder will be included here, since the symptom expression aligns more closely with serial killers' behavior.

Figure 3.14 Bipolar Disorder Symptoms

Bipolar I Disorder

Diagnostic Criteria[5]

For a diagnosis of bipolar I disorder, it is necessary to meet the following criteria for a manic episode. The manic episode may have been preceded by and may be followed by hypomanic or major depressive episodes.

Manic Episode

A. A distinct period of abnormally and persistently elevated, expansive, or irritable

5. Reprinted with permission from the Diagnostic and Statistical Manual of Mental Disorders, Fifth Edition, Text Revision (Copyright © 2022). American Psychiatric Association. All Rights Reserved.

mood and abnormally and persistently increased activity or energy, lasting at least 1 week and present most of the day, nearly every day (or any duration if hospitalization is necessary).

B. During the period of mood disturbance and increased energy or activity, three (or more) of the following symptoms (four if the mood is only irritable) are present to a significant degree and represent a noticeable change from usual behavior:
   1. Inflated self-esteem or grandiosity.
   2. Decreased need for sleep (e.g., feels rested after only 3 hours of sleep).
   3. More talkative than usual or pressure to keep talking.
   4. Flight of ideas or subjective experience that thoughts are racing.
   5. Distractibility (i.e., attention too easily drawn to unimportant or irrelevant external stimuli), as reported or observed.
   6. Increase in goal-directed activity (either socially, at work or school, or sexually) or psychomotor agitation (i.e., purposeless non-goal-directed activity).
   7. Excessive involvement in activities that have a high potential for painful consequences (e.g., engaging in unrestrained buying sprees, sexual indiscretions, or foolish business investments).

C. The mood disturbance is sufficiently severe to cause marked impairment in social or occupational functioning or to necessitate hospitalization to prevent harm to self or others, or there are psychotic features.

D. The episode is not attributable to the physiological effects of a substance (e.g., a drug of abuse, a medication, other treatment) or another medical condition. **Note:** A full manic episode that emerges during antidepressant treatment (e.g., medication, electroconvulsive therapy) but persists at a fully syndromal level beyond the physiological effect of that treatment is sufficient evidence for a manic episode and, therefore, a bipolar I diagnosis.

Note: Criteria A–D constitute a manic episode. At least one lifetime manic episode is required for the diagnosis of bipolar I disorder.

Hypomanic Episode

A. A distinct period of abnormally and persistently elevated, expansive, or irritable mood and abnormally and persistently increased activity or energy, lasting at least 4 consecutive days and present most of the day, nearly every day.

B. During the period of mood disturbance and increased energy and activity, three (or more) of the following symptoms (four if the mood is only irritable) have persisted, represent a noticeable change from usual behavior, and have been present to a significant degree:
   1. Inflated self-esteem or grandiosity.
   2. Decreased need for sleep (e.g., feels rested after only 3 hours of sleep).
   3. More talkative than usual or pressure to keep talking.
   4. Flight of ideas or subjective experience that thoughts are racing.
   5. Distractibility (i.e., attention too easily drawn to unimportant or irrelevant external stimuli), as reported or observed.

6. Increase in goal-directed activity (either socially, at work or school, or sexually) or psychomotor agitation.
7. Excessive involvement in activities that have a high potential for painful consequences (e.g., engaging in unrestrained buying sprees, sexual indiscretions, or foolish business investments).

C. The episode is associated with an unequivocal change in functioning that is uncharacteristic of the individual when not symptomatic.
D. The disturbance in mood and the change in functioning are observable by others.
E. The episode is not severe enough to cause marked impairment in social or occupational functioning or to necessitate hospitalization. If there are psychotic features, the episode is, by definition, manic.
F. The episode is not attributable to the physiological effects of a substance (e.g., a drug of abuse, a medication, other treatment) or another medical condition. **Note:** A full hypomanic episode that emerges during antidepressant treatment (e.g., medication, electroconvulsive therapy) but persists at a fully syndromal level beyond the physiological effect of that treatment is sufficient evidence for a hypomanic episode diagnosis. However, caution is indicated so that one or two symptoms (particularly increased irritability, edginess, or agitation following antidepressant use) are not taken as sufficient for diagnosis of a hypomanic episode, nor necessarily indicative of a bipolar diathesis.

Note: Criteria A–F constitute a hypomanic episode. Hypomanic episodes are common in bipolar I disorder but are not required for the diagnosis of bipolar I disorder.

Major Depressive Episode

A. Five (or more) of the following symptoms have been present during the same 2-week period and represent a change from previous functioning; at least one of the symptoms is either (1) depressed mood or (2) loss of interest or pleasure.
Note: Do not include symptoms that are clearly attributable to another medical condition.
    1. Depressed mood most of the day, nearly every day, as indicated by either subjective report (e.g., feels sad, empty, or hopeless) or observation made by others (e.g., appears tearful).
    (**Note**: In children and adolescents, can be irritable mood.)
    2. Markedly diminished interest or pleasure in all, or almost all, activities most of the day, nearly every day (as indicated by either subjective account or observation).
    3. Significant weight loss when not dieting or weight gain (e.g., a change of more than 5% of body weight in a month), or decrease or increase in appetite nearly every day. (**Note**: In children, consider failure to make expected weight gain.)
    4. Insomnia or hypersomnia nearly every day.
    5. Psychomotor agitation or retardation nearly every day (observable by others, not merely subjective feelings of restlessness or being slowed down).

6. Fatigue or loss of energy nearly every day.
7. Feelings of worthlessness or excessive or inappropriate guilt (which may be delusional) nearly every day (not merely self-reproach or guilt about being sick).
8. Diminished ability to think or concentrate, or indecisiveness, nearly every day (either by subjective account or as observed by others).
9. Recurrent thoughts of death (not just fear of dying); recurrent suicidal ideation without a specific plan; a specific suicide plan; or a suicide attempt.

B. The symptoms cause clinically significant distress or impairment in social, occupational, or other important areas of functioning.
C. The episode is not attributable to the physiological effects of a substance or another medical condition.

Note: Criteria A–C constitute a major depressive episode. Major depressive episodes are common in bipolar I disorder but are not required for the diagnosis of bipolar I disorder.

Note: Responses to a significant loss (e.g., bereavement, financial ruin, losses from a natural disaster, a serious medical illness or disability) may include the feelings of intense sadness, rumination about the loss, insomnia, poor appetite, and weight loss noted in Criterion A, which may resemble a depressive episode. Although such symptoms may be understandable or considered appropriate to the loss, the presence of a major depressive episode in addition to the normal response to a significant loss should also be carefully considered. This decision inevitably requires the exercise of clinical judgment based on the individual's history and the cultural norms for the expression of distress in the context of loss.

Bipolar I Disorder

A. Criteria have been met for at least one manic episode (Criteria A–D under "Manic Episode" above).
B. At least one manic episode is not better explained by schizoaffective disorder and is not superimposed on schizophrenia, schizophreniform disorder, delusional disorder, or other specified or unspecified schizophrenia spectrum and other psychotic disorder.

Coding and Recording Procedures

The diagnostic code for bipolar I disorder is based on type of current or most recent episode and its status with respect to current severity, presence of psychotic features, and remission status. Current severity and psychotic features are only indicated if full criteria are currently met for a manic or major depressive episode. Remission specifiers are only indicated if the full criteria are not currently met for a manic, hypomanic, or major depressive episode. Codes are as follows:

Bipolar I disorder	Current or most recent episode manic	Current or most recent episode hypomanic*	Current or most recent episode depressed	Current or most recent episode unspecified**
Mild (p. 175)	F31.11	NA	F31.31	NA
Moderate (p. 175)	F31.12	NA	F31.32	NA
Severe (p. 175)	F31.13	NA	F31.4	NA
With psychotic features*** (p. 173)	F31.2	NA	F31.5	NA
In partial remission (p. 175)	F31.73	F31.71	F31.75	NA
In full remission (p. 175)	F31.74	F31.72	F31.76	NA
Unspecified	F31.9	F31.9	F31.9	NA

**Severity and psychotic specifiers do not apply; code F31.0 for cases not in remission.*

***Severity, psychotic, and remission specifiers do not apply. Code F31.9.*

****If psychotic features are present, code the "with psychotic features" specifier irrespective of episode severity.*

In recording the name of a diagnosis, terms should be listed in the following order: bipolar I disorder, type of current episode (or most recent episode if bipolar I disorder is in partial or full remission), severity/psychotic/remission specifiers, followed by as many of the following specifiers without codes as apply to the current episode (or the most recent episode if bipolar I disorder is in partial or full remission). **Note:** The specifiers "with rapid cycling" and "with seasonal pattern" describe the pattern of mood episodes.

Specify if:

With anxious distress (pp. 169–170)
With mixed features (pp. 170–171)
With rapid cycling (p. 171)
With melancholic features (pp. 171–172)
With atypical features (pp. 172–173)
With mood-congruent psychotic features (p. 173; *applies to manic episode and/or major depressive episode*)
With mood-incongruent psychotic features (p. 173; *applies to manic episode and/or major depressive episode*)
With catatonia (p. 173). **Coding note:** Use additional code F06.1.

With peripartum onset (pp. 173–174)
With seasonal pattern (pp. 174–175)

Anthony Hardy

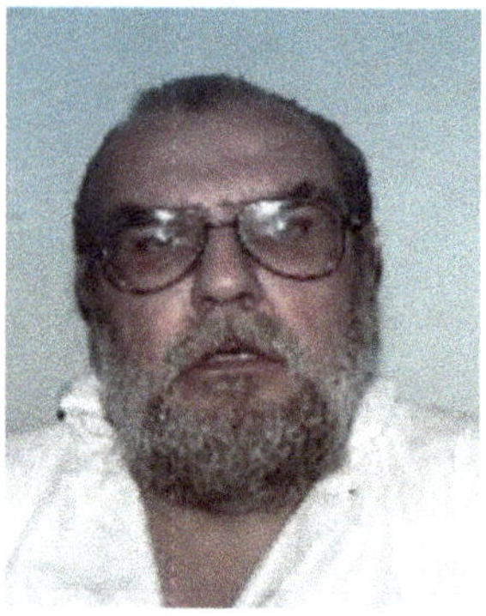

Figure 3.15 Anthony Hardy

Diagnosed with bipolar disorder, Anthony Hardy was an English serial killer who was active in the early 2000s. His crimes were brutal as he eviscerated and dismembered at least nine women who were sex workers, thus easy targets (Bell, n.d.). Full of energy from a manic episode, Hardy most likely killed during these periods. He would lure women to his apartment with offers of work only to strangle them to death (Bell, n.d.). Despite having a fairly normal childhood and excelling academically, Hardy struggled with mental health issues. He was in and out of psychiatric hospitals and was diagnosed with bipolar disorder and substance abuse disorder (Osley, 2023). Though he married and had four children, that relationship was tumultuous and ended with his wife leaving him; this only exacerbated his mental instability. Hardy became severely depressed as the dissolution of his marriage likely threw him into a major depressive episode.

Now on his own, Hardy rented a small flat and engaged in petty theft to make ends meet. Known as a derelict in this community, a neighbor called police to report vandalism and stated that Hardy was the likely culprit. When they entered his flat to question him about the incident, they discovered a dead woman (Osley, 2023). With the case wide open, authorities were able to connect him to other women whose bodies had been mutilated and dumped in the Thames River or in trash bins in an alley. Caught on CCTV returning to the trash bins to view his trophies, Hardy implicated himself by being associated with the crimes, validating his neighbor's concerns about his criminal activity (Bell, n.d.). The evidence against him mounted when police found lewd pictures of the deceased victims. Hardy was sentenced to life in prison and died from COVID in 2020 (Osley, 2023).

Sexual Sadism

Figure 3.16 Human Trafficking

A majority of serial killers fall into this category. While most sexually sadistic serial killers are male, a few are female. Often, the killer believes they require certain conditions to achieve sexual gratification. This may include having complete control and dominance over a nonconsenting victim (Morana et al., 2006; Ramsland, 2006). People with **sexual sadism** are sexually aroused when a victim is frightened, harmed, or even postmortem. This modus operandi usually starts in adolescence. In fact, research discovered that most serial killers under the age of 18 were sexual sadists (Garcia-Baamonde et al., 2022), though the low rates of child serial killers could simply be due to getting caught after one homicide

(Hickey, 2013). They exhibited predatory behaviors such as stalking rather than committing homicide due to self-defense or retaliation (Garcia-Baamonde et al., 2022). The fantasy of these acts has been mulled over for years, until the killer feels as though they can't hold it in any longer. Moreover, regardless of age, sexual sadists have a need to be up close and personal with their victims, preferring to strangle or stab rather than shoot to kill (Hickey, 2013). Part of their ritual may also include collecting trophies from their victims to touch them later and relive the sexual experience (Ramsland, 2006).

Sexual Sadism

Sexual Sadism Disorder, Diagnostic Criteria, F65.52[6]

A. Over a period of at least 6 months, recurrent and intense sexual arousal from the physical or psychological suffering of another person, as manifested by fantasies, urges, or behaviors.
B. The individual has acted on these sexual urges with a nonconsenting person, or the sexual urges or fantasies cause clinically significant distress or impairment in social, occupational, or other important areas of functioning.

Specify if:

In a controlled environment: This specifier is primarily applicable to individuals living in institutional or other settings where opportunities to engage in sadistic sexual behaviors are restricted.

In full remission: The individual has not acted on the urges with a nonconsenting person, and there has been no distress or impairment in social, occupational, or other areas of functioning, for at least 5 years while in an uncontrolled environment.

Video on sexual sadists:

QR Code 3.3

6. Reprinted with permission from the Diagnostic and Statistical Manual of Mental Disorders, Fifth Edition, Text Revision (Copyright © 2022). American Psychiatric Association. All Rights Reserved.

Andrei Chikatilo

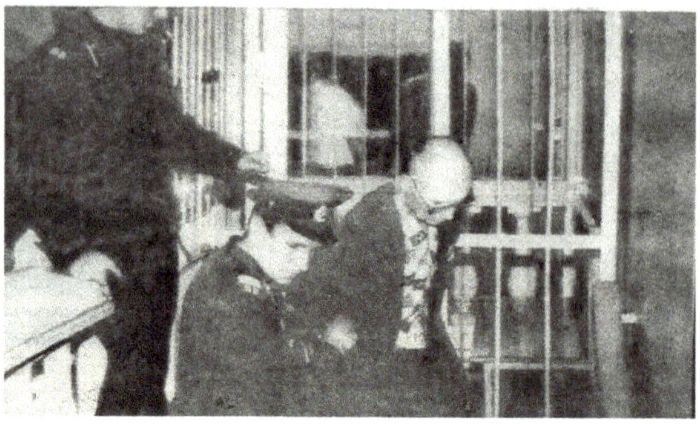

Figure 3.17 Andrei Chikatilo, Courtroom, 1992

Andrei Chikatilo was born in 1936 in Rostov, Russia (Garcia-Baamonde, et al., 1992). Bullied his whole life by his family, he was further insulted by his students when he was a teacher. Lacking any shred of confidence, he took the abuse and bottled it up. Despite graduating from a university, marrying, and fathering two children, he was always shy and insecure (Ramsland, 2006; Willmott et al., 2017). Chikatilo had difficulty performing as a husband, as a teacher, and sexually (Schechter, 2003). This may have stemmed from his first sexual encounter; when he was 17, he attempted to rape a young girl only to ejaculate immediately upon grabbing her (Garcia-Baamonde et al., 1992; Willmott et al., 2017). Impotence was a theme throughout his life. His rage arose later when he began to kidnap and stab children and women in the woods behind local train tracks. Citing sexual arousal as his motivation, Chikatilo noted that he experienced sexual gratification upon first cutting into his victim (Willmott et al., 2017). He managed to get away with murder a shocking 55 times over 12 years (Garcia-Baamonde et al., 1992).

He had been a suspect prior to his conviction, but since his blood type was different from other bodily fluids, which is exceedingly rare, he was removed from the suspect list (Biography.com, 2020). He was apprehended after walking out of the woods by the train station with blood on his hands in 1990, and his reign of terror on Rostov finally ended (Garcia-Baamonde et al., 1992). Deemed extremely dangerous by the judge, he was locked in a cage in the courtroom to protect everyone who attended his trial. While in the courtroom cage, he dropped his pants, showing everyone his genitals and stating that they were proof of his heterosexuality (Ramsland, 2006). He was executed in 1994 by a single bullet to the back of the head (Biography.com, 2020).

Summary

Mental illness is rampant and can affect anyone, regardless of gender, age, or race. When it is combined with a traumatic childhood, it can lead to antisocial behavior. The cases above illustrate the influence of mental disorders on behavior in the most macabre way. Mary Bell was severely abused and turned her rage onto other innocent children. Henry Lee Lucas was born into such abuse and neglect that his life seemed destined for destruction. Dennis Rader simply couldn't help himself and needed the notoriety that often comes with being a serial killer. Aileen Wuornos's family was rife with abuse and neglect. If only she'd had at least one appropriate caregiver, things may have turned out differently for all involved. Richard Chase couldn't escape the demons in his head, Anthony Hardy's mental disturbances paved the way for his life of crime, and Andrei Chikatilo's impotence ruined the lives of countless families. Understanding the mental disorders associated with these killers doesn't excuse their behavior, yet hopefully it provides a fraction of insight into the inner workings of their minds.

Keywords

Antisocial personality disorder (ASPD)

Bipolar disorder

Borderline personality disorder (BPD)

Conduct disorder (CD)

Narcissistic personality disorder (NPD)

Oppositional defiant disorder (ODD)

Schizophrenia

Sexual sadism

Chapter Review Questions

1. How might conduct disorder be a precursor to antisocial personality disorder?
2. Why might some disorders be more prevalent in males versus females?
3. What are some common links between mental illness and violent behavior?

References

American Psychiatric Association. (2022). *Diagnostic and statistical manual of mental disorders (5th ed., text revision).* https://doi.org/10.1176/appi.books.9780890425787

Arrigo, B. A., & Griffin, A. (2004). Serial murder and the case of Aileen Wuornos: Attachment theory, psychopathy, and predatory aggression. *Behavioral Sciences and the Law, 22*, 375–393.

Bell, R. (n.d.). *Anthony John Hardy, England's famous Camden Ripper.* Crime Library: Criminal Minds and Methods. https://www.crimelibrary.org/serial_killers/predators/anthony_hardy/5.html

Ben-Porath, Y. S., & Tellegen, A. (2020). *Minnesota Multiphasic Personality Inventory-3 (MMPI-3): Manual for administration, scoring, and interpretation*. University of Minnesota Press.

Bhambhani, L. P., Prakash, S., & Tripathi, M. A. (2021). Psychopathy and sociopathy: A modern understanding of antisocial personality disorder. *Indian Journal of Social Studies and Humanities, 1*(5), 17-23.

Biography.com. (2021, April 5). Henry Lee Lucas. https://www.biography.com/crime/henry-lee-lucas

Biography.com Editors. (2020, July 10). Andrei Chikatilo. http://www.biography.com/crime/andrei-chikatilo

Federal Bureau of Investigation (FBI). (1979). Richard Chase part 01. https://vault.fbi.gov/richard-chase/richard-chase-part-01

First, M. B., Spitzer, R. L., & Williams, J. B.W. (2015). *Structured clinical interview for DSM-5® personality disorders.* American Psychiatric Publishing.

Fouche, P., Nel, H., & Naidoo, P. (2015). The Dracula killer: A psychobiographical illustration of the Schahrair syndrome model for serial murder. *Journal of Psychology in Africa, 25*(5), 419–428.

Gao, Y., & Raine, A. (2010). Successful and unsuccessful psychopaths: A neurobiological model. *Behavioural Science and Law, 28*, 194-210.

Garcia-Baamonde, M. E., Blazquez-Alonso, M., Moreno-Manso, J. M., Guerrero-Barona, E., & Gray, M. (1992). Russia's ripper. *Maclean's, 105*(26), 38–40.

Garcia-Baamonde, M. E., Blazquez-Alonso, M., Moreno-Manso, J. M., Guerrero-Barona, E., & Guerrero-Molina, M. (2022). Youth serial killers: Psychological and criminal profiles. *International Journal of Environmental Research and Public Health, 19*(9), 5359.

Gudjonsson, G. (1999). The making of a serial false confessor: The confessions of Henry Lee Lucas. *Journal of Forensic Psychiatry, 10*(2), 416–427.

Hare, R. D., Harpur, T. J., Hakstian, A. R., Forth, A. E., & Hart, S. D. (1990). The revised psychopathy checklist: Reliability and factor structure. *Psychological Assessment, 2*(3), 338–341.

Hickey, E. W. (2013). *Serial murderers and their victims (7th ed.).* Wadsworth.

Jewel, T., & Raypole, C. (2024, February 8). *What it actually means to be a 'sociopath'.* Healthline. https://www.healthline.com/health/mental-health/sociopath

Kay, C. S., & Arrow, H. (2022). Taking an elemental approach to the conceptualization and measurement of Machiavellianism, narcissism, and psychopathy. *Social and Personality Psychology Compass, 16*(4),1–18.

Kolla, N. J., & Bortolato, M. (2020). The role of monoamine oxidase A in the neurobiology of aggressive, antisocial, and violent behavior: A tale of mice and men. *Progress in Neurobiology, 194,* 101875.

Luna, R. E. (2024). What are disruptive, impulse control and conduct disorders? *American Psychiatric Association.* https://www.psychiatry.org/patients-families/disruptive-impulse-control-and-conduct-disorders/what-are-disruptive-impulse-control-and-conduct

Mayo Clinic Staff. (2024). Borderline personality disorder. https://www.mayoclinic.org/diseases-conditions/borderline-personality-disorder/symptoms-causes/syc-20370237

Myers, W. C., Chan, H. C., Vo, E. J., & Lazarou, E. (2009). Sexual sadism, psychopathy, and recidivism in juvenile sexual murderers. *Journal of Investigative Psychology, 7*(2), 49-58.

Morana, H. C. P., Stone, M. H., & Abdalla-Filho, E. (2006). Personality disorders, psychopathy, and serial killers. *Brazilian Journal of Psychiatry, 28,* 74–79.

Osley, R. (2023, January 1). *20 years on from the 'Camden Ripper', nobody mentions the failure and freed serial killer to strike—now the case is pure clickbait. Camden New Journal.* https://www.camdennewjournal.co.uk/article/20-years-on-from-the-camden-ripper%E2%80%88nobody-mentions-the-failures-that-freed-serial-killer-to-strike-now-the-case-is-pure-clickbait

Pieperhoff, P., Hofhansel, L., Schneider, F., Muller, J., Amunts, K., Weber-Papen, S., Weidler, C., Clemens, B., Raine, A., & Habel, U. (2025). Associations of brain structure with psychopathy. *European Archives of Psychiatry and Clinical Neuroscience, 276*(1), 63-75.

Raine, A. (2013). *The anatomy of violence: The biological roots of crime.* Vintage.

Ramsland, K. (2006). *Inside the minds of serial killers: Why they kill.* Praeger.

Ramsland, K. (2016). *Confession of a serial killer: The untold story of Dennis Rader, the BTK killer.* University Press of New England.

Reid, S., Katan, A., Ellithy, A., Stua, R. D., & Denisov, E. V. (2019). The perfect storm: Mapping the life trajectories of serial killers. *International Journal of Offender Therapy and Comparative Criminology, 63*(9), 1621–1662.

Richard-Devantoy, S., Olie, J. P., & Gourevitch, R. (2009). Risk of homicide and major mental disorders: A critical review. *L'Encephale, 35*(6), 521–530.

Schechter, H. (2003). *The serial killer files: The who, what, where, how, and why of the world's most terrifying murders.* Ballantine Books.

Sereny, G. (1998). *Cries unheard: Why children kill: The story of Mary Bell.* Macmillan.

The Guardian. (1968). *Life detention for girl of 11.* https://www.theguardian.com/uk/1968/dec/18/ukcrime.childprotection

Viding, E., Blair, R. J. R., Moffitt, T. E., & Plomin, R. (2005). Evidence for substantial genetic risk for psychopathy in 7-year-olds. *Journal of Child Psychology and Psychiatry, 46*(6), 592–597.

Wechsler, D. (2008). *Wechsler Adult Intelligence Scale—Fourth Edition (WAIS-IV)* [Database record]. APA PsycTests. https://doi.org/10.1037/t15169-000

Willmott, D., Boduszek, D., & Robinson, R. (2017). A psychodynamic-behaviorist investigation of the Russian sexual serial killer Andrei Chikatilo. *The Journal of Forensic Psychiatry & Psychology, 29*(3), 498–507.

Image Credits

Fig. 3.1: Tahoe City Police Department, https://murderpedia.org/male.C/c/chase-richard.htm, 1978.

Fig. 3.2: Copyright © 2022 by R. J. R. Blair (CC BY-SA 4.0) at https://commons.wikimedia.org/wiki/File:Conduct_disorder_framework.png.

Fig. 3.3: Mary Flora Bell, https://www.youtube.com/watch?v=sxujUGSXdKM. Copyright © 1968 by Mary Flora Bell.

Fig. 3.4: Copyright © 2019 by MissLunaRose12 (CC BY-SA 4.0) at https://commons.wikimedia.org/wiki/File:Signs_of_AsPD_1.png.

Fig. 3.5: Rudigft, https://commons.wikimedia.org/wiki/File:Henry_Lee_Lucas.jpg, 2025.

Fig. 3.6: Copyright © by MissLunaRose12 (CC BY-SA 4.0) at https://commons.wikimedia.org/wiki/File:Word_Cloud_NPD.png.

Fig. 3.7: Copyright © by Melissa_Hogan (CC BY-SA 4.0) at https://commons.wikimedia.org/wiki/File:The_Dark_Triad_Traits.svg.

Fig. 3.8: Wichita Heights High School, https://commons.wikimedia.org/wiki/File:Dennis_Rader_1963.jpg, 1963.

Fig. 3.9: Dennis Rader/Osage County Sheriff's Office, https://www.cnn.com/2023/09/02/us/btk-drawings-serial-killer-investigation/index.html. Copyright © 2005 by Dennis Rader.

Fig. 3.10: Copyright © 2019 by MissLunaRose12 (CC BY-SA 4.0) at https://commons.wikimedia.org/wiki/File:Signs_of_BPD_1.png.

Fig. 3.11: Florida Department of Corrections, https://commons.wikimedia.org/wiki/File:Aileen_Wuornos.jpg, 2002.

Fig. 3.12: Copyright © 2023 by Sameem Arif (CC BY-SA 4.0) at https://commons.wikimedia.org/wiki/File:Schizophrenia_symptoms.png.

Fig. 3.13: Copyright © 2017 by Booyabazooka; adapted by The Anome (CC BY-SA 3.0) at https://commons.wikimedia.org/wiki/File:Comedy_and_tragedy_masks_without_background.svg.

Fig. 3.14: National Institute of Mental Health, https://www.nimh.nih.gov/sites/default/files/documents/health/publications/bipolar-disorder-in-children-and-teens/bipolar-disorder-in-teens-and-young-adults.pdf, National Institutes of Health, 2022.

Fig. 3.15: Screenshot from Cold Trace – True Crime Stories, "Catching The Camden Ripper | The Grisly Tale of Anthony Hardy," https://www.youtube.com/watch?v=d9FOXOKK5r8. Copyright © 2024 by Cold Trace – True Crime Stories.

Fig. 3.16: Copyright © 2022 Depositphotos/NewAfrica.

Fig. 3.17: Magazyn Kryminalny, Crime Magazine, https://commons.wikimedia.org/wiki/File:AndriejCzikatiloSad.png, 1993.

CHAPTER 4

THE BRAIN AND BEHAVIOR OF SERIAL KILLERS

A Neuropsychological Analysis

"I actually think I may be possessed with demons, I was dropped on my head as a kid."

Dennis Rader

This chapter will provide an overview of neuropsychology, with a focus on key brain structures involved in abnormal or psychopathic behavior, and how these influence the diathesis-stress model, or predisposition, toward becoming a serial killer. Indeed, the connections between genetics and the environment have been implicated in the neuropsychological routes of aggressive behavior (Kolla & Bortolato, 2020). Therefore, various regions of the brain work together to create the world we experience. When specific areas of the brain don't form correctly or are damaged, it influences the way individuals think and behave. Our increased knowledge of these interactions led psychologists to create the biological model of psychology (Raine, 2013). Such deficiencies or maladies in the brain can be caused by lack of nurturing as a child, inadequate nutrition, trauma, cysts, and cancer.

Figure 4.1 Dennis Rader, Airforce, 1966

One of the most well-known parts of the brain indicated in murderous behavior is the amygdala, as you will see below. Certainly, when several brain structures are deficient, including the concentration and flow of neurotransmitters, this can result in an inability to conform to society's ethical and moral standards. Indeed, when parts of the brain don't receive adequate blood, the neural connections die, leaving visible gaps in MRI and PET scans (Raine, 2013). Depending on the region of the brain in which this occurs, it impacts behavior specific to that area, such as executive functioning or the ability to make rational decisions based on available information. As such, the most common parts of the brain and neurotransmitters implicated in antisocial and psychopathic behavior will be explained.

Learning Outcomes

After reading this chapter, students will be able to do the following:

1. Understand how the brain affects behavior.
2. Connect brain function to specific serial killer behavior.
3. Comprehend the interplay between genetics and environmental stressors.

Biological Model of Serial Murder

Since the focus of this chapter is on biology and psychopathology, and their relation to overt and observable behavior, a brief explanation of the biological model of serial murder will provide a foundation for the information below. First, damage to neural networks can influence violent behavior (Darby et al., 2017). While neural plasticity is adaptive and allows humans to adjust to their environment, impairment to this process results in abnormal behavior (Chassy, 2017). In fact, research has discovered the influence of lesions in the brain on criminal behavior (Darby et al., 2017). Disruptions to the brain and neural pathways have been viewed in the brains of violent criminals; these deficits resulted in inaccurate appraisals of dangerous situations (Anderson & Kiehl, 2012). Indeed, psychopaths have a lower than average fear response (Anderson & Kiehl, 2012).

Moreover, sexually deviant fantasies can cement in a serial killer's brain, resulting in the intense memories of those fantasies (Chassy, 2017). In fact, roughly 50% of serial killers report rape fantasies as early as age 12 (Douglas & Olshaker, 2000). When thoughts of sexual sadism fail to satisfy and the killer takes his first victim, the neural network is strengthened and more salient, as the killer is able to connect lived experience to the fantasy he drummed up for years. Additionally, hormones are strong drivers of behavior. Testosterone, specifically, has been implicated in aggressive, dominant, imprudent, and harmful behavior (Miller, 2014; Raine, 2013). These biological factors result in a certain kind of personality—one that is hostile and antagonistic—and when that person lives in a neglectful and traumatic environment, it creates the worst-case scenario.

Neuropsychology

The concept of **neuropsychology** has a long evolution in the field of psychology (Kent, 2020). We have known that the brain affects behavior, but exactly how it does this still largely remains a mystery, despite medical advances. More recently, scientific research on neuropsychological deficits illustrates their influence on behavior, including psychopathy (Beaver et al., 2011; Raine, 2013). When your brain is under stimulated due to these deficits, you seek experiences to supplement and increase the creation and flow of neurotransmitters in an effort to essentially self-medicate (Miller, 2014). Importantly, these brain alterations related directly to psychopathy cannot be better explained for by environmental influences, such as childhood attachment and parenting style (Beaver et al., 2011). Often, however, someone becomes a serial killer as the result of nature *and* nurture.

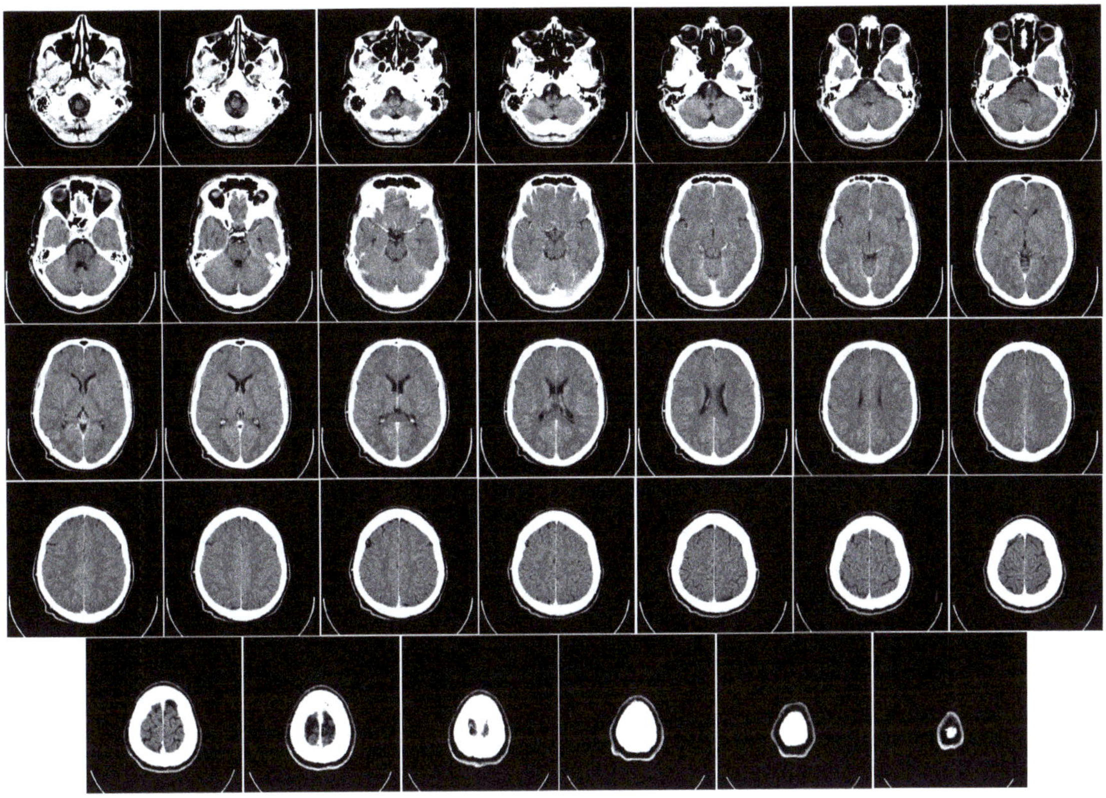

Figure 4.2 Tomography of Human Brain

In this chapter, the focus will be on nature, primarily. In fact, damage to the brain as a child can cause changes to the brain and has been shown to increase aggression. Likewise, neurochemical imbalances, specifically serotonin and dopamine, have been linked to violent behavior (Raine, 2013; Soderstrom et al., 2001; Wu & Barnes, 2013). Similarly, males with the low-functioning MAOA genotype, known as the warrior gene, and who reported traumatic early life experiences, are more sensitive to life stress as adults and have a higher risk for antisocial behaviors (Wells et al., 2017; Wermter et al., 2010).

Indeed, studies have found the heritability of antisocial behavior to be 40%–50% (Raine, 2013; Wright et al., 2008). Adoption studies have assessed the role of nature and nurture in an attempt to determine the amount of influence of each (Raine, 2013; Wermter et al., 2010). By assessing the likelihood that a child will commit homicide based on biological parent's criminal behavior, one large study found this increase to be 2.5%–10%, with higher rates of homicide correlating positively with increased criminal behavior by the biological parent (Raine, 2013). This presents a strong argument for the important role nature plays in our behavior, regardless of environment.

As noted in Chapter 2, prenatal influences, such as drug use, can alter and disrupt the regulation of neurotransmitters responsible for emotional and behavioral regulation (Reid et al., 2019). Specifically, serotonin and dopamine are reward pathways that thrive on situations that are stimulating and exciting, and at times prepare individuals for responding to threats in their environment (Miller, 2014). In serial killers, these responses are overly aggressive and disproportionate to the situation (Miller, 2014). Lower levels of these neurotransmitters result in feelings of depression and aggression, leading the individual to seek novel experiences (Reid et al., 2019).

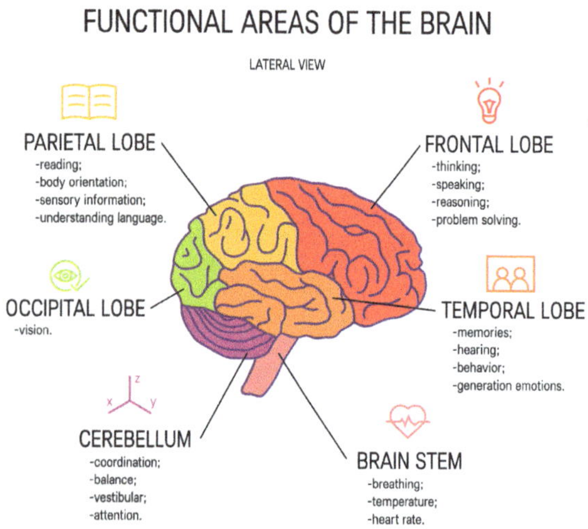

Figure 4.3 Human Brain Areas and Their Functions

Key Brain Structures and Their Functions

While the environment can bring about or suppress the expression of certain genes, organically dysfunctional regions of the brain have been shown to result in antisocial behavior. In some cases, people are born with these deficits or they occur in utero, while other dysfunctions are due to head trauma, such as traumatic brain injury, as noted in Chapter 2. Damaged or inadequately formed areas of the brain result in abnormal or unusual thoughts and behaviors that are linked directly to the function of that part of the brain. Therefore, the primary areas of the brain implicated in aggression and violence will be discussed, including the prefrontal cortex, amygdala, and limbic system.

Prefrontal Cortex

When a mother holds her child for the first time after birth, this creates positive neural pathways related to attachment. A lack of such skin conductance has been connected to maladaptive behavior; this vital connection is located in the **prefrontal cortex** region of the brain (Raine, 2002). The prefrontal cortex is involved in decision-making, impulse control, and moral reasoning (Gao & Raine, 2010). Specifically, disturbances in impulse control are associated with psychological pressure that builds and isn't sated until the individual completes the compulsive behavior (Miller, 2014). This region of the brain also includes the orbitofrontal cortex, which is responsible for social behavior, emotional regulation, and decision-making (Hanlon et al., 2013). Impairments in this area of the brain found in serial killers are specifically located in the "orbitofrontal cortex and middle frontal gyrus" (Gao & Raine, 2010, p. 199). Indeed, since the prefrontal cortex is responsible for decision-making, damage to that part of the brain can affect someone's ability to weigh options in a situation and choose the more appropriate action (Gao & Raine, 2010). Furthermore, damage to the ventral medial prefrontal cortex (vmPFC) results in psychopathic features and symptoms (Gao et al., 2009). When making moral judgments, those with vmPFC damage will endorse actions of highly emotionally aversive harm, suggesting that vmPFC mediates emotions that are important for moral judgments. Unsurprisingly, research has discovered associations between the volume of the prefrontal cortex and ratings on questions related to antisocial behavior on Hare's Psychopathy Checklist (2003), such that higher psychopathy scores are related to smaller prefrontal cortex volume (Pieperhoff et al., 2025).

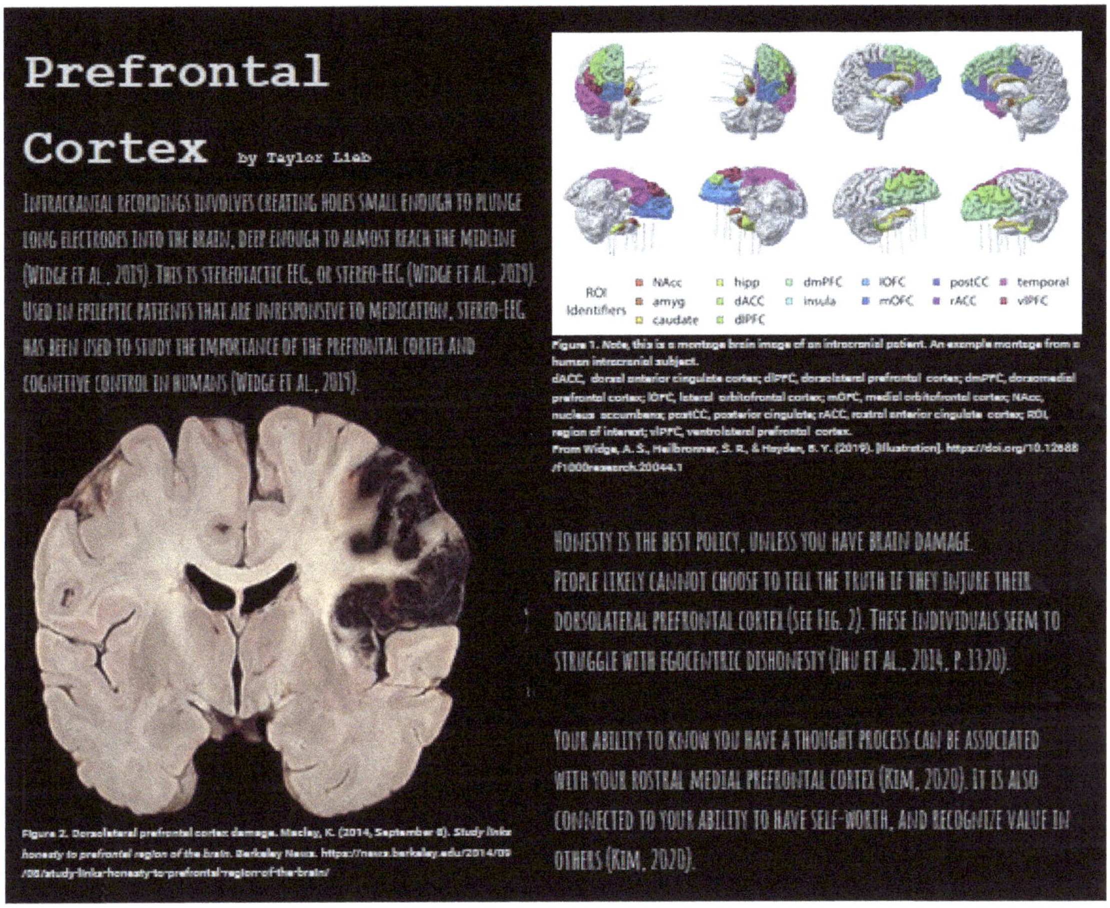

Figure 4.4 The Prefrontal Cortex and Its Role in Behavior

Moreover, reduced decision-making ability is closely connected to serotonin and dopamine levels, meaning that damage to this area of the brain, which is significantly regulated by these specific neurotransmitters, further results in aggression and addictive behaviors (Reid et al., 2019). People who have been convicted of homicide and attempted to use the *not guilty by reason of insanity* plea, and who have a severe mental disorder to back up that plea, have been found to have reduced glucose metabolism in their prefrontal cortex (Hanlon et al., 2013). Additional evidence for aggressive behavior related to lower levels of the MAOA-L gene is associated with changes in the structure and function of the amygdala and the medial prefrontal cortex (Wells et al., 2017). Though described to a degree in Chapter 2, this gene expression is also relevant to the overall discussion of neuropsychology, as it has neurobiological implications in relation to reactive and proactive aggression (Baum, 2011; Kolla & Bortolato, 2020). These types of aggression are related to responses to perceived insults and premeditated violence, respectively (Baum, 2011; Kolla & Bortolato, 2020). Such behavioral reactions to perceived threats are the direct result of MAOA's role in deconstructing and altering neurotransmitters related to emotion, such as serotonin (Kolla & Bortolato, 2020).

Albert Fish

Figure 4.5 Albert Fish Mugshot, 1903

We see the result of damage to the prefrontal cortex in several serial killers, including Albert Fish. Fish was born in 1870 in Washington, D.C.; his mother reportedly suffered from symptoms of schizophrenia and his father died when he was only 5 years old. Fish was sent to live at an orphanage by his mother, as she was unfit to care for him (Brown et al., 2013). During his time at the orphanage, Fish endured abuse at the hands of the staff. Ironically, he began to enjoy the pain he experienced while being abused (Schechter, 2003). That was the beginning of his interest in sadomasochism. In fact, once incarcerated and assessed, he was diagnosed by one doctor with several paraphilias, including fetishism, sadism, pedophilia, and cannibalism (Brown et al., 2013). To add insult to injury, Fish fell off a cherry tree as a child, incurring damage to his frontal lobe (Schechter, 2003). It was reported that his personality changed and he was unable to make appropriate decisions after that accident (Ramsland, 2006). In addition to sexual deviance, Fish was a small-time criminal, stealing and harassing neighbors.

Poor decision-making was at the center of his life, and he was unable to control his impulses. Upset following the dissolution of his marriage, his behavior continued to be erratic and he visited the Budds' house. They were a small, poor family who lived near Fish in Manhattan, New York. He told them he was looking for their son to help him with yardwork after the son had placed an ad in the newspaper looking for work, but then he saw their daughter Grace. He asked her parents if he could take her to his granddaughter's birthday party (Ramsland, 2006). Using the façade of a kind older man who gifted them with food and drink, her parents agreed, although reluctantly at first. Fish brought Grace to his house, murdered her, and ate her. If you're trying to get away with murder, meeting your victim's parents is not the ideal way to remain undetected. Indeed, his judgment was so poor that he wrote a letter to Grace's parents detailing what he did to her (Schechter, 2003). The letter was macabre and graphic, and explained how he murdered and ate their daughter. This resulted in his capture and conviction in 1935 when authorities were able to connect the specific paper used for the letter (Brown et al., 2013). He boasted of killing at least 15 children and molesting several hundred more. Following a trial and years in jail, Fish was executed in 1936.

Amygdala

The **amygdala** is an important brain region implicated in serial killing. It affects our emotion processing, specifically related to fear and aggression responses (Moul et al., 2012). The visual cortex interprets visual stimuli and signals the amygdala, which jump-starts the fight or flight response (Raine, 2013). Information from the senses reaches the amygdala twice as fast as it does to the frontal lobe. Before your frontal cortex can rein back the amygdala's aggressive response, fight or flight kicks in. Smaller amygdala volume and structural abnormalities often result in impaired responses to external stimuli (Moul et al., 2012).

Such deficits in cognitive and emotional regulation related to reduced gray matter volume in the amygdala are often found in serial killers (Gao & Raine, 2010). Insufficiencies in the amygdala-hippocampal area have been associated with emotional defects such as shallow affect and a lack of remorse, as well as social dysfunction that includes pathological lying and "superficial charm" (Gao et al., 2009). For example, reduced amygdala volume (Tiihonen et al., 2015) and delayed response to words with neutral and negative associations (Kiehl et al., 2001) were also found in individuals with high levels of psychopathy. These findings suggest that amygdala impairment affects socialization, especially by influencing aversive conditioning and instrumental learning (Blair, 2003). Indeed, impairment in the development of the amygdala may result in the individual perceiving benign social cues as aggressive.

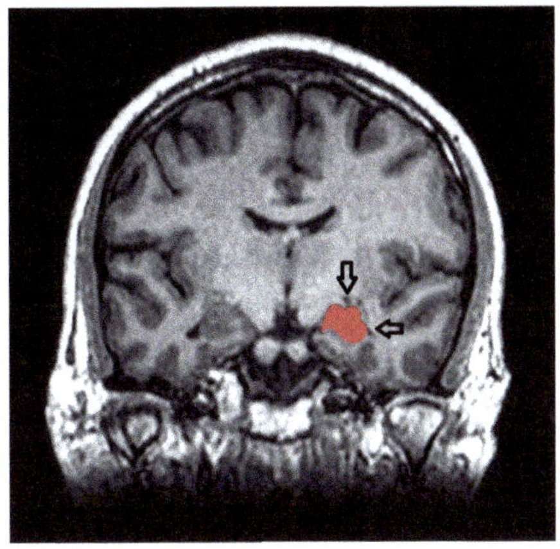

Figure 4.6 The Amygdala

Essentially, psychopaths, aka most serial killers, are not negatively affected by the punishment associated with their antisocial behavior; thus, they continue those behaviors because they are reinforcing in other ways, such as having more control and dominance over others. For example, when presented with a story, psychopaths with reduced amygdala volume could not correctly match feelings of guilt experienced by the characters (Kiehl, 2009). Further, reduced amygdala volume has been found in "unsuccessful psychopaths" (i.e., those who were caught; Gao & Raine, 2010). From the few brain scans and dissections, researchers believe that many serial killers have reduced amygdala volume of 5%–10% as compared to normal brains (Raine, 2013). Since brain scans pre- or postmortem have not been performed on most serial killers, I will choose a case not yet discussed in this text to connect to amygdala dysfunction.

Myra Hindley

One could surmise that Myra Hindley had a smaller than average amygdala. She was easily swayed and convinced to torture and kill children by her boyfriend, Ian Brady (Clark, 2019). Born in London in 1942, she was sent away to live with her grandmother after her parents had a second daughter. Unwanted by her parents, Hindley didn't return to her home often (Biography, 2023). This may have been for the better, since they regularly fought and drank. Scholastically, she was subpar, fought with peers at school, and was viewed as callous (Clark, 2019), all signs of impaired socialization typical of someone with a smaller than average amygdala (Blair, 2003). Demonstrating insight, Hindley eventually explained the "effects of her physically violent and abusive father on her emotional development. This, she suggests, taught her to be tough and hide her emotions" (Clark, 2019, p. 466). The neglect and abuse she experienced and witnessed as a young child made a lasting impression on her.

On her own as an adult, Hindley met and fell in love with Ian Brady, though their relationship was unusual; Brady would beat her during sex and even drugged and raped her in her sleep (Biography, 2023). Her shallow emotions didn't allow her to feel the true depth of this kind of abuse. Her brain's fight or flight response was not adequately activated in relation to the abuse, and she continued her relationship with Brady (Biography, 2023). The violence in their relationship ensued and expanded to those outside the relationship, including children. The couple kidnapped, tortured, raped, and murdered several young children in 1963 and 1964 (Clark, 2019). Their terror ended when Hindley's brother-in-law witnessed Brady killing a child with an axe and contacted police (Biography, 2023). Hindley and Brady were arrested and convicted of rape and murder. At that time, Hindley attempted to clear her name, stating that Brady forced her to harm the children. Her pleas went unanswered and she served two life terms until her death in 2002.

Limbic System

A third brain region connected to serial killing is the **limbic system**. It is responsible for our fight or flight reactions to immediate threat. It plays a central role in emotional regulation and memory (Calzada-Reyes et al., 2021; Raine, 2013). Evidence indicates that disruptions in the limbic system might contribute to violent tendencies (Raine, 2013). In fact, research has shown increases in beta activity in those with violent behaviors (Calzada-Reyes et al., 2021). Beta activity is associated with alertness, attention, and cognitive processing (Blair, 2012). This may lead someone with abnormalities in that region to over or underreact. Indeed, alterations related to these abilities may be more prevalent in disorganized serial killers, or those who did not get away with it three or more times to meet the definition of serial killer. Further, a lack of cortical thickness in this area of the brain may result in more reported traits of psychopathy (Blair, 2012; Calzada-Reyes et al., 2021).

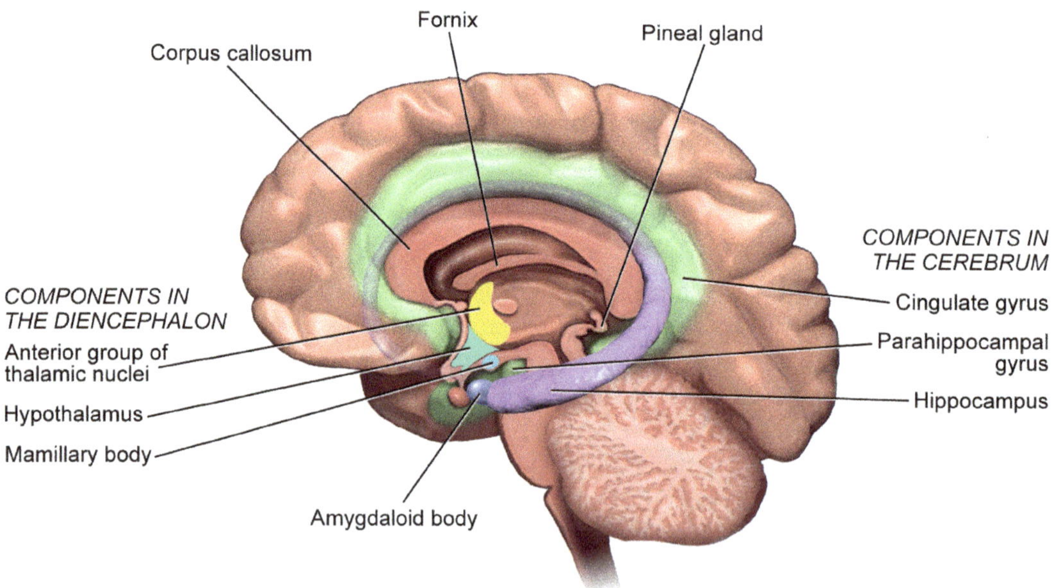

Figure 4.7 The Limbic System

The **paralimbic system**, which includes the orbitofrontal cortex and amygdala, has also been indicated in violent and psychopathic behavior (Calzada-Reyes et al., 2021; Ermer et al., 2012). Dysfunction in this area of the brain has been linked to difficulty recognizing and understanding others' emotions, which can result in inappropriate social responses (Calzada-Reyes et al., 2021). This lack of appropriate social behavior is common in serial killers. The inability to understand others' emotions is one of the reasons serial killers are often loners, or are able to compartmentalize their own feelings about others; interactions with people are primarily based on their own emotions.

Joseph Duncan

When there is damage to your limbic system or it is dysfunctional, as was the case with the violent sexual predator Joseph Duncan, your ability to regulate your emotions and compulsions is compromised. Indeed, reduced activity in the orbitofrontal context has been implicated in pedophilia, as it impairs the ability to inhibit inappropriate desires (Wondery, 2022). Sadistic child molesters like Duncan derive satisfaction from inflicting pain on children. Lacking impulse control, Duncan had his mind set on killing the parents of two young children in 2005 so he could kidnap, torture, and sexually assault them (Ramsland, 2006; Wondery, 2022). This train of thought was nothing new to him; his adolescent years were marred by deviant behavior and criminal activity (Gordon, 2021; Wondery, 2022). His childhood was filled with abuse, resulting in helplessness and insecurity, which he then enacted on the two innocent children. As he moved in and out of prison for sexual offenses, his impulse to engage in sexually explicit activities remained (Gordon, 2021).

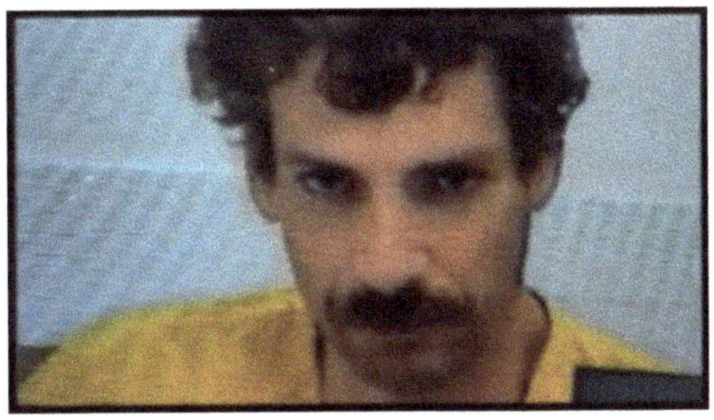

Figure 4.8 Joseph Edward Duncan

Figure 4.9 Presentation of evidence

Further, he created a blog titled *The Fifth Nail* where his writings provided ample insights into his psyche (Wondery, 2022). There his narrative was one of grandiosity and the illogical notion that the devil chose him to perpetrate these crimes. Instead of keeping one of the children out of sight to conceal his actions, he took her to Denny's for a late-night meal (*The Spokesman-Review*, 2005). Believing he was invincible, he focused on his hunger at the expense of getting caught, compartmentalizing his emotions and feelings while ignoring those of the restaurant patrons and, of course, the children he abducted. This resulted in his demise when restaurant managers and patrons recognized him and the little girl, and called 911 (*The Spokesman-Review*, 2005). He was finally caught and convicted of sexually assaulting and murdering six children (Ramsland, 2006). Sentenced to death in 2008, he died on death row of brain cancer in 2021 (U.S. Attorney's Office, District of Idaho, 2021).

Discussion question: How does one child become a serial killer while their siblings do not?

Diathesis-Stress Model

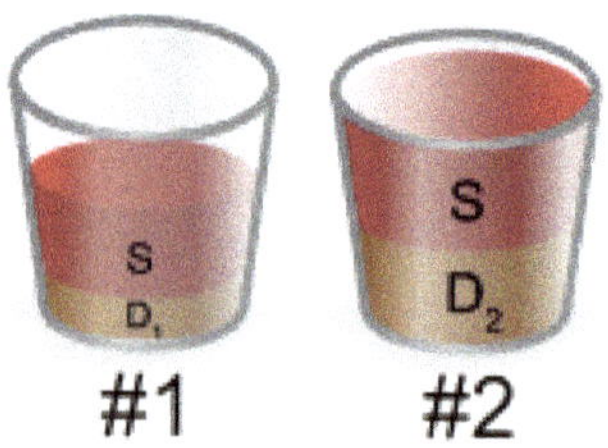

Figure 4.10 A cup analogy demonstrating the diathesis-stress model that under the same amount of stressors, person 2 is more vulnerable than person 1 because of their genetic predisposition for expression of the trait

What sets us apart? How does one sibling become a serial killer while the other is a constructive member of society? This is where the **diathesis-stress model** comes into play. Broadly, the diathesis-stress model (Stoltz et al., 2017; Zuckerman, 1999) assumes that people are genetically predisposed to certain personality traits and behaviors (diathesis); stressors in their environment result in the expression of some traits and not others. Chronic stress results in hyperarousal of our nervous system, and when these areas are activated for extended periods of time it leads to serious negative health problems, such as cancer and heart disease (Reid et al., 2019). Therefore, when someone has a genetic predisposition to kill, which may be evidenced by their parents' violent and socially maladaptive behaviors, and then they are raised in a household full of chronic stress in the form of trauma, abuse, and neglect, it's almost a wonder how they could turn out to be productive members of society. "This combination leads to the development of self-esteem, self-control, and sexual dysfunction problems. These problems feedback on one another and lead to the development of maladaptive social skills, which moves the person to retreat into his private pornographic world" (Walsh & Hemmens, 2008, p. 369). However, rarely do they end up becoming serial killers like the example below.

Richard Ramirez

Richard Ramirez didn't have it easy growing up. Born in El Paso, Texas, in 1960, he was the youngest of five siblings. His father was physically abusive towards him, his mother, and his siblings (Learish, 2021). There are reports that his mother faced complications during pregnancy, resulting in birth defects in her children. The culprit was likely exposure to the harmful chemicals at a factory where she worked (Cullen, 2020). Ramirez also sustained head injuries at a young age when a dresser fell on his head and another time when he was knocked out in a fight at school on the playground. Ramirez said he never felt the same after those incidents (Learish, 2021). To make matters worse, in his teenage years he became close with a cousin who was known for violence and cruel behavior (Cullen, 2020). Indeed, Ramirez saw his cousin shoot his wife to death (Ramsland, 2006). This excited him sexually and he believed that violence was necessary for him to become sexually aroused (Cullen, 2020).

With an abusive father, and absent mother, he likely had a genetic predisposition toward psychopathy. That coupled with a chaotic and abusive environment are possibly what led him to become a serial killer, known as the Night Stalker. His criminal activity started with burglary in his early teens and escalated to indiscriminate murder in his 20s. He raped and killed at least 13 people, who ranged from age 9 to 79, stating Satan prompted him to commit these crimes (Learish, 2021; Ramsland, 2006). Ramirez was finally captured in 1985 when police discovered a single shoe print in his latest victim's home and a young victim escaped, providing a description of Ramirez. After being in custody for four years, Ramirez was convicted of 13 murders and sentenced to death. He served 24 years behind bars before dying of lymphoma in 2013 (Cullen, 2020).

Figure 4.11 Richard Ramirez Mugshot, 2007

Figure 4.12 Ramirez in Court, 1986

Video of the Richard Ramirez case:

QR Code 4.1

Summary

The aforementioned data and cases "explain" the role of neuropsychology on the behavior of serial killers. Indeed, less gray matter volume in the prefrontal cortex and a smaller amygdala (Cope et al., 2012; Yang et al., 2009) result in deficits apparent in serial killers' ability to control emotions, make decisions, and control behavior (Raine, 2013). Further, ineffectual limbic and paralimbic systems can result in deficits related to social interactions, such as realizing another person is experiencing fear (Calzada-Reyes et al., 2021), which may lead a serial killer with these deficits to incorrectly interpret their victim's emotional state. For example, a serial killer with a prefrontal cortex that isn't formed correctly or is deficient in some way will not be able to control their emotional responses; the limbic system overcompensates in a sense and leads the individual to commit heinous acts that they potentially would not otherwise.

Keywords

Amygdala

Diathesis-stress model

Limbic system

Neuropsychology

Paralimbic system

Prefrontal cortex

Chapter Review Questions

1. How do specific regions of the brain affect serial killer behavior?
2. What role does the autonomic system play in the development or expression of psychopathic traits?

3. How does the diathesis-stress model "explain" how some people become serial killers while others do not?

References

Anderson, N. E., & Kiehl, K. A. (2012). The psychopath magnetized: Insights from brain imaging. *Trends in Cognitive Science, 16*(1), 52–60.

Baum, M. L. (2011). The monoamine oxidase A (MAOA) genetic predisposition to impulsive violence: Is it relevant to criminal trials? *Neuroethics, 6,* 287–306. https://doi.org/10.1007/s12152-011-9108-6

Beaver, K. M., Vaughn, M. G., DeLisi, M., Barnes, J. C., & Boutwell, B. B. (2011). The neuropsychological underpinnings to psychopathic personality traits in a nationally representative and longitudinal sample. *Psychiatry Quarterly, 83, 145–159.*

Biography.com Editors. (2023, October 03). *Myra Hindley*. Biography.com. https://www.biography.com/crime/myra-hindley

Blair, R. J. R. (2003). Neurobiological basis of psychopathy. *The British Journal of Psychiatry, 182*(1), 3-7.

Blair, R. J. R. (2012). Cortical thinning and functional connectivity in psychopathy. *American Journal of Psychiatry, 169*(7), 684–687.

Brown, J., Harris, B. R., & Daniels, S. (2013). Psychology of Albert Fish. *Behavioral Health, 1*(1), 1–6.

Calzada-Reyes, A., Alvarez-Amador, A., Galan-Garcia, L., & Valdes-Sosa, M. (2021). Electroencephalographic and morphometric abnormalities in psychopath offenders. *Behavioral Sciences & the Law, 39*, 597–610.

Chassy, P. (2017). The neural signature of emotional memories in serial crimes. *Medical Hypotheses, 108,* 31–34.

Clark, T. (2019). "Normal Happy Girl" interrupted: An auto/biographical analysis of Myra Hindley's public confession. *Deviant Behavior, 42*(4), 458–472. https://doi.org/10.1080/01639625.2019.1689047

Cope, L. M., Shane, M. S., Segall, J. M., Nyalakanti, P. K., Stevens, M. C., Godfrey, D. P., Calhoun, V. D., & Kiehl, K. A. (2012). Examining the effect of psychopathic traits on gray matter volume in a community substance abuse sample. *Psychiatry Research, 204*(2-3), 91-100.

Cullen, E. (2020). *American evil: The psychology of serial killers*. Waterside Press.

Darby, R. R., Laganiere, S., Pascual-Leone, A., Prasad, S., & Fox, M. D. (2017). Finding the imposter: Brain connectivity of lesions causing delusional misidentifications. *Brain, 140*(2), 497–507.

Douglas, J., & Olshaker, M. (2000). *The anatomy of motive*. Pocket Books.

Ermer, E., Cope, L. M., Nyalakanti, P. K., Calhoun, V. D., & Kiehl, K. A. (2012). Aberrant paralimbic gray matter in criminal psychopathy. *Journal of Abnormal Psychology, 121*(3), 649–658.

Gao, Y., Glenn, A. L., Schug, R. A., Yang, Y., & Raine, A. (2009). The neurobiology of psychopathy: A neurodevelopmental perspective. *Canadian Journal of Psychiatry, 54*(12), 813–823.

Gao, Y., & Raine, A. (2010). Successful and unsuccessful psychopaths: A neurobiological model. *Behavioral Sciences and Law, 28*(2), 194–210.

Gordon, L. (2021). *Sicko: The true story of Joseph Duncan III.* Trellis Publishing.

Hanlon, R. E., Brook, M., Stratton, J., Jensen, M., & Rubin, L. H. (2013). Neuropsychological and affective differences between types of murderers: Affective/impulsive vs predatory/instrumental (premeditated) homicide. *Criminal Justice & Behavior, 40*(8), 933–948.

Hare, R. D. (2003). *The Hare Psychopathy Checklist-Revised* (2nd ed.). Multi-Health Systems.

Kent, P. L. (2020). Evolution of clinical neuropsychology: Four challenges. *Applied Neuropsychology Adult, 27*(2), 121-133.

Kiehl, K. (2009). The criminal psychopath revealed: Assessment, recidivism, treatment and neuroscience. Gruter Institute Squaw Valley Conference 2009. *Law, Behavior & the Brain*.

Kiehl, K. A., Smith, A. M., Hare, R. D., Mendrek, A., Forster, B. B., Brink, J., & Liddle, P. F. (2001). Limbic abnormalities in affective processing by criminal psychopaths as revealed by functional magnetic resonance imaging. *Biological Psychiatry, 50*(9), 677-684.

Kolla, N. J., & Bortolato, M. (2020). The role of monoamine oxidase A in the neurobiology of aggressive, antisocial, and violent behavior: A tale of mice and men. *Progress in Neurobiology, 194,* 101875.

Learish, J. (2021, June 29). Richard Ramirez: The story, the evidence, the night stalker. *CBS News*. https://www.cbsnews.com/pictures/richard-ramirez-night-stalker-murders/2/

Miller, L. (2014). Serial killers: I. Subtypes, patterns, and motives. *Aggression and Violent Behavior, 19*(1), 1-11.

Moul, C., Killcross, S., & Dadds, M. R. (2012). A model of differential amygdala activation in psychopathy. *Psychological Review, 119*(4), 789–806.

Pieperhoff, P., Hofhansel, L., Schneider, F., Muller, J., Amunts, K., Weber-Papen, S., Weidler, C., Clemens, B., Raine, A., & Habel, U. (2025). Associations of brain structure with psychopathy. *European Archives of Psychiatry and Clinical Neuroscience, 276*(1), 63-75.

Raine, A. (2002). Biosocial studies of antisocial and violent behavior in children and adults: A review. *Journal of Abnormal Child Psychology, 30*(4), 311–26.

Raine, A. (2013). *The anatomy of violence: The biological roots of crime.* Pantheon Books.

Ramsland, K. (2006). *Inside the minds of serial killers: Why they kill*. Praeger.

Reid, S., Katan, A., Ellithy, A., Stua, R. D., & Denisov, E. V. (2019). The perfect storm: Mapping the life trajectories of serial killers. *International Journal of Offender Therapy and Comparative Criminology, 63*(9), 1621–1662.

Schechter, H. (2003). *The serial killer files: The who, what, where, how, and why of the world's most terrifying murderers.* Ballantine Books.

Soderstrom, H., Blennow, K., Manhem, A., & Forsman, A. (2001). CSF studies in violent offenders. L 5-HIAA as a negative and HVA as a positive predictor of psychopathy. *Journal of Neural Transmission, 108*, 869–878.

Stoltz, S., Beijers, R., Smeekens, S., & Dekovic, M. (2017). Diathesis stress or differential susceptibility? Testing longitudinal associations between parenting, temperament, and children's problem behavior. *Social Development, 26*, 783–796.

The Spokesman-Review. (2005, July 3). Tense late-night drama ends quietly, safely. https://www.spokesman.com/stories/2005/jul/03/tense-late-night-drama-ends-quietly-safely/

Tiihonen, J., Rautiainen, M-R., Ollila, H. M., Repo-Tiihonen, E., Virkkunen, M., Palotie, A., Pietilainen, O., Kristiansson, K., Joukamaa, M., Lauerma, H., Saarela, J., Tyni, S., Vartiainen, H., Paananen, J., Goldman, D., & Paunio, T. (2015). Genetic background of extreme violent behavior. *Molecular Psychiatry, 20*, 786-792.

United States Attorney's Office, District of Idaho (2021, March 28). Convicted child murderer Joseph Edward Duncan, III, dies on death row. https://www.justice.gov/usao-id/pr/convicted-child-murderer-joseph-edward-duncan-iii-dies-death-row

Walsh, A., & Hemmens, C. T. (2008). *Introduction to criminology: A text/reader.* Sage.

Wells, J., Armstrong, T., Boisvert, D., Lewis, R., Gangitano, D., & Hughes-Stamm, S. (2017). Stress, genes, and generalizability across gender: Effects of MAOA and stress sensitivity on crime and delinquency. *American Society of Criminology, 55*(3), 548–574. https://doi.org/10.1111/1745-9125.12147

Wermter, A. K., Laucht, M., Schimmelmann, B. G., Banaschweski, T., Sonuga-Barke, E. J., Rietschel, M., & Becker, K. (2010). From nature versus nurture, via nature and nurture, to gene x environment interactions in mental disorders. *European Child Adolescent Psychiatry, 19*, 199–210.

Wondery. (2022, April 15). Joseph Edward Duncan | Killer Psyche | Full Episode [Video]. YouTube. https://www.youtube.com/watch?v=ge55-MrUYj0

Wright, J. P., Tibbitts, S. G., & Daigle, L. E. (2008). *Criminals in the making: Criminality across the life course.* Sage.

Wu, T., & Barnes, J. C. (2013). Two dopamine receptor genes (DRD2 and DRD4) predict psychopathic personality traits in a sample of American adults. *Journal of Criminal Justice, 41*, 188–195.

Yang, Y., Raine, A., Colletti, P., Toga, A. W., & Narr, K. L. (2009). Abnormal temporal and prefrontal cortical gray matter thinning in psychopaths. *Molecular Psychiatry, 14*(6), 561–562.

Zuckerman, M. (1999). *Vulnerability to psychopathology: A biosocial model.* American Psychological Association.

Image Credits

Fig. 4.1: U.S. Air Force, https://commons.wikimedia.org/wiki/File:Dennis_Rader_Airman_Portrait.jpg, 1966.

Fig. 4.2: Department of Radiology, Uppsala University Hospital, https://commons.wikimedia.org/wiki/File:Computed_tomography_of_human_brain_-_large.png, 2008.

Fig. 4.3: Copyright © 2018 Depositphotos/marina_ua.

Fig. 4.4: Copyright © 2021 by Liebtaylor (CC BY-SA 4.0) at https://commons.wikimedia.org/wiki/File:PrefrontalCortexinfo.png.

Fig. 4.5: Source: https://commons.wikimedia.org/wiki/File:Albert_Fish_1903.JPG.

Fig. 4.6: Amber Rieder and Jenna Traynor, https://commons.wikimedia.org/wiki/File:MRI_Location_Hippocampus_up..png, 2011.

Fig. 4.7: Copyright © 2014 by BruceBlaus (CC BY 3.0) at https://commons.wikimedia.org/wiki/File:Blausen_0614_LimbicSystem.png.

Fig. 4.8: Screenshot from 4 News Now, “Duncan Jury Shown the Video,” https://www.youtube.com/watch?v=-FkA0XifMbo, 2008.

Fig. 4.9: Copyright © 2015 Depositphotos/Couperfield.

Fig. 4.10: Copyright © 2019 by Blacktc (CC BY 4.0) at https://commons.wikimedia.org/wiki/File:Diathesis_stress_model_cup_analogy.svg.

Fig. 4.11: San Quentin State Prison, California Department of Corrections and Rehabilitation, https://commons.wikimedia.org/wiki/File:Richard_Ramirez_CDCR.jpg, 2007.

Fig. 4.12: Copyright © 1986 by Lacy Atkins, LA Times (CC BY 4.0) at https://commons.wikimedia.org/wiki/File:Richard_Ramirez_escorted_by_sheriffs_from_court.jpg.

CHAPTER 5

THE ADDICTIVE BRAIN

Serial Murder and Substance Use in a Neurobehavioral Context

"The first time I killed somebody, it was such a rush. It was just like that, a shot of dope every time I did it."

-Tommy Sells

Addiction is powerful. Individuals can be addicted to nicotine, caffeine, illegal drugs, exercise, food, and power, to name a few. Furthermore, an individual who is already expressing psychopathy might use alcohol and drugs to self-medicate. Conversely, someone may start using drugs, not realizing that they are exacerbating an existing mental illness, or creating drug-induced psychosis. The fantasy of luring and killing victims only fuels and maintains the addictive behaviors (Malizia, 2017). Indeed, the physiological and psychological pathways of addiction, whether it be to alcohol, gambling, pornography, or murder, are insidious and change lives for the worse.

Figure 5.1 Tommy Sells, Texas Department of Criminal Justice, 2000

Addiction is defined as "the fact of being addicted to a particular substance, thing, or activity" (Merriam-Webster, n.d.). **Addiction** can be psychological and/or physiological. When our body craves the substance and we experience withdrawal symptoms (headache, shakes, sweating) without the drug in our system, this indicates physiological addiction (American Psychiatric Association [APA], 2022). Psychological addiction involves thinking about the substance, thing, or activity most of the time almost every day (APA, 2022). The same can be said for serial killing—the killers crave the experience of murder, think about it incessantly, and feel depressed during the cooling-off periods.

Since serial killer accounts of drug use can't always be confirmed, some inferences must be made. Additionally, substance use results in cognitive and behavioral changes and at times it can be assumed that those changes are the direct result of the drug, but there is no way to confirm that. Those changes could be due to unknown physiological and/or environmental factors. Therefore, while we know that the use of some substances exacerbates aggressive tendencies, we can only make interpretations, as correlation doesn't necessarily equal causation.

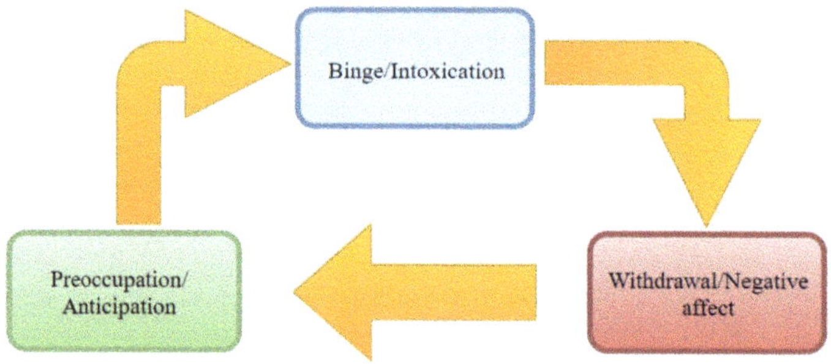

Figure 5.2 The Cycle of Addiction

Learning Outcomes

After reading this chapter, students will be able to do the following:

1. Critically assess the similarities between drug addiction and serial murder.
2. Understand the physiological and psychological underpinnings of addictive behavior.
3. Relate serial killer cases to addiction.

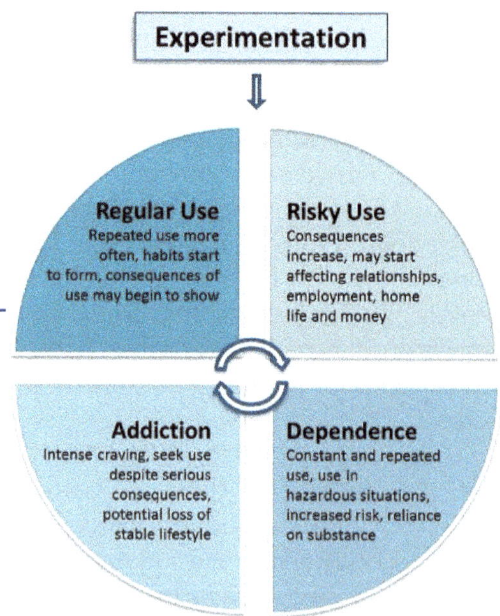

Figure 5.3 The Stages of Addiction

Addiction to Substances

Addiction is a word that is used often, though frequently incorrectly. It is vital to understand exactly what addiction *is* and what it is *not*. There are standard addictive behaviors, regardless of the drug/object/activity of choice. Addiction incorporates constant thoughts about the substance, hiding it or concealing behaviors associated with its use, interference with daily functioning, and withdrawal symptoms. These actions are not due to being "weak"; they are deeply rooted in our physiology. "All drugs that are taken in excess have in common direct activation of the brain reward system, which is involved in the reinforcement of behaviors and the production of memories" (APA, 2022, p. 481). Regardless of the substance, object, or activity, addictive behavior is caused and sustained by the neurotransmitter **dopamine** (APA, 2022). Research has confirmed this over and over again. In fact, Anselme and Robinson (2016) found that the longer you use the drug, the greater the negative impact it has on your dopamine stores, leading to the requirement of the drug to bring the levels of it in your brain back up to their original baseline. In fact, higher doses of the drug may not even result in the same high they used to achieve (Anselme & Robinson, 2016).

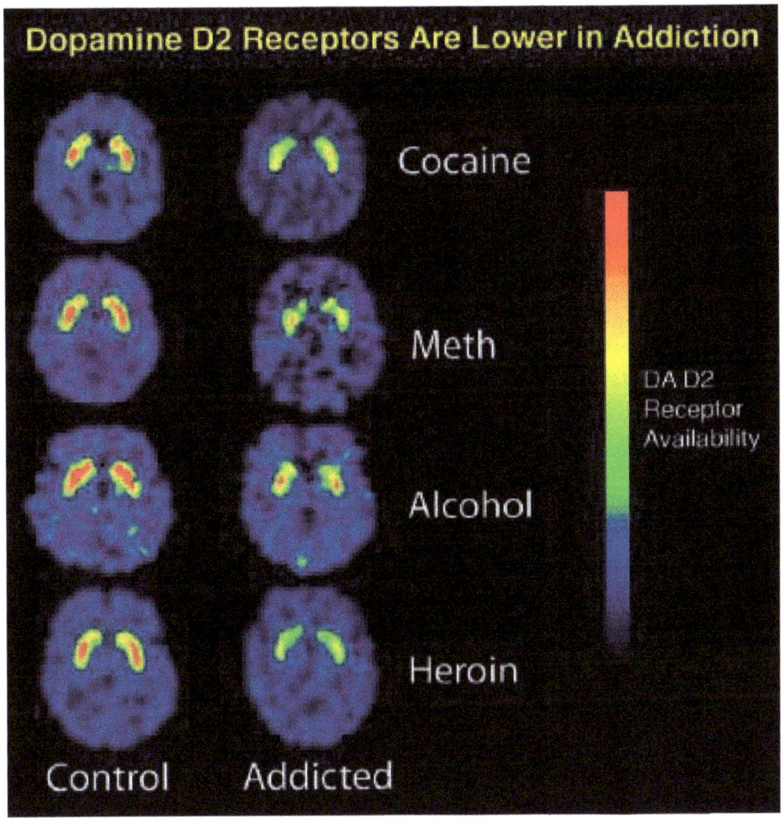

Figure 5.4 PET Images Depicting How Consistent Drug Use Negatively Impacts the Brain, Specifically Reducing Dopamine Levels

Substance Use Disorders

Substance use disorders are diagnosed when the individual meets the diagnostic criteria and the symptoms cause significant distress (APA, 2022). The physiological effects of drugs on the brain and body can be long lasting, especially when coupled with environmental influence, such as spending time with other substance users. In fact, women who experienced childhood sexual abuse had a higher prevalence of developing alcohol use disorder (Kolla & Bortolato, 2020). Furthermore, the impediment of the addiction is evidenced by their constant focus on the substance—they are thinking about it, focusing on whether they have enough, and when they are going to get it again. They may choose to spend their time and money on the drug, object, or activity rather than working, paying bills, enjoying hobbies, or spending time with friends and family (APA, 2022). The user also exhibits tolerance for the drug (they need larger doses to feel its effects) and withdrawal symptoms in its absence. The substance use categories most commonly seen in serial killers are discussed below. Oftentimes, use starts in the home, where the drug may be easily accessible and its use socially acceptable.

Parental Substance Abuse

Social modeling occurs at a very young age (Bandura, 1977). When our parents or guardians engage in adaptive behaviors, the result is our ability to model those behaviors and lead a successful and healthy life. However, when caretakers abuse alcohol and other drugs, it normalizes that behavior for children. Unless they have other adults who model less harmful behavior, this is all they know. Coupled with these environmental factors is the fact that addiction can be genetic, thus the child is more likely to develop addictive behaviors.

Not only does parental **substance abuse** influence children through social modeling (Bandura, 1977), it also affects the parent's ability to be an effective caretaker. When parents are high on drugs or coming down from that high, their ability to be present and adequately meet the child's needs are reduced. This can result in neglect, both physical and emotional, and abuse, as you will see with Albert DeSalvo (below). Further, parental substance abuse means the drugs of choice are likely in the house and more readily available to the child than they would be otherwise. Ease of access to alcohol, marijuana, and heroin, to name a few, in addition to social modeling and the normalizing of substance abuse, increases the likelihood of a child using and possibly abusing the drugs (Ducci & Goldman, 2008).

Albert DeSalvo

Figure 5.5 Albert DeSalvo's Arrest, 1967

Albert DeSalvo, born in 1931 in Massachusetts, is more commonly known as the Boston Strangler (Ferrarin, 2021; Ramsland, 2006; Schechter, 2003). He terrorized Boston, Massachusetts, from 1962 to 1965. Raping and strangling his victims, he initially chose older women and later murdered younger women. By pretending to be a worker or modeling scout, he gained access to their homes where he enacted his fantasies on unsuspecting women (Schechter, 2003). Several women reported sexual assaults during photo shoots and DeSalvo was imprisoned for 18 months. As a child, he endured his father's alcoholic aggression. His dad would drink until he was blindly drunk and then beat his wife and children. In fact, DeSalvo watched his dad knock his mother's teeth out and break her finger before beating him with a pipe (Schechter, 2003). Additionally, his father brought home sex workers and made the family watch. Likely due to the influence of seeing daily alcohol and drug use in the home, he partook of substances and even ran drugs in prison (Ferrarin, 2021).

As an adult, DeSalvo held various factory jobs while engaging in petty crime to supplement his income (Biography Editors & Donica, 2023). He even met and married a German woman who he met while in the Army. In 1964 he was arrested again for burglary and sexual assault, and confessed to 13 murders while awaiting trial. Perhaps his system was cleared of the mind-altering substances and he experienced a moment of clarity that resulted in the confession. With ample detail of the crimes, a jury quickly convicted DeSalvo to life in prison in 1967. While incarcerated, he continued to consume and sell drugs, which resulted in a reported drug deal gone bad; the affected inmate stabbed DeSalvo to death in 1972 (Biography Editors & Donica, 2023).

Discussion question: How does addiction influence people's behavior?

Substance Abuse's Influence on Murder

Substance use can facilitate serial murder. The similarities between addiction to substances and violence include the escalation of consumption and perceived need due to physical or psychological withdrawal symptoms. An individual needs more of the "drug" to satiate their physiological and physical needs as time progresses. Physiologically, they have exhausted the dopamine in their brain and are trying to restore it back to baseline (Raine, 2013). This requires amplification of the addictive behaviors to achieve homeostasis, just as described earlier in this chapter in relation to substances. "The prepotent role of dopamine-induced 'wanting' in controlling approach behavior is not surprising if we consider its importance for survival (in particular, feeding and reproduction)" (Anselme & Robinson, 2016, p.126). This process results in the activation of the brain's reward system, as shown in Figure 5.6.

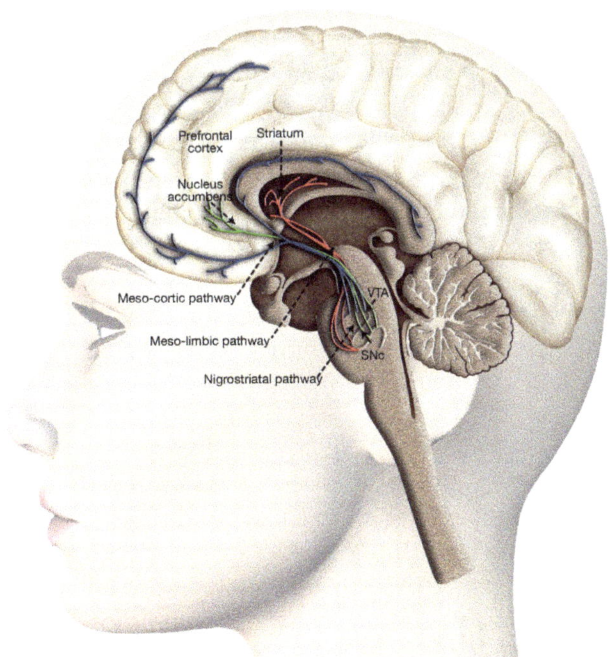

Figure 5.6 Dopaminergic Neural System and Its Impact on Reward Processing

In fact, combining antisocial behavior with substance abuse increases the risk of violent behavior (Botelho & Gonçalves, 2016; Nigel et al., 2018). Substance abuse is listed as a key contributor to homicide, with alcohol and drugs impairing judgment, increasing impulsivity, and fostering aggression. The connection between addiction and violence manifests through psychopharmacological effects and economic compulsion (e.g., crimes to fund addiction; Botelho & Gonçalves, 2016). Intoxicated individuals are more likely to engage in high-risk activities, while those with co-occurring mental health disorders may exhibit heightened aggression during crises or medication lapses. Sociocultural factors, such as poverty, unemployment, and unstable environments, can impact mental health in addition to the influence of community and cultural factors, increasing stress and the likelihood of addiction and violence (Botelho & Gonçalves, 2016; Nigel et al., 2018).

Psychological Impacts of Drug Classes on Violent Behavior

While drug use and abuse can aggravate preexisting behavioral tendencies, it is usually not the only cause of the serial killer's murderous behavior (Lee & Choi, 2014; Yarvis, 1994). Instead, drug use appears to be a method of anxiety reduction utilized by serial killers to lower their inhibitions prior to a homicide. While substance use is only one of myriads of factors involved in the creation of a serial killer, its influence can still be a powerful precipitating factor in their homicidal inclinations. Therefore, the most common classes of drugs will be explored in their relation to violent and hostile behavior.

Hallucinogens

This class of drugs includes lysergic acid diethylamide (LSD), psilocybin ("magic mushrooms"), 3–4 methylenedioxymethamphetamine (MDMA), etc. While use of hallucinogens most often does not result in violent behavior, there have been incidents where their consumption has been directly linked to aggressive behavior and even homicide (Holoyda, 2020; Sayrafizadeh et al., 2025). Certainly, these actions may have been confounded by concurrent substance abuse or underlying mental illness. For instance, research has found that high doses or chronic use of MDMA or LSD in combination with other drugs, such as alcohol, can reduce impulse control and lead to paranoia and violent behavior (Sayrafizadeh et al., 2025). Few instances of such behavior have been associated with psilocybin, and they almost always occur when the individual has a preexisting mental illness (Hendricks et al., 2018).

Depressants

The most common depressant is alcohol. It is consumed by one-third of the world population (Griswold et al., 2018), and is present in 42% of serial murder cases (Shaw et al., 2006). Alcohol can cause people to focus on the present moment rather than the future costs of their current behaviors (Dearden & Payne, 2009). It reduces inhibitions and cognitive faculties needed for decision-making (Griswold et al., 2018). Alcohol use is common amongst those with antisocial personality traits (Aamodt et al., 2023; Raine, 2013). We know that alcohol has been implicated in violent behavior; people have had direct experiences with the negative impact of this drug on relationships, especially within families (Dearden & Payne, 2009; Eriksson et al., 2021). In Australia, over one-third to just under half of all homicides involved alcohol use by the perpetrator prior to the offense (Dearden & Payne, 2009), in addition to excessive alcohol and other substance use in the year prior to the homicide (Eriksson et al., 2021). Indeed, one study found that roughly 17% of homicide perpetrators (information regarding serial murder cases was unavailable) had substance use and mental health problems (Shaw et al., 2006).

Table 5.1 Lifestyle at Time of First Homicide: Substance Abuse

	United States		**International**		**Total**	
	N	**%**	***N***	**%**	***N***	**%**
Alcohol	620		190		810	
No	128	20.6	52	27.4	180	22.2
Yes	492	79.4	138	72.6	630	77.8
Drugs	836		169		1,005	
No	174	20.8	67	39.6	241	24.0
Yes	662	79.2	102	60.4	764	76.0

Note. This is only part of the table.

Source: Michael G. Aamodt, Terence Leary, and Senthil Girimurugan, Selection from Radford/FGCU Annual Report on Serial Killer Statistics: 2023, p. 59. Copyright © 2023 by Radford University.

Addiction to Killing

Ed Kemper explained addiction to serial killing as follows: "It's a daring kind of a thing. … And this craving, this awful raging, eating feeling inside. I could feel it consuming my insides, this fantastic passion. Uh, it was overwhelming me. It was like drugs" (Ramsland, 2011, p. 102). Just like a drug addict, serial killers are constantly fantasizing about their next victims and how they will kill them. The addictive aspect of their behaviors is evident in their compulsive need to kill, which often escalates due to various influences such as unresolved trauma, substance abuse, or profound feelings of inadequacy and isolation. Indeed, research has shown that while sexual motivations are common, other motives such as profit, anger, and revenge frequently intertwine, further complicating the understanding of their addictive and compulsive actions (Beasley, 2004; Taylor, 2014). Their behaviors follow a cyclical pattern, reinforcing the need for continued study into the complex dynamics of serial murder and the addictive elements driving such violence. In fact, "serial killers and addicts may both (1) experiment until they find their preferred high, (2) have substitute addictions when they cannot get their preferred high, (3) refuse to accept responsibility for their destructive behavior, and (4) engage in cycles of sobriety and binges that get worse over time" (Lankford & Hayes, 2022, p. 5). Further, serial killers covet the memories of their murders and, if they chose to keep trophies, revisit them to maintain the "high."

Definition

Addiction to serial murder is evidenced by the buildup of fantasy, practice on objects/animals, and then the need for "more," or acts that are closer to the real fantasy (Taylor, 2014). Once they commit murder and achieve the high they desire, they are satiated for a while, hence the cooling-off period. After a while, the need slowly grows in intensity until the killer can't wait any longer, the withdrawal is too much, so they kill again to satisfy their urges.

Childhood Exposure to Violence

Viewing violence daily in your home as a child makes you think it's commonplace. It seems "normal." Unfortunately, exposure to family members' altercations at a young age may result in desensitization to and modeling of the behavior. It is a risk factor for addiction to physical and psychological harm to others (Mash & Wolfe, 2018). Poverty and limited resources compound this effect, resulting in reduced brain formation and social skills, which we see often in serial killers. Further, living in a community where violence and crime are rampant can lead to the development of mental health disorders, such as posttraumatic stress disorder, which puts a child at a disadvantage in their ability to cope with stressors (Mash & Wolfe, 2018). This may result in rash decisions and impulsive behavior; this would be typical of the disorganized serial killer (Ramsland, 2006). Punishment for such behaviors may lead a serial killer to turn inward and keep their murderous thoughts to themselves.

Fantasy

Fantasy starts in the mind (Ramsland, 2006). Serial killers often begin with a deeply rooted reliance on fantasy as a coping mechanism stemming from childhood trauma and dysfunctional environments. Over time, this reliance evolves into an obsessive need to transform violent fantasies into reality through murder (Malizia, 2017). The addictive nature of this cycle is comparable to substance dependency, with each act of murder reinforcing the fantasy and increasing the need to kill again to achieve a psychological "high." This is fueled by isolation, antisocial behavior, and a distorted sense of control, ultimately leading to a pattern of violence that persists in the absence of external intervention (Malizia, 2017). This behavior, while complex, is not merely a result of innate evil but rather a manifestation of an addiction to fantasies that offer temporary relief and bolster self-esteem.

Specifically, in connection with Jeffrey Dahmer's case, his behaviors met the criteria for physiological and physical addiction to substances and murder (Lankford & Hayes, 2022). He used alcohol and drugs to numb the pain he felt as an unwanted child who was bullied at school. Jeffrey felt it was easier to submit to his urges when he reduced his inhibitions with alcohol. This allowed him to follow through with his fantasies and urges to kill in an attempt to create a zombie-like sex slave (Lankford & Hayes, 2022).

Tommy Lynn Sells

Likewise, Tommy Sells's innate addictive behavior was unmistakable; he eagerly drank the alcohol his grandfather offered him when he was only 7 years old (Ramsland, 2011). Born into a negligent household, where his twin sister died as a baby, he wasn't given the love and attention needed to thrive as a child. With no dad, an absent mother, and his clearly maladroit grandfather as his only father figure, Sells quickly advanced from alcohol to harder drugs to escape his life and mute his feelings. After being kicked out by his family at 13, he was on his own and left to fend for himself. Having already found solace in drugs, he continued to use them and steal to pay for his habit, since his eighth-grade education would only afford him access to low-paying jobs. This resulted in his first murder in 1979 at only age 15 (Ramsland, 2011). Upon Sells breaking and entering, the owner of the home confronted Sells, who then shot him dead. His anger toward the world and addictive behavior led him to kill *at least* 12 more people, including pregnant women and children. "Usually, a murder had the effect of dampening his hunger for violence, but it always returned. For him, murder was a fix, like heroin to a drug addict" (Ramsland, 2011, p. 174). Once he had a taste for it, he fantasized about killing more innocent people; this led to a deeper addiction to drugs and murder. This eventually resulted in his capture in 1999 after he murdered a teenage girl and slit the throat of another one, who thankfully escaped and informed police. He was executed in Texas in 2014. While Sells's focus was rage fantasy turned to reality, other killers find sexual gratification in the act of murder.

Paraphilia

Paraphilias, such as voyeurism, exhibitionism, frotteurism, sexual sadism, pedophilia, and fetishes are rooted in feelings of lust and sexual compulsion (APA, 2022). They involve sexual interest and behaviors outside of culturally appropriate sex norms with a consenting partner (APA, 2022). Someone with a paraphilic disorder or tendencies has sexual interest in objects, situations, or activities rather than humans (Ramsland, 2006). Indeed, paraphilia can include activities, such as sadomasochism, or specific types of people or objects, such as dead bodies or underwear (APA, 2022).

Sexually addicted lust killers' behaviors are reflective of a progressive sexual addiction that escalates into violent crimes (Blanchard, 1995; Myers et al., 2006). These types of murderers, often driven by intense sexually violent fantasies, escalate from less severe sexual acts to egregious crimes, such as rape and murder. These acts serve as compulsive rituals to fulfill their cravings. Much like traditional addicts, these offenders demonstrate an amplified intensity in their crimes as they seek greater levels of excitement and dominance (Blanchard, 1995). Traumatic childhoods and dysfunctional relationships frequently serve as precursors, shaping their obsessive and macabre behaviors.

Their crimes are propelled by unresolved psychological trauma, profound feelings of inadequacy, and a need for control, leading to an addiction-like cycle where murder becomes compulsive (Blanchard, 1995; Myers et al., 2006). This pathological cycle is compounded by their inability to regulate or manage their compulsive behaviors, resulting in the repeated enactment of violent fantasies. The progression of their crimes highlights a parallel between sexual addiction and lust murderers, suggesting that for these individuals, each violent act temporarily satiates their cravings and ultimately propels them toward more extreme behaviors to experience the euphoric high once again.

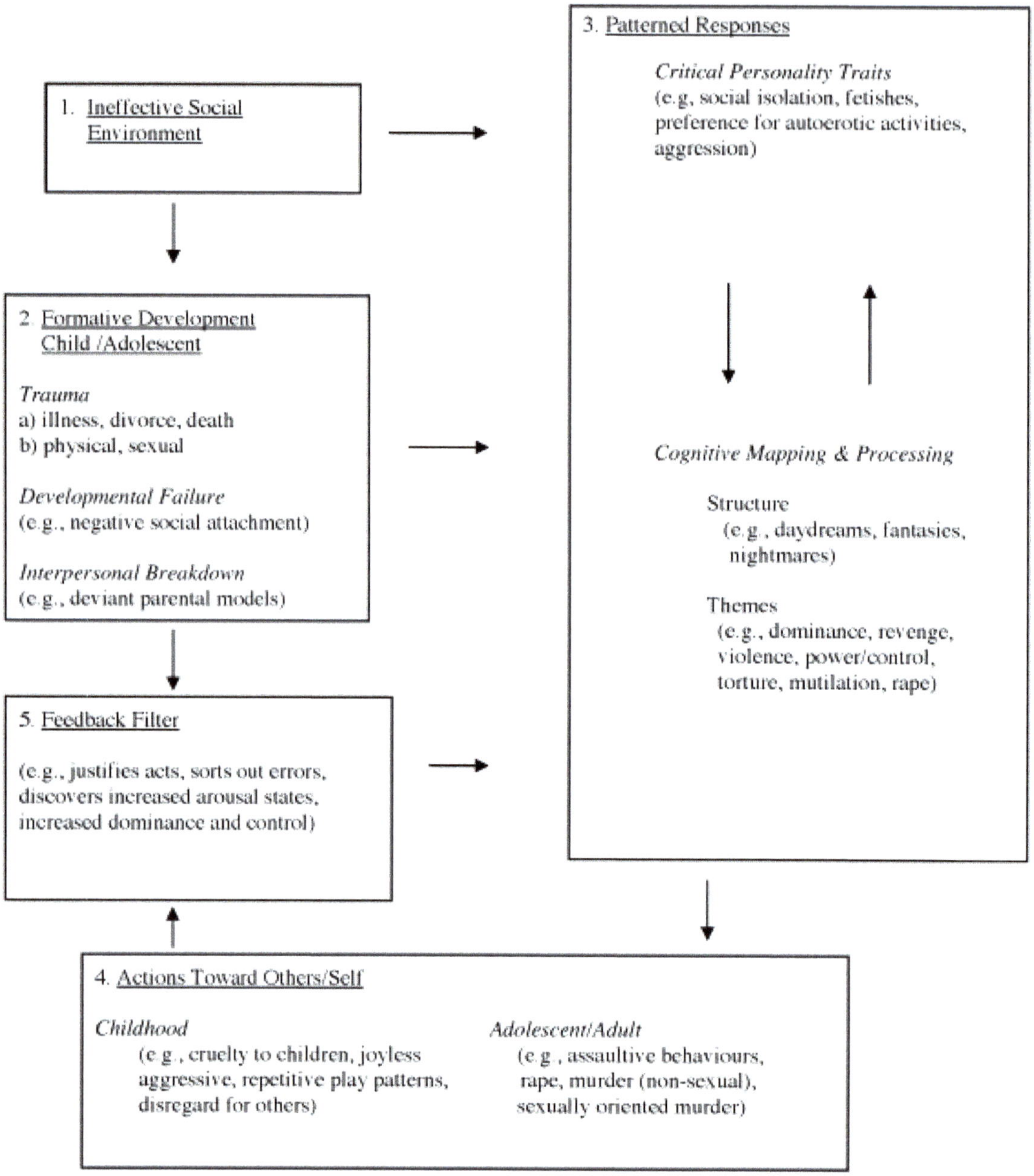

Figure 5.7 Psychosocial Development of Atypical Sexuality

Jerry Brudos

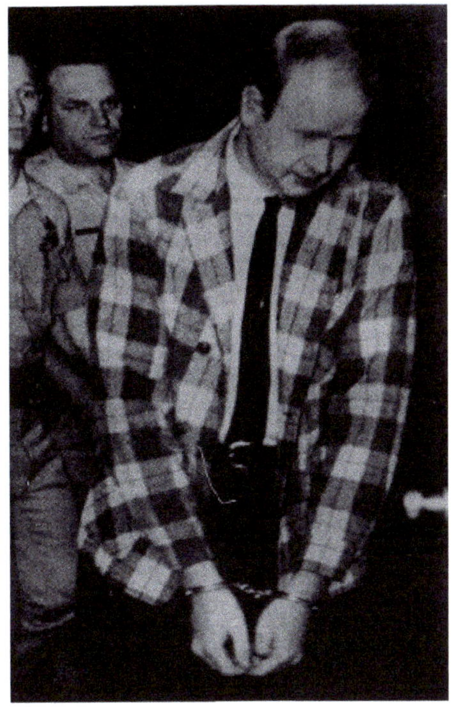

Figure 5.8 Jerry Brudos Arrested, 1969

Feet and shoes are common fetish choices. Jerry Brudos was an innocent boy wandering around his neighborhood when came upon discarded shoes, and brought them home (Schechter, 2003). He thought they were pretty and liked the style of the high heels. When he wore them to show his mother his exciting new toys, he endured a severe beating. Back in the 1940s, and likely even today in many households, little boys were scolded for wearing any attire deemed "feminine." Brudos's unusual behavior continued through adolescence. Indeed, he would lure girls into a barn to take pictures of them naked (Ressler & Schachtman, 1992). These early behaviors were disturbing and traumatic for the young girls, but that didn't bother Brudos, and his fetish for women's shoes and clothing continued throughout his life. He was enamored by women's clothes, so much so that he wore bras, lacy panties, and pretty shoes around his house, much to the chagrin of his wife (Schechter, 2003). Unfortunately, his paraphilia escalated and he began breaking into houses to steal shoes or luring women to a hotel room with promises of money in exchange for pictures of their feet in various footwear (Ressler & Schachtman, 1992). While some of these women were allowed to leave or were unharmed, he eventually raped and murdered three women, some of whom he photographed post-mortem in various lingerie. After he solicited college-aged women for dates, several notified campus police due to his age and creepy demeanor. When he was questioned and his house searched, authorities found ample evidence of the murders, and he received three life sentences in 1969 and died in prison in 2006. Though much of the focus of this chapter has been on men, women are not immune to addiction to substances and murder.

Female Serial Killers

Addictive behaviors present in female serial killers (FSKs) are similarly apparent through patterns of repeated murder that often escalate in frequency and intensity (Harrison et al., 2015). FSKs exhibit compulsive tendencies through serial killings to maintain a sense of power, control, or fulfillment of desires, akin to the cycle of addiction. Indeed, their killing careers tend to last longer than men's, in part due to the sociocultural norms under which they can hide (sweet, innocent woman), in addition to the more covert methods of murder, such as poison (Wilson & Hilton, 1998). Many FSKs engage in patterns of behavior that could be seen as ritualistic or compulsive, targeting vulnerable victims. They use methods that allow them to maintain a façade of normalcy, such as poisoning or financial gain due to the loss of a husband. In some respects, continuing to financially improve their lives with the deaths of husbands and children could be viewed as a type of gambling. Eliminating the burden of children could also be reinforcing in a disturbing sense. This compulsivity reflects an element of addictive behavior, where the cycle of killing provides a form of psychological gratification, reinforcing these acts (Harrison et al., 2015).

Dorothea Puente

When we picture a serial killer, an elderly woman usually does not come to mind. However, that is the perfect disguise. Dorothea Puente used her image as a sweet old lady to mask her murderous behaviors. Hiding under the mask of a concerned and caring mother figure, she ran a boarding house in California in the 1980s for disenfranchised individuals (Ramsland, 2006). Her boarders often didn't have close family members or anyone else who watched over them; they were addicts or elderly. This allowed her to cash in her boarders' welfare checks, even after they were dead, and capitalize on their misfortune (Ramsland, 2006). Puente poisoned her ailing tenants and buried them in her backyard to cover her tracks. It is estimated that she stole between $87,000 and $100,000.

Figure 5.9 Dorothea Puente Mugshot, 1988

Her behaviors were akin to gambling addiction; she kept rolling the dice, addicted to the money she stole from the lives she took. Though there is no report of her alcohol or drug use, both of her parents were alcoholics, indicating a likelihood that she inherited a propensity for addictive behavior. Further, she underwent traumatic events in childhood, including her mother's frequent suicide attempts (Ramsland, 2006). With little education and negligent parents, Puente sold her body to make ends meet in her teens and 20s. After depositing several boarders' checks, her greed intensified and she modified her modus operandi, switching from her home to a local bar in search of new victims. She couldn't get enough. Upon a social worker checking in on one of her boarders whose family member had not heard from him in a while, police were called to investigate and she was finally caught (Ramsland, 2006). While on the scene, authorities noticed that the soil in her backyard was disturbed and decided to take a closer look—the bodies of nine victims were found buried in her garden (Ramsland, 2006). Convicted of serial murder, Puente spent the rest of her life in prison before she died in 2011.

Summary

Addiction and addictive behaviors often begin in childhood, with parental influence or as a way to cope with severe abuse and neglect. Addiction to drugs alters our brain's reward system and may result in reduced inhibitions for murderous fantasies, leading to serial killing. The high of dope and murder leads the serial killer to continue their murderous rampage over the course of months or years. Indeed, serial killers may be drunk or high on other substances when they commit murder. Childhood exposure to violence and disturbing sexual fantasies and fetishes fuel their addiction to killing, especially when finding a willing partner proves difficult. When physiological and psychological addiction reign supreme, you never know who will end up giving in to their addictive impulses.

Keywords

Addiction

Dopamine

Paraphilia

Substance abuse

Chapter Review Questions

1. Are addictive behaviors the product of nature or nurture? Explain why.
2. What role does dopamine play in addiction?
3. How are paraphilias representative of addictive behavior?

References

Aamodt, M. G., Leary, T., & Girimurugan, S. (2023). *Radford/FGCU Annual Report on Serial Killer Statistics*. Radford University.

American Psychiatric Association. (2022). *Diagnostic and statistical manual of mental disorders (5th ed., Text Revision).* https://doi.org/10.1176/appi.books.9780890425787

Anselme, P., & Robinson, M. J. F. (2016). "Wanting," "liking," and their relation to consciousness. *Journal of Experimental Psychology: Animal Learning and Cognition, 42(2)*, 123–140. https://doi.org/10.1037/xan0000090

Bandura, A. (1977). *Social learning theory.* Prentice-Hall.

Beasley, J. O. (2004). Serial murder in America: Case studies of seven offenders. *Behavioral Sciences & the Law, 22*(3), 395–414. https://doi.org/10.1002/bsl.595

Biography.com Editors & Donica, A. (2023, March 17). Albert DeSalvo.*Biography.* https://www.biography.com/crime/albert-de-salvo

Blanchard, G. T. (1995). Sexually addicted lust murderers. *Sexual Addiction & Compulsivity: The Journal of Treatment & Prevention, 2*(1), 62–71. https://doi.org/10.1080/10720169508400067

Botelho, M., & Gonçalves, R. A. (2016). Why do people kill? A critical review of the literature on factors associated with homicide. *Aggression and Violent Behavior, 26*, 9–15. https://doi.org/10.1016/j.avb.2015.11.001

Dearden, J., & Payne, J. (2009). Alcohol and homicide in Australia. *Trends & Issues in Crime and Criminal Justice*, 372, 1-6. https://www.aic.gov.au/publications/tandi/tandi372

Ducci, F., & Goldman, D. (2008). Genetic approaches to addiction: Genes and alcohol. *Addiction, 103*, 1414–1428.

Eriksson, L., Bryant, S., McPhedran, S., Mazerolle, P., & Wortley, R. (2021). Alcohol and drug problems among Australian homicide offenders. *Addiction, 116*(3), 618–631.

Ferrarin, E. (2021). *Did an abusive childhood turn Albert DeSalvo into the 'Boston Strangler' serial killer? A&E*. https://www.aetv.com/real-crime/boston-strangler-abusive-childhood

Griswold, M. G., Fullman, N., & Gakidou, E. (2018). Alcohol use and burden for 195 countries and territories, 1990–2016: A systematic analysis for the Global Burden of Disease Study 2016. *The Lancet, 392*(10152), 1015–1035.

Harrison, M. A., Murphy, E. A., Ho, L. Y., Bowers, T. G., & Flaherty, C. V. (2015). Female serial killers in the United States: Means, motives, and makings. *The Journal of Forensic Psychiatry & Psychology, 26*(3), 383–406. https://doi.org/10.1080/14789949.2015.1007516

Hendricks, P. S., Crawford, M. S., Cropsey, K. L., Copes, H., Sweat, N. W., Walsh, Z., & Pavela, G. (2018). The relationships of classic psychedelic use with criminal behavior in the United States adult population. *Journal of Psychopharmacology, 32*(1), 37–48.

Holoyda, B. (2020). The psychedelic renaissance and its forensic implications. *Journal of the American Academy of Psychiatry and the Law, 53*(1), 1–11.

Kolla, N. J., & Bortolato, M. (2020). The role of monoamine oxidase A in the neurobiology of aggressive, antisocial, and violent behavior: A tale of mice and men. *Progress in Neurobiology, 194*, 101875.

Lankford, A., & Hayes, J. K. (2022). Could serial killing actually be addictive? A close examination of compulsion and escalation in the Jeffery Dahmer case. *Sexual Health & Compulsivity, 29*(3–4), 1–27.

Lee, J-L., & Choi, K. (2014). Serial murder: An exploration and evaluation of theories and perspectives. *American International Journal of Contemporary Research, 4*(3), 99–106.

Malizia, N. (2017). Serial killer: The mechanism from imagination to the murder phases. *Sociology Mind, 7*(2), 44–59. https://doi.org/10.4236/sm.2017.72004

Mash, E. J., & Wolfe, D. A. (2018). *Abnormal child psychology (7th ed)*. Cengage.

Merriam-Webster. (n.d.). Addiction. In *Merriam-Webster.com dictionary*. Retrieved January 11, 2024, from https://www.merriam-webster.com/dictionary/addiction

Myers, W. C., Husted, D. S., Safarik, M. E., & O-Toole, M. E. (2006). The motivation behind serial sexual homicide: Is it sex, power, and control, or anger? *Journal of Forensic Science, 51*(4), 900–907.

Nigel, S. M., Dudeck, M., Otte, S., Knauer, K., Klein, V., Böttcher, T., Maaß, C., Vasic, N., & Streb, J. (2018). Psychopathy, the big five and empathy as predictors of violence in a forensic sample of substance abusers. *The Journal of Forensic Psychiatry & Psychology, 29*(6), 882–900. https://doi.org/10.1080/14789949.2018.1439993

Raine, A. (2013). *The anatomy of violence: Biological roots of crime*. Vintage.

Ramsland, K. (2006). *Inside the minds of serial killers: Why they kill*. Praeger.

Ramsland, K. (2011). *The mind of a murderer: Privileged access to the demons that drive extreme violence*. Praeger.

Ressler, R. K., & Schachtman, T. (1992). *Whoever fights monsters: My twenty years tracking serial killers for the FBI*. St. Martin's.

Sayrafizadeh, N., Ledwos, N., Husain, M. I., & Castle, D. J. (2025). Aggressive behaviours associated with MDMA and psychedelics: A narrative review. *Acta Neuropsychiatrica, 37*, e30.

Schechter, H. (2003). *The serial killer files: The who, what, where, how, and why of the world's most terrifying murders*. Ballantine Books.

Shaw, J., Hunt, I. M., Flynn, S., Amos, T., Meehan, J., Robinson, J., Bickley, H., Parsons, R., McCann, K., Burns, J., Kapur, N., & Appleby, L. (2006). The role of alcohol and drugs in homicides in England and Wales. *Addiction, 101*(8), 1117–1124.

Taylor, T. (2014). Is serial killing an addiction? *IOL*. https://www.iol.co.za/news/is-serial-killing-an-addiction-1673542

Wilson, W., & Hilton, T, (1998). Modus operandi of female serial killers. *Psychological Reports, 82*(2), 495–498.

Yarvis R. M. (1994). Patterns of substance abuse and intoxication among murderers. *The Bulletin of the American Academy of Psychiatry and the Law, 22*(1), 133–144.

Image Credits

Fig. 5.1: Texas Department of Criminal Justice, https://www.tdcj.texas.gov/death_row/dr_info/sellstommy.html. Copyright © 2014 by Texas Department of Criminal Justice.

Fig. 5.2: Copyright © 2018 by U3143109 (CC BY-SA 4.0) at https://commons.wikimedia.org/wiki/File:Addiction_Cycle.jpg.

Fig. 5.3: Fiona Guy, "Addicted To Killing: Serial Killers and The Addiction Cycle," https://web.archive.org/web/20250521181228/https://www.crimetraveller.org/2018/06/addicted-to-killing-serial-killers-addiction-cycle/. Copyright © 2018 by Crime Traveller.

Fig. 5.4: Debra P. Davis, https://commons.wikimedia.org/wiki/File:Dopamine_D2_Receptors_in_Addiction.jpg, 2007.

Fig. 5.5: Federal Bureau of Investigation (FBI) – Strangler Bureau, https://commons.wikimedia.org/wiki/File:Albert_deSalvo.jpg, 2009.

Fig. 5.6: Copyright © 2010 by Oscar Arias-Carrión et al. (CC BY 4.0) at https://commons.wikimedia.org/wiki/File:Dopaminergic_system_and_reward_processing.jpg.

Fig. 5.7: Copyright © 2010 by CEB and Jtneill (CC BY 3.0) at https://commons.wikimedia.org/wiki/File:Development_of_deviant_sexuality.png.

Fig. 5.8: John Ericksen, https://commons.wikimedia.org/wiki/File:Jerry_Brudos_Arrested_Statesman_Journal_June_28_1969.jpg, 1969.

Fig. 5.9: Center for Sacramento History, https://www.sactownmag.com/a-killers-instincts/, 1988.

CHAPTER 6

SERIAL KILLING ACROSS CULTURES

A Global Perspective

"I did not kill either people I hated, or people I loved. I killed whoever crossed my path at the moment my urge for murder took hold of me."

-Peter Kürten

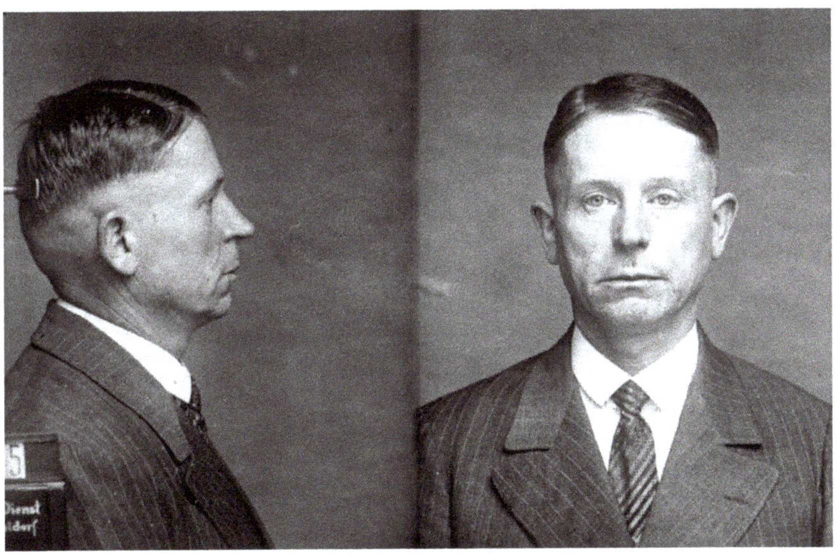

Figure 6.1 Peter Kürten Mugshot, Dusseldorf, Germany, 1930

This chapter will discuss the similarities and differences present in serial killer behavior and convictions in various countries. Research has discovered cultural variations in victim selection, modus operandi, and other factors, which could be due to societal norms (Bourrie et al., 2016; Dalal et al., 2009; Harbort & Mokros, 2001). There are inherent limitations to this endeavor in that countries define serial killing in ways that differ from the United

States. Additionally, record keeping and sharing amongst countries isn't always appropriate or accurate, and may even be considered taboo. Often, few resources are allocated to classifying and documenting serial murder. In fact, many countries do not have access to or utilize the latest DNA technology to solve crimes. This may be one of the reasons for lower prevalence rates amongst various countries, in addition to other cultural norms. Indeed, many instances of murder or serial murder are viewed differently across countries.

Accounts vary based on the publication, but the United States has always had the most documented serial killers. Other countries with high serial murder rates include Germany, South Africa, Canada, Japan, India, Ireland, and the American Indian/Alaska Native population in North America. While there are undoubtedly serial killers in other countries, literature on the cultural norms and prevalence rates and peer-reviewed manuscripts are sparse. Therefore, one or two case examples will be provided for each country/population of focus.

Learning Outcomes

After reading this chapter, students will be able to do the following:

1. Describe how the conceptualization of serial murder differs around the world.
2. Explain case examples from various countries.
3. Comprehend how systemic failings can result in serial killers' ability to continue to kill.

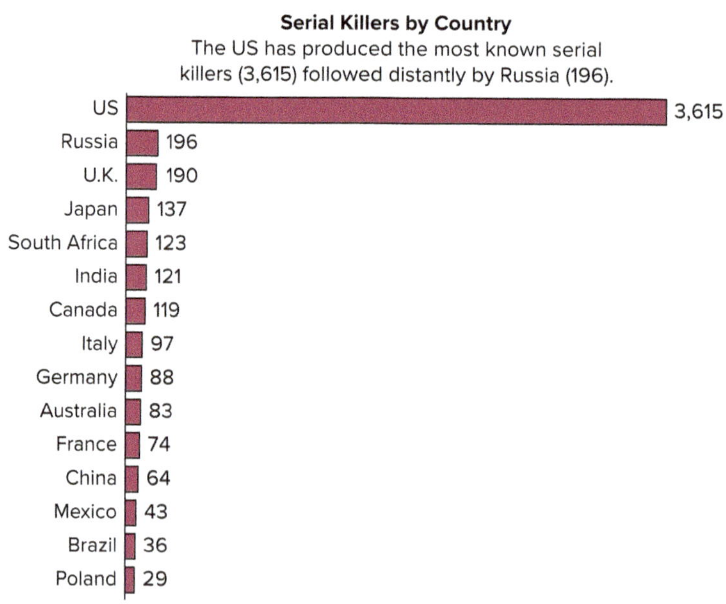

Figure 6.2 Serial Killers by Country

Germany

As is the case with many countries, serial killing is more commonly called serial murder in Germany. Specifically, in Germany it is defined as when "the fully or partially culpable perpetrator commits alone or with accomplice(s) at least three completed murders, each of which have to be premeditated and characterized through a new, hostile intent" (Harbort & Mokros, 2001, p. 313). Germany has a national database that catalogues DNA from criminals to aid in capturing serial murderers (Forensics, 2017). With decidedly few overall incidents of serial murder—only 61 *caught* between 1945 and 1995 (54 of those were men and 7 were women)—research has pinpointed several commonalities amongst German killers (Harbort & Mokros, 2001). These traits are fairly universal, such as male gender, mental disorders, troubled homes, difficulty with peer relationships, lower socioeconomic status, and brain damage. Some characteristics appear to be more common in German serial killers, however, including premeditation. Moreover, the average IQ of German murderers was slightly above average (100–110), yet many struggled in school. A majority of the serial killers studied also had difficulty maintaining steady employment (Harbort & Mokros, 2001). The average age at which they committed their first murder ranged from age 14 to 53. Additionally, high rates of suicide attempts and suicide completion were also common. As such, serial murderers in Germany are fairly typical in many regards to serial killers in other countries.

Fritz Haarmann

One notorious German serial killer was Fritz Haarmann. Born in 1879 in Hanover, Germany, his childhood was marred by neglect and trauma, save for the close relationship with his mother (Murray, 2007; Schechter, 2003). Haarmann's father belittled and berated him, telling him he wasn't tough. This resulted in Haarmann being shipped off to the military. Times were hard after World War I and Haarmann was largely left to fend for himself. To make ends meet as an adult with a rap sheet for petty crime, he became a butcher, as other employment options weren't available to him (Warren, 2021). He also began a romantic relationship with a man named Hans Grans, who eventually became his accomplice. Together, they lured young boys from their neighborhoods or at the train station, sexually assaulting and murdering them. Haarmann became so sexually excited by the murders that he bit into his victims in his fit of passion, which led to his moniker, the **Vampire** of Hanover (Ramsland, 2006; Schechter, 2003). Once he murdered his victim, he often ate the body or sold it on the black market as pork or beef; meat was a high commodity in those days. This was never officially confirmed and any knowledge of this was ignored, as he was an informant for the police for a time. He was eventually caught in 1924 after a victim's family recognized the jacket he was wearing as their son's and confronted him. Haarmann broke down once arrested and confessed to killing 27 boys and young men (Ramsland, 2006). The trial was swift and Haarmann was executed in April 1925. Justice was served differently 100 years ago.

Figure 6.3 Fritz Haarmann Being Arrested, 1924

Peter Kürten

Figure 6.4 Police Photograph of Peter Kürten, 1931

Another serial killer who was born and raised in Germany was Peter Kürten. Raised in Dusseldorf, Germany, in the early 1900s, Kürten was a sexual sadist who used scissors to stab, mutilate, and end his victims' lives (Ramsland, 2006). Kürten came from a lower socioeconomic status family, where his father was an abusive drunk (Serena, 2024). Not only did Kürten experience physical abuse, his parents made him watch them have sex, which undoubtedly skewed his view of the act. This led him to engage in one of the more classic serial childhood behaviors—harm to animals, including bestiality (Serena, 2024). Most of his life was spent robbing, killing, and living behind bars. Later, he married and outwardly lived a rather normal existence, while continuing to murder and drink the blood of children. His victims were mainly young, innocent girls. This behavior resulted in him being dubbed the Vampire of Dusseldorf (Serena, 2024). Kürten was finally arrested after a victim escaped and sent a letter to a friend about the incident; the letter was mailed to the wrong address, and, thankfully, the recipients informed the police. In 1930, he was convicted of killing 29 people (Schechter, 2003). No remorse was shown for the victims; rather he blamed those who had hurt him for his actions, including his father and society. He was executed by guillotine in 1931.

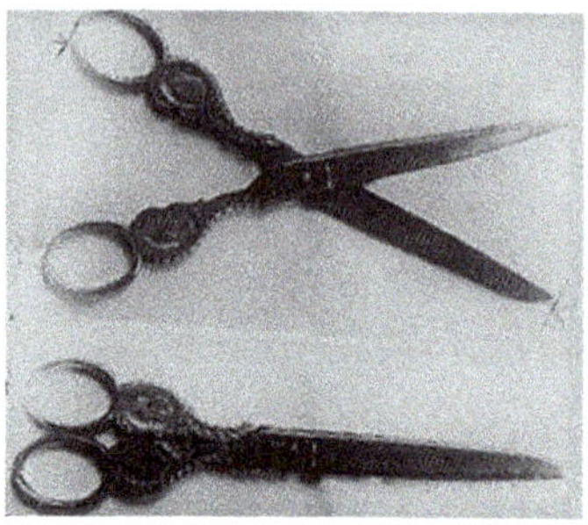

Figure 6.5 Scissors Used by Peter Kürten to Kill His Victims, 1930

American Indian/Alaska Native

There are numerous American Indian/Alaska Native (AI/AN) tribes and cultures. This makes it difficult to determine one overarching definition of serial murder amongst this population. Indeed, given the levels of historical trauma due to colonization and continued underrepresentation in the literature and media, one must view cases where the serial killer is American Indian on an individual basis. Thus, no general description of serial killing per American Indian culture is available in the literature. Indeed, underreporting and scant media attention given to cases involving AI/AN perpetrators and victims has resulted in inadequate knowledge of the depth and breadth of these atrocities either on or off of reservations. With higher than average violent crime amongst AI/AN women especially (Indian Affairs, n.d.) and approximately half of AI/AN murder cases still cold (Hilleary, 2019), one could surmise that the prevalence of serial murder in these communities is higher than recorded and/or publicly distributed.

Leonard Peltier

Although he was only convicted of two murders in 1977, the case of Leonard Peltier, of the Turtle Mountain Band of Chippewa Indians, is poignant in that he murdered two White FBI agents. The murders could have had political and cultural motivations, especially given the time in history. In fact, Peltier was an activist for Native American rights (Dewan, 2025). While most serial killers murder within their own ethnicity, this case was different, and was precipitated by non-natives patrolling the Pine Ridge Indian Reservation, located in South Dakota. The two FBI agents were looking for a man (not Peltier) on the reservation. In their attempt to detain the suspect, other men on the reservation became upset about outsiders attempting to penalize one of their own; the men didn't feel it was the FBI agents' place to do so. This led to a shootout that resulted in the two agents' murders. Despite numerous armed persons present, all of whom were declared innocent, Peltier was the only one who was an activist and who a jury found guilty. Many in the community believed evidence was destroyed, resulting in an unfair trial. Indeed, Peltier continued to state his innocence and his two life sentences were commuted in 2025 to home confinement by President Biden (Dewan, 2025).

Figure 6.6 Leonard Peltier Mugshot, 1972

Discussion question: Do you think Peltier meets the true definition of a serial killer?

James Allen Red Dog

James Allen Red Dog was another American Indian serial killer. He was born in 1954 and raised on the Fort Peck Indian Reservation in Montana (Supreme Court of Delaware, 1992; UPI Archives, 1993). Red Dog was (Dakota) Sioux and Assiniboine. Stuck in poverty from the beginning of his life, he became dismayed with the lack of opportunity afforded on the reservation and for American Indians in general (UPI Archives, 1993). To get by, per Red Dog, he stole food and alcohol. In 1972, one robbery led to the murder of the store owner; Red Dog was arrested and convicted of the man's murder (Supreme Court of Delaware, 1992). His criminal behavior, all he knew in life, resumed in prison, where he sold drugs. This led to an overdose by a fellow inmate who Red Dog supplied with his drugs of choice. Despite these incidents, Red Dog was allowed temporary release for ceremonial purposes. However, he didn't return to the prison as outlined in his temporary release requirements, and instead killed two men who welcomed him into their home to sleep for a night (Supreme Court of Delaware, 1992). Once caught and brought back to jail, he was able to gain favor with law enforcement using charm and manipulation. Prison officials offered him a deal as a snitch, providing inside information about gangs and the American Indian Movement to officials. These actions resulted in his parole in 1990. However, it took little to aggravate him to the point of murder once again, and he murdered his wife's friend in his basement in a fit of rage. Incarcerated for the last time, Red Dog asked to be put to death due to his warrior's code rather than put his family through a long trial. After being blessed by a medicine man, he was executed in 1992 in Delaware (Supreme Court of Delaware, 1992).

Discussion question: What are some cultural variations of serial murder around the world?

South Africa

Available data indicates that there have been around 160 serial killers in South Africa, and of course that number will continue to increase (Labuschange, 2021). Accurate prevalence rates are aided by the South African Police Service, where information is aggregated and disseminated globally (Labuschange, 2021). This practice is not the norm globally. Moreover, the definition of serial killing in South Africa is "the unlawful killing of two or more victims by the same offender(s), in separate events" (Hodgskiss, 2003). This definition is similar to many of the other serial killer/murderer definitions around the world. Commonalities with other countries regarding serial killer cases include being male (there are no recorded cases of female serial murderers), childhood trauma, social isolation, and mental illness. Prevalence data indicate that 67% of serial killers in South Africa are Black and 24% are White, those being the two predominant ethnic groups (Labuschange, 2021). However, research revealed that South African serial murderers are more likely to kill in rural locations, lure victims with promises of employment (Labuschange, 2021), and commit cross-ethnic crimes; are rarely part of a "team"; kill fewer victims over a shorter period of time; and do not report *violent* sexual fantasies (Hodgskiss, 2003). Moreover, research on cases in South Africa suggest a strong focus on power, control, and financial gain. Additionally, a rise in serial murder cases in South Africa occurred during the 1990s. The 1990s was a period of significant political and social change. In fact, in 1995 the death penalty was overturned and is still illegal. Further, urbanization, economic hardship, and high crime rates created conditions that may have contributed to the rise in serial killings in the 1990s. As such, researchers point out that serial murder should not be viewed as a separate category of crime but rather as part of a broader crime pattern influenced by societal factors (Hodgskiss, 2003).

Moses Sithole

Many of these systemic issues were the catalyst for Moses Sithole's violent behavior. Born in Vosloorus, Gauteng, South Africa, in 1964, Sithole had a tumultuous life from the start (Criminalminds, n.d.). His father died when he was a young child, and his mother left him and his siblings to the wills of foster care; she didn't want them. The foster homes weren't much better and he was abused, leaving him to distrust caregivers and people in general (Yesufu, 2022). As an adult, Sithole worked in the gold mines in Johannesburg to make a living. Using his narcissistic charm, he seduced Black women, only to rape and strangle them, often with their own personal items, such as underwear or purse strap (Yesufu, 2022). Apparently, he had disdain for Black women and targeted them specifically. One could hypothesize that this relates to his mother abandoning him as a child. Sithole was first incarcerated for rape, and received some comeuppance in prison (he was repeatedly raped). Once released from prison, his rage and crimes only intensified. He wasted no time before committing his first murder, killing 38 people in two years (Yesufu, 2022). He committed most of his murders in the mid-1990s and was called the ABC killer due to killing in the following three cities in South Africa: Atteridgeville, Boksburg, and Cleveland. Authorities finally determined that Sithole was a suspect, when he was identified by a victim. An operation to capture him was arranged after Sithole called a journalist to brag about the murders. This resulted in a "meet-up," where he wielded an axe in a standoff with police; he was shot as he attempted to run away and was finally caught for good. After admitting to the crimes while in custody, Sithole was convicted and sentenced for his crimes in 1997; he received 2,410 years in prison and sits there to this day (Criminalminds, n.d.).

Image 6.1

Canada

When it comes to punishment for murder, the Canadian government doesn't mess around. "Under paragraph 745(a) of the *Criminal Code of Canada* (CCC), an offender serving life for 1st degree murder is eligible for full parole 25 years after the date they were taken into custody. Eligibility does not mean automatic release. Full parole must be granted by the Parole Board of Canada" (Government of Canada, 2022). This rule is consistent for single and multiple murders. Serial murder is defined the same way as it is in the United States, requiring three or more murders over a period of time with cooling-off periods between each murder. As with most other countries, obtaining statistics on serial murder in Canada is difficult, as police are reticent to discuss the topic and provide information (InFocus, 2019). Further, a Canadian serial killer or homicide database doesn't exist, adding to the limitations of the full understanding of this problem and its affects (InFocus, 2019).

Peter Woodcock

Peter Woodcock, born in 1939 in Toronto, Canada, was abused by his biological and foster parents as a young child (Bourrie et al., 2016). He was eventually placed in an affluent and loving foster home where he attended private school and was given a bicycle to expend his youthful energy. Despite these affordances, Woodcock began showing signs of psychopathy at a young age. Using the newfound freedom of his bike, which he rode around the neighborhood, he lured young children with the promise of an exciting bike ride, only to take them away from their family, rape, mutilate, and murder them (Bourrie et al., 2016; Hier, 2019). In 1956 and 1957, he sexually assaulted and killed three children all under the age of 10 when he was only a teenager. Biting the legs of his victims, he left behind teeth marks that were used to identify Woodcock as the killer (Hier, 2019). Additionally, witnesses provided information about the suspect's appearance and bike, ultimately leading to his capture. He was arrested and sent to a psychiatric ward after being granted a rare not guilty by reason of insanity plea. Woodcock was relatively placid at the institution, until a fellow inmate whom he had a fancy for rejected him sexually. When finally given a day pass from the psychiatric ward, he wasted no time and killed the man a shocking 34 years after being admitted to the facility (Bourrie et al., 2016). Assuming the murder would be connected to him, Woodcock immediately confessed to his last murder. His disturbed existence finally ended when he passed away in 2010 at age 71 (Bourrie et al., 2016; Hier, 2019).

Elizabeth Wettlaufer

Figure 6.7 Elizabeth Wettlaufer Being Arrested, 2016

Another Canadian serial killer, Elizabeth Wettlaufer, chose her place of work in the health care industry to murder her unsuspecting victims (Foong-Reichert et al., 2021; Frank, 2020). As noted previously in this book, this is a classic modus operandi for female serial killers especially; they more commonly than men work in the health care field and also utilize poison and medications to end the life of their victim. Wettlaufer, born in 1967 in Ontario, endured bullying and confusion about her sexuality as a child (McIntosh, 2019). She was a nurse between 2007 and 2016 who misused insulin to kill residents in long-term care homes (Foong-Reichert et al., 2021). Working the night shift helped her remain undetected for years. Indeed, she had a long history of making careless mistakes at work, drug diversion, and unprofessional behavior that should have raised warning signs. In fact, she was suspended for pocketing opioids from work (Frank, 2020). Wettlaufer ended up murdering eight patients over seven years; four patients weren't given a dose high enough to kill them, so they were spared. She was finally arrested in 2016 when she confessed while living in an in-patient facility for addiction and mental health, where she was diagnosed with major depressive disorder, borderline personality disorder, and antisocial traits (Foong-Reichert et al., 2021; McIntosh, 2019). She explained that the reason for the murders was due to the patients being inappropriate and that she was so unhappy with herself and her life. Some of this distress might have been due to conflicts between her strict Baptist upbringing and her sexual interest in women (McIntosh, 2019).

Japan

Secrecy and silence prevail over serial murder in Japan. With lack of consensus in a definition for serial murder, Japan uses the United States's definition (Kantha, 2024). Most serial killers who have been caught and convicted in Japan acted alone (Kantha, 2024). Further, psychopathy and sexual sadism are prominent, and most killers fit into the organized category, which corresponds to the methodical cultural prototype. In cases where an individual has been convicted of serial murder, execution may be the ultimate punishment for their crimes. However, the death penalty has always been controversial in Japan; instead of abolishing it, the government allows it on a case-by-case basis (Kantha, 2024; Metraux, 2024). The government does not announce pending executions nor confirm that they even occurred after the event. Indeed, knowledge of the execution is only due to details being leaked to the press by family members or lawyers of the deceased, if at all. Between 1945 and 2000, Japan executed 584 people (Metraux, 2024). Furthermore, hanging is the only method used for all executions in Japan (Kantha, 2024).

Norio Nagayama

Norio Nagayama was born in 1949 in Abashiri, Hokkaido. Nagayama's father died at a young age and his mother abandoned him; he grew up very poor and frequently changed jobs as an adult (Metraux, 2024). Nagayama admitted to robbing and killing four men across the nation in 1968 with an American-made pistol stolen from the American Air Force Base in Japan; strict gun laws in Japan impede easy access to firearms (Kantha, 2024). He was arrested in 1969 after attempting to enter a Tokyo school. He pled for mercy at his trial, saying his crimes were due to "poverty and ignorance." Despite only being 19 years old at the time of his arrest, and considered a minor at that age, he was sentenced to death due to the depravity of his crimes. Given the death penalty initially, his sentence was reduced two years later due acknowledgement of the failings of Japanese governmental welfare and assistance (Kantha, 2024; Metraux, 2024). This change didn't last long though, and in 1997 he was sentenced to death yet again.

During his time in prison, Nagayama became a successful novelist and donated his earnings to the victims' families and a charity that assisted children living in poverty. His family begged for leniency for him but was unsuccessful. His case, however, resulted in a change in the law related to murder called the "Nagayama Criteria." The criteria included the nature of the crimes, motivation, the method used to kill, number of victims, the feelings the family has toward the killer, magnitude of social implications, age of the killer, criminal record, and degree of remorse that has been demonstrated by the killer (Metraux, 2024). This set of nine factors is used by Japanese judges to determine whether a case warrants the death penalty. Despite his rehabilitation efforts, Japanese courts upheld his execution, emphasizing the brutality of his crimes. Nagayama's execution in 1997 sparked debate about Japan's death penalty system, particularly the secrecy surrounding executions and the conditions of death row inmates.

Video of Nagayama Norio and the death penalty:

QR Code 6.1

India

In India, "the word 'murder' is defined under Section 300 IPC wherein an injury is caused to a person which is sufficient to cause death in the ordinary course of nature, with the intention to cause such injury, and if the bodily injury is intended to be inflicted is likely to cause death, it is labelled as 'culpable homicide' under Section 299 IPC" (Dalal et al., 2009, p. 110). Interestingly, there are no laws that outline the punishment for serial killing in India. In fact, some states in India do not acknowledge such crimes, perhaps to avoid an increase in reported violence. Another possible reason for sparse information about serial killing in India is due to their concern about an increased likelihood of copycats, which can increase crime rates. Thus, the lack of reporting and undefined punishment may be a strategy by government officials to keep the crimes at bay (Dalal et al., 2009).

Additionally, sociocultural norms affect the view of serial killing in India. Indeed, their religious philosophy of aggression is based on Hindu scripts (Balodhi, 2001). Adherence to the scripts and **dharma** (duty) are the ways in which to control feelings and acts of violence, including murder. Moreover, deities in Indian culture represent the phenomenology of anger and the desire to engage in destructive behaviors (Balodhi, 2001). It is argued that aggression can and should be controlled. However, when an individual is aggressive and is disciplined, thoughts of revenge arise, reducing the impact of the punishment. Therefore, per beliefs in India, punishment does not mitigate **recidivism**; in other words, it does not serve as a form of prevention against subsequent criminal activity. The belief is that spirituality should be used to overcome mental disorders and aggression. Self-examination and meditation techniques can be used as well, such as reciting prayers, energy transference, yoga, and rituals (Balodhi, 2001).

Surinder Koli

Surinder Koli, one of India's most well-known serial killers, was responsible for murdering 19 children in Nithari between 2005 and 2007 (BBC, 2023; Dogra et al., 2012). He was servant and accomplice to Moninder Singh. Just like many of the cases above, Koli was influenced by many factors, including traumatic childhood experiences and mental illness. At a young age,

Koli showed signs of antisocial personality disorder. If you remember from Chapter 3, this disorder includes criteria such as a lack of empathy, deceptive behavior, manipulation of others, and violent tendencies (Dogra et al., 2012). Indeed, he had disturbing thoughts about killing and harming others as a child. Unfortunately, Indian cultural factors, such as the avoidance of violence, may have helped Koli avoid detection. However, when rumors about missing children whose bodies were discarded in bags were spread to neighboring communities, authorities discovered the victims' corpses near his home in Nithari. Disturbingly, he also engaged in necrophilia and cannibalism (BBC, 2023).

During the investigation, Surinder Koli was secretive and uncooperative, often pretending not to understand questions. Even though his crimes were extremely violent, brain scans found no abnormalities (Dogra et al., 2012). However, the Rorschach Inkblot Test and Thematic Apperception Test indicated that he avoided showing emotions and had deep-seated violent thoughts. While Koli claimed not to remember luring his victims with candy, strangling, raping, and murdering them, the evidence showed his crimes were premeditated and he was cognizant of his actions (Dogra et al., 2012). In a shocking twist, a judge reviewed the case and determined that there was insufficient evidence to convict Koli of the murders. Further, Koli stated that his confession was the result of torture and he was truly innocent of the crimes. This led to his release from prison in 2023 (BBC, 2023).

Ireland

Ireland is a small country with a population of 5.3 million (United States Census Bureau, 2025). Even though murder rates in Ireland have changed over time, the country has had one of the lowest murder rates in Europe, even lower than Japan and Singapore (Wilbanks, 1996). There was an uptick in murder and serial murder per police records in the 1800s during the potato famine, but prevalence rates have dropped significantly since then (Wilbanks, 1996). Indeed, in the 1960s, the murder rate remained low and stable. A common thread amongst serial murder in Ireland is that the perpetrator and victim often know one another. Additionally, very few murders in Ireland were related to robbery or gangs (Wilbanks, 1996).

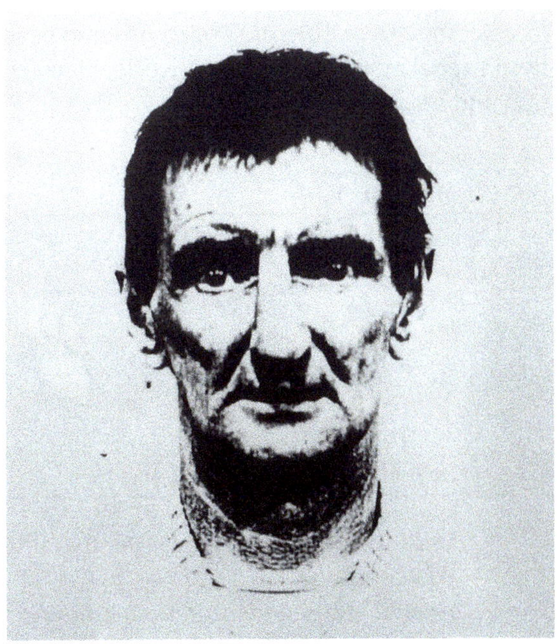

Figure 6.8 Kieran Kelly, n.d.

Kieran Kelly

Kieran Kelly was one of the few Irish serial killers where sufficient information was available to properly include the case in this book. Kelly was born in Rathdowney, County Laois, in Ireland in 1930 (Platt, 1988). He grew up poor and spent most of his free time at church. Homeless and destitute for most of his adult life, he wandered around London after moving there following a failed marriage while he resided in Dublin. With few skills to secure a decent job, he drank away his time with thoughts of homosexual acts. Another failed marriage and abandonment by that wife and their children left Kelly in even worse spirits. Struggling to keep warm in the cold London winters, he loitered in the underground subway, where he pushed unsuspecting victims off the platform and onto the tracks right before a train approached (Platt, 1988). To silence one of his victims who had discovered that Kelly had engaged in sex with men, he pushed him in front of a train, quickly ending his life. In fact, he did this eight times and was arrested each time, only to continue to murder while in prison. There is no explanation as to how he was released each of these times. The final conviction occurred in 1983 (Platt, 1988) and the rest of his life was spent in prison until he passed away in 2001 at age 71.

Summary

Certainly, there are additional countries and with countless other serial killer cases, but these are some fascinating ones, as is the information about each country's view of murder or serial murder. It's not surprising that cultural norms greatly influence how each country evaluates homicide and its view of the appropriate punishment. This fact affects reported numbers of serial killing in each country. Further, few countries have the infrastructure and interest in pooling resources to maintain databases on serial killer statistics. Indeed, many countries don't have DNA databases that could aid in the capture of many at-large serial killers (Labuschange, 2021). It's important to understand that these variations exist and influence reporting of cases, thus leading to inaccurate and missing data that could provide us with a more complete picture of serial murder in several countries. Ultimately, there are commonalities in serial murder around the world. Many killers' motives are connected to sexual gratification and power.

Keywords

Dharma

Recidivism

Vampire

Chapter Review Questions

1. Describe Japanese serial killer characteristics based on the information provided in this chapter.
2. How might historical trauma influence one's desire to kill?
3. What is unique about Japan's rules regarding their conviction and execution of serial murderers?

References

Balodhi, J. P. (2001). Phenomenology of aggression: Indian context. *Indian Journal of Psychological Medicine, 24*(1), 11–15.

BBC. (2023). *Nithari killings: Men jailed for India 'house of horrors' murders freed.* https://www.bbc.com/news/world-asia-india-67119737

Bourrie, M., Vronsky, P., & Parker, R. J. (2016). *Peter Woodcock: Canada's youngest serial killer.* RJ Parker Publishing Inc.

Criminalminds. (n.d.). *Moses Sithole.* https://criminalminds.fandom.com/wiki/Moses_Sithole

Dalal, J. S., Aggarwal, K. K., Bhullar, D. S., & Sharma, M. (2009). A case study of serial killers. *Journal of Punjab Academy of Forensic Medicine & Toxicology, 9*, 109–113.

Dewan, S. (2025, February 18). *Native American activist Leonard Peltier released from prison. The New York Times.* https://www.nytimes.com/2025/02/18/us/leonard-peltier-released-prison.html

Dogra, T. D., Leenaars, A. A., Chadha, R. K., Manju, M., Lalwani, S., Sood, M., Lester, D., Raina, A., & Behera, C. (2012). A psychological profile of a serial killer: A case report. *OMEGA—Journal of Death and Dying, 65*(4), 299–316. https://doi.org/10.2190/om.65.4.d

Foong-Reichert, A., Grindrod, K. A., & Houle, S. K. D. (2021).Exploring health professional criminality and competence using the case of Canadian health care serial killer Elizabeth Wettlaufer. *Journal of Medical Regulation, 107*(3), 19–27.

Forensics: Germany considers wider use of DNA evidence in criminal cases [Editorial]. (2017). *Nature, 543*, 589–590. https://doi.org/10.1038/543589b

Frank, C. (2020). Health care serial murder. *Canadian Family Physician, 66*(10), 719–722.

Government of Canada. (2022). *Sentence calculation: Fast facts: Offender serving life sentence for 1st degree murder. https://www.publicsafety.gc.ca/cnt/rsrcs/pblctns/2021-sntnc-clcltn-fstfcts-02/index-en.aspx*

Harbort, S., & Mokros, A. (2001). Serial murderers in Germany from 1945–1995: A descriptive study. *Homicide Studies, 5*(4), 311–334.

Hier, S. (2019). Almost famous: Peter Woodcock, media framing, and obscurity in the cultural construction of a serial killer. *Crime, Media, Culture: An International Journal, 16*(3), 375–394.

Hilleary, C. (2019, November 15). *Data suggest serial killers active in Indian country. Voice of America (VOA).* https://www.voanews.com/a/usa_data-suggest-serial-killers-active-indian-country/6179327.html

Hodgskiss, B. (2003). Lessons from serial murder in South Africa. *Journal of Investigative Psychology and Offender Profiling, 1*(1), 67–94. https://doi.org/10.1002/jip.2

Indian Affairs. (n.d.). *Missing and murdered indigenous people crisis: Violence against Native Americans and Alaska Natives far exceed national averages*. U.S. Department of the Interior. https://www.bia.gov/service/mmu/missing-and-murdered-indigenous-people-crisis

InFocus. (2019, May 1). *Serial killers hunting large swaths of Canada: Criminologist. APTN News.* https://www.aptnnews.ca/national-news/serial-killers-hunting-large-swaths-of-canada-criminologist/

Kantha, S. S. (2024). Serial murderers in Japan (1882–2017): A narrative analysis. *Jaffna Medical Journal, 36*(1), 33–37.

Labuschange, G. N. (2001). An overview of serial murder and its investigation in South Africa. In Chan H. C. O., & Adjorlolo, S. (Eds.). Crime, mental health and the criminal justice system in Africa (pp. 121-148). Palgrave Macmillan.

McIntosh, E. (2019, August 19). *Elizabeth Wettlaufer case*. Historica Canada. https://thecanadianencyclopedia.ca/en/article/elizabeth-wettlaufer-case

Metraux, D. A. (2024). *The Nagayama Criteria for assessing the death penalty in Japan: Reflections of a case suspect.* The Free Library. https://www.thefreelibrary.com/The+Nagayama+criteria+for+assessing+the+death+penalty+in+Japan%3A...-a0213529570

Murray, W. (2007). *Serial killers: Notorious killers who lived among us*. Canary Press.

Platt, G. (1988). *London underground serial killer: The life of Kieran Kelly.* Pen & Sword Books Ltd.

Ramsland, K. (2006). *Inside the minds of serial killers: Why they kill*. Praeger

Red Dog v. State, 616 A.2d 298 (1992). https://law.justia.com/cases/delaware/supreme-court/1992/616-a-2d-298-1.html

Schechter, H. (2003). *The serial killer files: The who, what, where, how, and why of the world's most terrifying murderers.* Ballantine Books.

Serena, K. (2024, November 3). *Peter Kürten, the 'Vampire of Dusseldorf' who murdered young girls for sexual pleasure—and sometimes drank their blood*. Retrieved March 12, 2025, from https://allthatsinteresting.com/peter-kurten

United States Census Bureau. (2025). Ireland. https://www.census.gov/popclock/world/ei

UPI Archives. (1993). Delaware executes five-time killer James Allen Red Dog. https://www.upi.com/Archives/1993/03/03/Delaware-executes-five-time-killer-James-Allen-Red-Dog/8000731134800/

Warren, A. R. (2021). *Butcher of Hanover: Fritz Haarmann.* House of Mystery.

Wilbanks, W. (1996). Homicide in Ireland. *International Journal of Comparative and Applied Criminal Justice, 20*(1), 59–75. https://doi.org/10.1080/01924036.1996.9678562

Yesufu, S. (2022). An insight into the socio-psycho contexts and modus operandi of South Africa's worst serial killers over time. *EUREKA: Social and Humanities, 4*, 103–112.

Image Credits

Fig. 6.1: Copyright © 1931 by Bundesarchiv, Bild 102-11502 (CC BY-SA 3.0) at https://commons.wikimedia.org/wiki/File:Bundesarchiv_Bild_102-11502,_Polizeiaufnahme_eines_Massenm%C3%B6rders.jpg.

Fig. 6.2: Data Source: https://www.worldatlas.com/crime/countries-that-have-produced-the-most-serial-killers.html

Fig. 6.3: Copyright © by Aktuelle-Bilder-Centrale, Georg Pahl (Bild 102) (CC BY-SA 3.0) at https://commons.wikimedia.org/wiki/File:Bundesarchiv_Bild_102-00881,_Hannover,_Proze%C3%9F_gegen_Friedrich_Haarmann.jpg.

Fig. 6.4: German Weimar Republic, https://commons.wikimedia.org/wiki/File:Mugshot-K%C3%BCrten.jpg, 1931.

Fig. 6.5: German Weimar Republic, https://commons.wikimedia.org/wiki/File:PeterK%C3%BCrtenScissorsAttacksWeimar1929c.jpg, 1929.

Fig. 6.6: Federal Bureau of Investigation, https://commons.wikimedia.org/wiki/File:Leonard_Peltier_mug_shot_(cropped2).jpg, 1972.

IMG 6.1: Copyright © 2020 Depositphotos/HandmadePicture.

Fig. 6.7: Screenshot from Annie Elise, "Nurse Turned Serial Killer: The Elizabeth Wettlaufer Story," https://www.youtube.com/shorts/hWU3DsDekFw, 2025.

Fig. 6.8: Copyright © 1980 by Scotland Yard, OGLv3.0 at: https://commons.wikimedia.org/wiki/File:Kieran_Patrick_Kelly.jpg. A copy of the license can be found here: https://www.nationalarchives.gov.uk/doc/open-government-licence/version/3/.

CHAPTER 7

KILLING PATTERNS

Analyzing the Modus Operandi of Serial Killers

"I liked to drive by the 'clusters' around the county and think about the women I placed there."

-Gary Ridgway

Figure 7.1 Gary Ridgway Mugshot, 2001

Modus operandi is "a distinct pattern or method of operation that indicates or suggests the work of a single criminal in more than one crime" (Merriam-Webster, 2024). Crime scenes provide information about the killer's psychological state and the fantasy that led to their actions, including how they kill their victims and where they dispose of the bodies. The site(s) tend to echo elements of the killer's fantasy in such manners as the placement and condition of the body (Ressler et al., 1988). Serial killers often continue the same patterns in their method of killing. This could be due to the comfortability and assurance of knowing they can get away with murder through these specific approaches. Often, part of the thrill is the "signature" that marks their territory, so to speak; it provides abundant information about the killer's psychological state before, during, and after the murder, providing information as to *why* they did it.

Ultimately, it all starts with motive. What drives the individual toward committing the cruelest acts imaginable? The most common motives are power, money, sexual sadism, fame, and mental illness. The next step in their minds is how to locate and lure victims. Do they choose easy targets (sex workers, runaway children), victims who resemble the ex-lover who scorned them, or do they pick an unlucky woman who is in the wrong place at the wrong time? Once they have chosen a target, do they have a weapon in hand or do they plan to use the victim's clothing to strangle them, or rely on brute strength to overpower them? Post-kill, there are additional strategies and perversions that these killers engage in, such as dumping the body in a river to remove evidence, or having sex with the corpse and then cooking and eating the meat. Whichever modus operandi the serial killer chooses, it helps profilers understand more about the killer, which ideally results in capture and end of their reign of havoc.

Learning Outcomes

After reading this chapter, students will be able to do the following:

1. Assess patterns in the ways serial killers choose victims.
2. Distinguish variations in the ways in which serial killers end their victims' lives.
3. Understand how modus operandi is created and maintained by serial killers.

Gender Variations in Modus Operandi

Women and men are vastly different in many regards. One of these is the way in which they exhibit patterns as serial killers, including victim choice, method of murder, and post-kill behavior (Wilson & Hilton, 1998). One hypothesis that utilizes evolutionary psychology notes that, conventionally, men have been providers, killing prey to feed their family (Harrison et al., 2019). Indeed, male serial killers demonstrate a wider range or geographical disbursement for trolling and stalking their victims. Meanwhile, women historically stayed home to tend to the children and gather food or harvest crops. These traditional roles could explain the higher prevalence of male serial killers and also their pattern of stalking victims/prey. Additionally, men tend to use physical force to murder strangers, while women methodically choose those close to them, including spouses and children, as a means toward a more financially secure end (Harrison et al., 2019). As you will see, this modus operandi, and others, including women's use of poison and men's preference for sexual sadism, hold true for many of the following case examples.

Motive

There are abundant personal motives expressed by serial killers. Some may be more covert, while others are extremely apparent. Oftentimes our childhood shapes our future needs, wants, and desires, as noted in Chapter 2. Other times our current sociocultural situation isn't ideal and we need to make ends meet at any cost. Ultimately, the most common motives for serial killing include power, sexual sadism, money, anger, fame, and mental illness (Haggerty, 2009; Harrison et al., 2019; Morton et al., 2005; Myers et al., 2006). These are certainly not mutually exclusive and are most often intertwined to create a sick killer.

Table 7.1 Motive, Method, and Number of Kills

	Men		Women	
Primary motive	***N***	**%**	***N***	**%**
Financial gain	1,238	28.3	302	69.6
Enjoyment—rape	1,209	27.7	16	3.7
Anger	779	17.8	76	17.5
Multiple motives	532	12.2	15	3.5
Enjoyment—no rape	360	8.2	23	5.3
Gang/criminal enterprise	254	5.8	2	0.5
	Men		**Women**	
Killing method	**N**	**%**	**N**	**%**
Shoot	1,434	**35.2**	76	19.1
Strangle	626	15.3	18	4.5
Stab	459	11.3	31	7.8
Stab/shoot	315	7.7	14	3.5
Bludgeon	310	7.6	15	3.8
Strangle/stab	196	4.8	4	1.0
Bludgeon/stab	191	4.7	13	3.3
Bludgeon/shoot	160	3.9	5	1.3
Strangle/bludgeon	163	4.0	2	0.5
Strangle/shoot	117	2.9	3	0.8
Poison	98	2.4	217	**54.5**
Bomb	10	0.2	0	0.0

Source: Michael G. Aamodt, Terence Leary, and Senthil Girimurugan, Selection from Radford/FGCU Annual Report on Serial Killer Statistics: 2023, p. 30. Copyright © 2023 by Radford University.

Power

When you lacked **power** and control as a child, and even into adulthood, you want to take back what you weren't initially afforded. Serial killers enjoy the power they have over others; they are finally in that role, rather than on the receiving end, as mentioned at length in Chapter 2. While power and control may assist a serial killer in overpowering their victims (Myers et al., 2006), thus may be a necessity in and of itself, psychological power in the sense of knowing the victim is frightened and willing to comply with their requests in order to reduce harm is its own source of satisfaction for the killer (Holmes et al., 1991). In fact, power is one of the most motivating factors behind serial killing. It is a foundational way of viewing and thinking about the world. The world isn't safe, as is evidenced by childhood trauma, and this leads an individual to adopt a power-orientation thinking style (Culhane et al., 2019). In other cases, political power is attained through the systematic removal of those deemed outsiders.

Peter Mangs

Figure 7.2 Peter Mangs in Court, 2012

Indeed, this was the case for Peter Mangs, a serial killer born in Sweden in 1972 who sought power through the killing of non-Whites (Gardell, 2018). His childhood was typical in many ways, with strict parents who withheld affection and never said I love you. Growing up, Mangs was influenced by the writings of Nietzsche and Hitler; Mangs believed in power, immorality, and eugenics (Belles, 2025). He was methodical in his study of their philosophies as well as music and nursing. Therefore, propelled by his sociopolitical ideals, Mangs desired to rid Sweden of those he felt didn't belong there. His reign of terror began in 2003 when he shot and killed his first victims based solely on their ethnicity (Gardell, 2018). By all accounts, he could have been a very productive member of society if not for his hatred of anyone unlike himself. He lived in Florida for a time before returning to Sweden to "clean it out." Stalking and shooting at least three people, and attempting to shoot 12 others, Mangs enacted his need for power while capitalizing on the fact that law enforcement assumed the killings were done by those in the Muslim, Jewish, or other minority communities, thereby offering him freedom to continue killing (Belles, 2025; Gardell, 2018). Finally, police realized that all of the victims were minorities and that's what truly connected them. Mangs was arrested in 2010 and convicted of only two of the murders. He was sentenced to life in prison, where he remains today.

Sexual Sadism

While power and control are often at the root of serial killing, so is sexual sadism, though these are certainly not mutually exclusive (Ressler & Shachtman, 1992). Though not the motive behind all serial killing, it is commonly at the root of the fantasy and final sadistic acts (Myers et al., 2006; Schechter, 2003). Childhood sexual desires build and grow into unfulfilled fantasy, which eventually escalates to, in the serial killer's mind, a need for sadism in order to achieve sexual gratification (Schechter, 2003), as noted in Chapter 3. Research has attempted to ascertain whether sexual murder differs from other types of murder (Healey et al., 2014). It was hypothesized that the sexual serial killer is a unique type of offender compared to those who sexually assault without killing their victim(s). The study found that sexual murderers' motive *is* the act of homicide and/or the sexual enjoyment of mutilating corpses (Healey et al., 2014). In fact, additional research pointed out that sexual sadism most often begins with manipulative behavior in adolescence, with some of the most common sadistic acts being vaginal rape and necrophilia (Myers et al., 2006).

John Christie

A sexual sadist and psychopath, John Christie raped and murdered his wife and several other women in his home in London, England, in the 1940s and 1950s (Schechter, 2003). As a reserved and mild-mannered man, Christie was unassuming and used this to his advantage when luring women into his home. His seemingly calm demeanor arose from a childhood full of neuroses that resulted in his selective mutism for several years as an adolescent (Schechter, 2003). Despite this façade, he fantasized about strangling and raping women. Though approachable enough to find a woman to marry, he went on to kill her and hide her body under the floorboards of their flat along with the other women. When he ran out of room in his flat, he buried his last two victims in his garden/backyard (Ramsland, 2006). Christie enjoyed sexual excitement from luring these unsuspecting women with promises of help with medical issues so he could gas or strangle them prior to engaging in necrophilia with their lifeless bodies (Lynes & Wilson, 2015; Schechter, 2003). He believed that he needed the women to be unconscious before he could achieve sexual arousal (Ramsland, 2006). He was finally caught when he moved out of his flat and the new tenants remodeled, only to find the bodies of the missing women, tying Christie to the murders. When he was hanged in 1953, the world was finally relieved of his evil.

Figure 7.3 John Christie Mugshot, 1953

Money

Women tend to kill for **money** more often than men. Several female serial killers have rid themselves of their husbands and children to cash in insurance policies. This, in part, explains why women begin killing at an older age than men, typically. Many of these female serial killers marry repeatedly as a way to collect their husbands' financial assets (Harrison et al., 2019; Wilson & Hilton, 1998). Historically, women have been at the whim of their husbands' ability to provide for the family, as they were unable to own homes or open bank accounts without their husbands' signature (U.S. Justice Department, 2011). This left them with few other choices for meeting their financial needs. Obviously, that doesn't justify killing your husband, but puts it in context, especially in relation to the case example below. Though times have thankfully changed, women still tend to kill for financial gain, at times searching for wealthy elderly victims (Holmes et al., 1991).

Belle Gunness

Figure 7.4 Belle Gunness and Her Three Children, 1908

One prime example of serial murder for financial gain is the case of Belle Gunness. Gunness was born in Norway in 1859. Not much is known about her childhood, though one could speculate that it consisted of abuse. Once an adult, fire and death followed Gunness everywhere she went. She met and married a man named Mads Sorenson. Together they had two children and owned a convenience store (Ramsland, 2006). When the store burned down, they collected the insurance money. This may have been Gunness's first taste of the fruits of fraud, and became a pattern with which she grew quite familiar. Not long after the fire, her husband and children became ill and passed away (Schechter, 2003). As the only family member remaining, the insurance money was all hers. She bought a farm in the country in Illinois, where she solicited suitors through want ads. Several men came to call, only to never be seen again. Between those men and their children, Gunness murdered around 40 people, dismembered them to remove evidence, and buried them on her expansive farm (Schechter, 2003). Eventually, a worker on her farm became suspicious, which led her to reportedly set her house on fire with her foster children in it. Police also found an adult woman's body in the house fire, but the head was never recovered, which led those in town to hypothesize that Gunness plotted the whole thing and escaped, never to be seen again (Ramsland, 2006). Clearly, she wasn't interested in being known, but rather getting away with it, unlike the next serial killer.

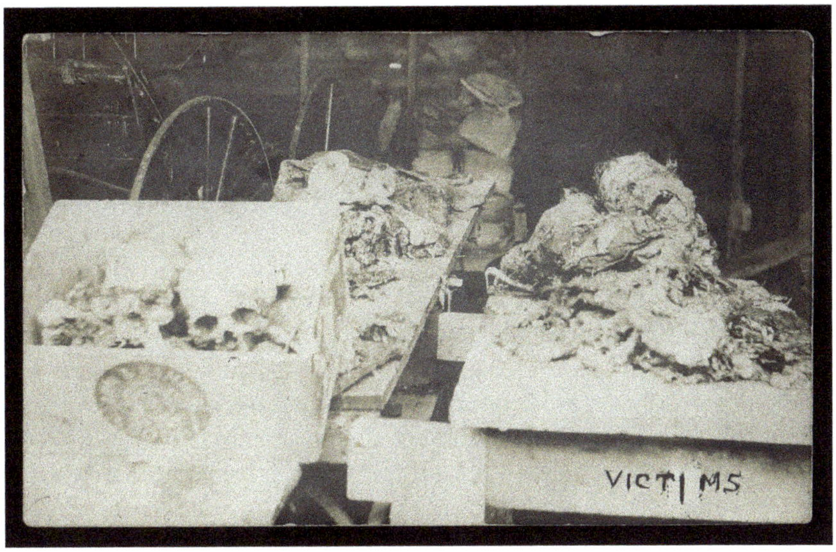

Figure 7.5 Victims' Bones Found on Gunness's Farm

Figure 7.6 Belle Gunness's Burned House

Discussion question: Why might people seek fame for criminal acts rather than prosocial accomplishments?

Fame

We all want to be seen and acknowledged by others, but some serial killers take this too far. They don't just want to be famous, but infamous, for committing horrendous crimes. Due to a lack of attention as a child, and likely as an adult as well, these individuals crave attention and hope to receive media coverage for their crimes; they want people to remember their name and face for years after they are put to death by the justice system (Haggerty, 2009). Historically, newspapers printed information about crimes, but not everyone received the paper or read it, which is a stark difference to the world we live in today. Further, we knew our neighbors; anonymity was virtually nonexistent. Now, our world is a juxtaposition to that life as we walk in mass amongst strangers. Nearly everyone has instant access to news and various other types of media. For those who aspire to achieve **fame** through murder, these changes have only fueled their fire.

Daniel Gonzalez

While many serial killers clearly enjoy the attention they receive from the media and fans, few kill solely for notoriety. Daniel Gonzalez is one of those. His goal in life was to terrorize those who resided in London and Sussex, England (BBC, 2006; Bowcott, 2006). Most serial killers extend their rage over months or years; Gonzalez, in contrast, killed four people within the span of three days in September 2004 (Bowcott, 2006). He stabbed and killed elderly individuals in particular due to his desire for easy victims. Outrageous acts were not uncommon for Gonzalez, who reportedly ran around local shops naked on one occasion (Bowcott, 2006). Despite this, his mother declares that help for her son never came, regardless of her numerous pleas for help (BBC, 2006). With no mental health care, Gonzalez continued to fantasize about achieving fame in the most shocking way possible. Hence, the murders were premeditated, as Gonzalez's sole goal in life was to be a famous killer and, in his mind, emulate Freddy Krueger from *A Nightmare on Elm Street* (Bowcott, 2006). Once caught and convicted, his outlandish antics continued. In an attempt to reduce his sentence, he feigned mental illness, stating he heard voices. While this led to a diagnosis of schizophrenia, he was still considered competent to stand trial and was sentenced to life in prison for murder. Perhaps in a last-ditch attempt to gain more media attention and notoriety, he committed suicide in 2007 (Bowcott, 2006).

Mental Illness

Mental illness can be insidious and lead people to act in ways they normally wouldn't. A large percentage of serial killers have been diagnosed with one or more mental disorders, as noted in Chapter 3. Since mental disorders were discussed at length previously, we will dive right into a case example.

Figure 7.7 David Berkowitz Being Arrested, 1977

David Berkowitz

David Berkowitz is one of the more well-known serial killers. He frightened New York City residents back in the late 1970s. Born in Brooklyn, New York, in 1953, he was unwanted, and his parents split up and put him up for adoption (Alcatraz East Crime Museum, n.d.). From the get-go, he enjoyed pushing the envelope and getting into trouble. He also enjoyed setting fires, a typical serial killer trait. Not only did he enjoy the infamy, but he was diagnosed with paranoid schizophrenia, which clouded his cognitive judgment (Raine, 2013). Stating he only killed attractive women (who often were with their boyfriends, parked at the local make-out spot) due to being ordered to by his neighbor's barking dog, Sam (hence his moniker Son of Sam), he lacked lucidity. He was suspicious of others and enjoyed the power he had over couples unable to safely leave their vehicle while he shot them to death (Schechter, 2003). In total, he killed six people and wounded several others. He had taunted the police with disturbing letters, reveling in his crimes and authorities' inability to capture him. However, ballistics from the same .44 caliber Bulldog used in several murders were traced back to Berkowitz (Alcatraz East Crime Museum, n.d.). He was finally caught due to surviving victims' description of his vehicle, which police traced back to Berkowitz. In his car they found ample evidence to connect him to the murders, including another letter he intended to send to police. On trial, psychologists deemed him unfit to stand trial (Schechter, 2003), yet the judge overruled that and he was sentenced to life in prison.

Figure 7.8 Drawing of David Berkowitz in Court

Victim Selection

When your mother has berated you your entire life and told you women are sinful, this negatively impacts your view of women and skews your relationship with them. Sometimes people are lonely and want company, whether they are dead or alive. While there are other reasons for victim choice, such as opportunity and sexual attraction, these are some of the most common motives and explanations for our understanding of *why* they killed these specific types of victims. Serial killers often dehumanize their victims to the point of thinking they are pests or vermin; this is how they justify their actions (Haggerty, 2009). Society tends to not see all people as equal. Some are seen as better and others as less than. The populations most commonly prone to denigration include the homeless, homosexuals, women, prostitutes, the mentally ill, racial minorities, and children. Serial killers are able to take advantage of this societal viewpoint and target people from these marginalized groups, knowing they are less likely to be reported missing, not including children.

Familiarity

Some serial killers have a particular type of victim they stalk, gain access to, and kill. This provides insight into their psychological state, especially when they are motivated to kill due to being scorned by a past lover or abusive mother (Kumkaria & Tiwari, 2024). Several cases already mentioned in this book tie directly into this type of victim selection. Ted Bundy, whose case was discussed in Chapter 2, chose women who looked much like his first girlfriend who rejected him; they all had long brunette hair that was parted down the middle (though that was the most typical hairstyle at the time). Was his ego so fragile that he couldn't bear the thought of being rejected? Did he think he would never find another woman like her? Bundy admitted to turning to pornography to satisfy his fantasies and fetishes, so perhaps the breakup spurred anger and the need to dominate women (Ramsland, 2006). Likewise, Ed Kemper, also described in Chapter 2, killed women who attended the college where his mother worked, as he associated that location with her (Schechter, 2003). After growing up in a household where he was dominated by his mother and grandmother, Kemper formed a hatred for women. Furthermore, he was unsure of how to interact with them since he lacked healthy experience in that realm. Feeling as though his mother took away his ability to form romantic relationships, he slowly attempted to have contact with women, which escalated into killing several of them, yet his mother was his real target, and he admits it (Ramsland, 2006). This level of scorn and spite can only arise from true disdain for the person, or people, who did you wrong. They are unable to ever let it go or move past it in adaptive ways with coping skills. Though they may be intelligent in some areas (Bundy was a law school student, Kemper is reported to have an IQ of 145), their emotional intelligence is greatly lacking.

Vulnerability

Another unfortunate modus operandi related to victim choice is disenfranchised members of society, such as sex workers, the homeless, indigenous individuals, and runaway children. With few family ties and a society that devalues them, those who are most vulnerable in so many regards in life are also prey for serial killers (Jiwani & Young, 2006; Haritaworn, 2019; Wttis, 2017). They are viewed as criminals and drug addicts who are responsible for their own demise, thus resulting in society's view of them as "less than" and unworthy of police resources and media coverage (Jiwani & Young, 2006; Wattis, 2017). When you want to get away with harming someone, this is group that will allow you to do so for much, much longer than you should. One man who knew this well was Gary Ridgway.

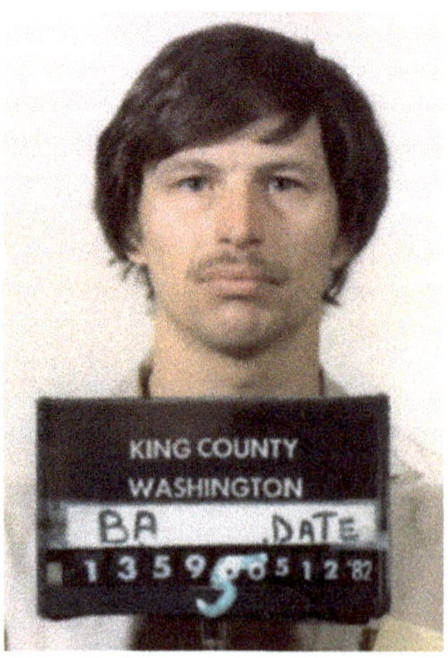

Figure 7.9 Gary Ridgway Mugshot, 1982

Gary Ridgway

Although many serial killers have chosen sex workers as their victims, none were as prolific as Gary Ridgway. Between 1982 and 2001, he killed at least 49 women in and around Seattle, Washington, most of whom were prostitutes (Levi-Minzi & Shields, 2007). Growing up, his father would often talk about necrophilia while his mother would berate him in front of his siblings for being a chronic bed wetter. Additionally, his mother was abusive towards his father, who never stood up for himself, modeling female dominance and male passivity (Levi-Minzi & Shields, 2007). Despite having a low IQ, Ridgway knew that killing prostitutes was the best way for him to get away with serial murder (Rossouw & Palys, 2024). In fact, he said, "[They] were easy to pick up without being noticed. I knew they would not be reported missing right away and might never be reported missing. I picked prostitutes because I thought I could kill as many of them as I wanted without getting caught" (Piccotti & Bertram, 2023, para. 14). Due to Ridgeway's non-threatening demeanor and status as a family man, often showing pictures of his son to prostitutes while negotiating, the women felt they were safe, and he used that to his advantage. However, after the sexual encounter, Ridgway would become angry and violent (Levi-Minzi & Shields, 2007). Finally, after murdering and disposing of the women in the Green River, he went about his life with one of his three wives, before DNA technology advanced and he was finally caught when he was linked to a victim (Piccotti & Bertram, 2023). He was sentenced to life in prison in 2001 and then linked to two more victims with the help of DNA technology.

Figure 7.10 After Agreeing to a Secret Plea Deal, Gary Ridgway Took Investigators to Several Remote Sites Where He Said He'd Dumped His Victims' Bodies.

Health Care Serial Killers

Another vulnerable population, yet in a different way, hospital patients are often elderly or infirm and unable to defend themselves. This makes them sitting ducks. While serial killers who work in health care professions aren't always women, they are more commonly represented in this field (Yardley & Wilson, 2016; Wilson & Hilton, 1998). When these health care serial killers (HCSKs) tend to always be on shift before, during, and after a patient's death, more than other doctors and nurses, it's a red flag. Other warning signs are when these same individuals make coworkers feel anxious, prefer to work the night shift, have a history of depression or mental instability, and possess of drugs at work or home, to name a few (Frank, 2020; Yardley & Wilson, 2016). With easy access to medication, overdose or poisoning is the most common method used to kill their victims (Yardley & Wilson, 2016). Once the victim count piles up, HCSK's often move to another hospital to remove themselves from the scene. Some of these killers claim to rid the world of dead weight, while others delight in the excitement of the emergency.

Kristen Gilbert

Figure 7.11 Kristen Gilbert Mugshot, 2001

One well-known HCSK is Kristen Gilbert. A nurse at the Veterans Affairs Medical Center in Northampton, Massachusetts, in the 1990s, she was the common denominator in a string of patient deaths at the hospital (Ramsland, 2006). Born in 1967, she had the makings of a budding psychopath, as evidenced by lying and scamming others to get what she wanted as an adolescent (Dover, 2023). Additionally, she was bright and used her intellect to manipulate others as well as to enter nursing school (Dover, 2023). With easy access to epinephrine, she was able to induce heart attacks in patients that were already admitted for heart troubles (Ramsland, 2006). This was an easy cover up, though when other nurses went looking for epinephrine and found the supply low, that was a sign that someone had been using more than required. In addition, deaths increased at an alarming rate during her shifts, which caused suspicion (Dover, 2023). Apparently, Gilbert reported enjoying the thrill of emergency situations, relishing in the chaos she created (Ramsland, 2006). She had victims at her disposal and took full advantage. Eventually, coworkers contacted officials to investigate Gilbert and they found high levels of epinephrine in four of her deceased patients, even though some hadn't been prescribed the medication (Dover, 2023). This resulted in a conviction and life in prison (Frank, 2020).

BBC article on Health Care and Serial Killers:

QR Code 7.1

Method by Which They Kill

Prior to ending their victims' lives, serial killers often perfect the way in which they attack them. Then, they enact one or more methods to end the victim's life. They may pretend to need help by feigning a broken arm, or seem like a friendly neighbor offering them a ride out of the rain/cold. Other serial killers hide and ambush their victims, using the element of surprise to throw them off guard. In some cases, no tactic was needed to lure the victims, since they were family members. Once their victim is obtained, serial killers choose specific ways to incapacitate them. This method is connected to the type of rage or fetish, a string of thoughts that leads them toward the need to watch their victims die. Given the various serial killers already discussed in this book, the psychology behind each method and reference to serial killers who used this method will be mentioned, but in-depth case examples will not be utilized.

Stabbing

Figure 7.12 Knife Blade

You must be up close to someone in order to stab them. When it comes to serial killing, this often translates to rage and/or sexual gratification. Some killers want to see the life leave the eyes of their victims; it gives them a thrill. Additionally, when a serial killer "overkills" and stabs the victim more times than is necessary to kill the person, it indicates extreme anger and frustration, and perhaps dissociation. Indeed, these killers often devalue their victims, especially when they are women and/or sex workers (Wattis, 2017). Within this category we could include rippers, who eviscerate their victims and may expose or remove their organs (Schechter, 2003). Serial killers who stab as part of their modus operandi tend to be more violent in other areas of their life (Douglas & Olshaker, 2019). Specifically, one study found that male serial killers tend to stab their victims 17% of the time, while female serial killers did so 5.5% of the time (Harrison et al., 2019). Examples of serial killers who used this modus operandi include Jack the Ripper, Peter Sutcliffe, and Andrei Chikatilo, to name a few.

Shooting

Figure 7.13 Gun and Ammunition

The utilization of firearms is more common among male serial killers, with men using this method 20.8% of the time and women 9.1% of the time (Harrison et al., 2019). This method is associated with serial killers who are more cowardly and unsure of their ability to physically overpower their victims. Also, this allows them to be more removed from the crime scene, leave less physical evidence (except the bullet, of course), and feel more confident their victims will die. While less commonly used as a method of murder, there are still several notable serial killers who shot and killed their victims. Some of these include David Berkowitz, Dean Corll, Pedro Lopez, and Lawrence Bittaker.

Strangulation/Asphyxiation

Strangulation is personal. The killers' hands are directly on the victim, and those hands are responsible for the death of the person. This translates to power and control. Indeed, those are both strongly correlated with sexual gratification, as noted previously in this book. True hate for human beings seems to be a central factor for these killers. Strangulation is the murder method of choice for approximately 47% of men and 31% of female serial killers. Examples of serial killers who strangled their victims to death include Dennis Rader, Arthur Shawcross, Albert DeSalvo, Samuel Little, and Gary Ridgway.

Beating/Torture

Along the lines of stabbing and strangulation, and often coupled with it, is physically beating up victims. This may be used to subdue victims and also render them unconscious. The level of anger is high with these killers. They want to inflict pain and suffering on their victims, perhaps in response to the suffering they have endured in their lives. This method is utilized around 7.5% of the time by men and 1.8% by women (Harrison et al., 2019). Examples include H. H. Holmes, Joel Rifkin, Robert Berdella, Charles Ng, and Maury Travis.

Poison

Figure 7.14 Bottles of Poison

As noted before, and overwhelmingly validated by one study, women tend to poison their victims much more often than men (47.3% and 7.5%, respectively; Harrison et al., 2019). Poisoning a victim involves little physical force and isn't as detectable as the above-mentioned forms of killing, for obvious reasons. When the options are limited and you are unable to overpower your victim, poison is one of the only choices left. It is covert and doesn't leave a mess, save for frothing of the mouth and eventual removal of the body. It is also often a slow death, taking an hour or more for the victim's body to succumb to the poison (Schechter, 2003). During this time, they are incapacitated and the killer gets to watch in delight. The victim is unable to defend themselves and retaliate, which, again, makes it a safe option for women especially. In fact, strychnine only takes 15–60 minutes to take effect once ingested (Centers for Disease Control and Prevention, 2024). Several serial killers who used poison to expire their victims include Belle Gunness, Jane Toppan, and Dorothea Puente.

Table 7.2 Offender Behaviors

		Men	Women		Chi-square	
Crime behavior	***N***	**%**	***N***	**%**		***p* level**
Tortured victims No	3,820	90.1	521	92.2	2.52	0.1126
Yes	419	9.9	44	7.8		

		Men	Women		Chi-square	
Crime behavior	***N***	**%**	***N***	**%**		***p* level**
Overkill No	3,271	81.9	478	93.2	41.23	0.0000
Yes	722	18.1	35	6.8		
Body muti-lated No	3,997	90.7	541	96.4	20.84	0.0000
Yes	411	9.3	20	3.6		
Necrophilia No	4,638	96.6	583	99.7	16.12	0.0001
Yes	161	3.4	2	0.3		
Ate body No	4,720	98.1	579	98.8	1.29	0.2566
Yes	89	1.9	7	1.2		
Drank blood No	4,769	99.3	583	99.7	1.14	0.2849
Yes	35	0.7	2	0.3		

Note. "Tortured victims," "ate body," and "drank blood" were not statistically significant.

Source: Michael G. Aamodt, Terence Leary, and Senthil Girimurugan, Selection from Radford/FGCU Annual Report on Serial Killer Statistics: 2023, p. 32. Copyright © 2023 by Radford University.

Crime Location

Where a serial killer chooses to commit their crime is often a personal choice and a location they know well. When they get away with murder at this location the first time, it reinforces the pattern and they choose the same or similar locations in the future. Evidence from research on this topic confirms this assumption; crime location is not random and serial killers make conscious decisions about where to commit the crime and where to dispose of the body, which will be discussed in more depth below (Synnott et al., 2018). One facet of this is that serial killers who left the body at the murder site (rather than moving it to a different location) usually lived closer to the area and had a smaller crime range location. In fact, they often commit these crimes closer to one of their previous homes rather than their current home to dodge detection. Also, and not surprising, most serial killers who live in rural areas traveled further from their home to find a victim, as compared to those who operated in urban areas (Synnott et al., 2018). This should come as no surprise given the scarcity of people, and therefore potential victims, in more rural areas.

Table 7.3 Murder and Disposal Location

Variables	Murder location % (*n*)	Disposal location % (*n*)
Indoor		
Own dwelling	26.4 (33)	22.4 (28)
Other dwelling	24.0 (30)	12.0 (15)
Other	6.4 (8)	4.8 (6)
Outdoor		
Other dwelling	3.2 (4)	4.8 (6)
Water	0.0 (0)	4.8 (6)
Open	17.6 (22)	24.8 (31)
Closed	13.6 (17)	26.4 (33)
Car	8.8 (11)	0.0 (0)

Source: Brendan Chapman, Cody Raymer, and Davide Keatley, Selection from "Death and Disposal Locations of Serial Homicides: The Effect on Recovery Timeframes," Homicide Studies, vol. 26, no. 2. Copyright © 2022 by SAGE Publications.

Dean Corll

However, sometimes it's easier to bring victims to you rather than go out and hunt them. That's exactly what Dean Corll did. He had the luxury of owning multiple homes, where he lured young boys with candy, then tortured and killed them (Schechter, 2003). Born in 1939 in Fort Wayne, Indiana, his childhood was tumultuous and he endured an on and off again relationship between his parents, with much verbal and physical abuse in the household (Schechter, 2003). With a sexual interest in boys that started young, Corll looked for ways to satisfy his urges. His neighborhood was rife with young boys playing outside in the summer sun (Myers et al., 2006). Corll capitalized on that and offered them candy in his home. Though not the most intelligent idea, since all of the boys would be last seen near his home(s), his urges to torture were apparently too strong to contain. In fact, to increase his chances of luring a victim, he enlisted the help of two boys, David Brooks and Elmer Wayne Henley (Myers et al., 2006). He compensated them well and they kept their mouths shut ... for a while. Finally, Henley had enough and he shot and killed Corll during one of their luring escapades in 1972.

So, then, what happens next? Now that the deed is done, what are serial killers' subsequent actions?

Post-Kill Modus Operandi

What happens when the victim has expired? Where does the serial killer put the body? Do they position it? Do they revisit it? For sexual purposes? Cannibalism? Learning the answers to these questions tells us so much about who the killer is and the reasons for their actions. Visiting disposal sites to relive the murder demonstrates emotional connections to their actions and pride in their "work." The body continues to be a trophy of sorts, allowing the serial killer to continue to feel power and control over the situation. It may be the one place in life where they don't feel like a failure. It could also be arousing, and provide sexual release without having to kill again. Other killers choose to cannibalize their victims to keep the victim with them or out of sheer curiosity.

Disposal Site

Not all serial killers pose or stage the body post-mortem. Yet for some, it's part of their modus operandi and a ritual that brings them joy. For others, it's a tactic to avoid capture; they pose the body in a way that alters the crime scene, indicating that they are likely an organized type of killer (Pettigrew, 2022). Some of the ways in which serial killers may do this is through evidence planting or altering or fabricating suicide notes in an attempt to make victims' deaths appear to be an overdose or suicide. Such manipulations have diverted police attention and allowed the offender to continue killing undetected for a prolonged period (Pettigrew, 2022).

Generally, serial killers rely on experience and familiarity with an area when selecting crime locations. Indeed, another way in which these murderers avoid detection is by killing the victim in one location and then placing the body in another. Serial killers who moved the body to another location post-mortem traveled far from their home (Synnott et al., 2018). Furthermore, researchers discovered that serial killers who dispose of their first victims but not subsequent ones demonstrate more conscious thinking, proving that there may be more planning involved in the role of serial killing. Another factor in the modus operandi of victim disposal is the landscape of the dumping site. Certain environmental conditions aid in the decomposition process, removing DNA evidence from the victim and providing a temporary respite from detection (Chapman et al., 2022; Synnott et al., 2018). Bodies of water, whether lake or river, have been popular body disposal sites due to these very factors. Arthur Shawcross, the Genesee River Killer, left his victims' bodies by the river to decompose quickly, as did Gary Ridgway, hence his moniker, the Green River Killer. These acts were deliberate and calculated ways in which to remove evidence so they would remain free to kill again.

Necrophilia

Though most serial killers do not engage in **necrophilia**, it is part of the modus operandi for others, and they would feel incomplete without engaging in sexual acts with their victims post-mortem. In fact, research has found that, in some countries, murderers (not only serial killers) have sexual relations with their victims post-mortem, on average, 22% of the time (Chopin & Beauregard, 2021). There even is a term for these killers—necrophiliac sexual homicide offenders (Chopin & Beauregard, 2021). Further, these killers are always unmarried men who have a history of arrests and choose strangers as their victims. Additionally, vaginal and anal sex were preferred by these offenders. One hypothesis is that these sexual sadists are looking to push the envelope and try something new. There is also evidence, unsurprisingly, of early childhood trauma by a domineering and abusive mother in the cases where serial killers choose to violate their victims in this way (Lester et al., 2015).

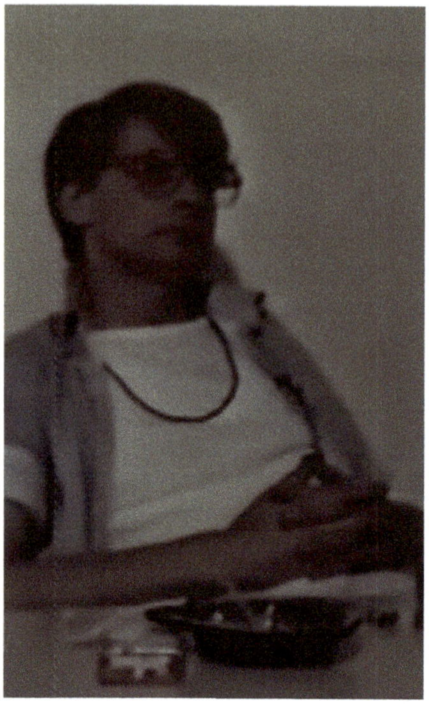

Figure 7.15 Dennis Nilsen

Dennis Nilsen

One necrophiliac serial killer that fits this profile is Dennis Nilsen. Born in Scotland in 1945, Nilsen, his mother, and his siblings lived with his grandfather (Biography.com Editors, 2023). He had a close bond with his grandfather and became extremely distraught when he passed away, noting that seeing his grandfather dead at the funeral made a lasting impression on him. So too did his desire for other boys, which was quite taboo in the 1950s. With his grandfather gone and his interests a far cry from other boys his age, he felt lonely and largely kept to himself (Biography.com Editors, 2023). As an adult, Nilsen couldn't shake his need for company, though he was awkward and found it difficult to initiate and maintain relationships, so he lured men from gay bars to his home with promises of booze and sex. He came through with both of those promises, though the latter often occurred after the man was dead. Nilsen was so fascinated with death that he would lay in front of the mirror with only his body showing to mimic a dead and unwilling stranger, and masturbate (Schechter, 2003). Furthermore, his desire for disinclined victims went so far that he kept the corpses in his apartment at his kitchen table and ate meals with them for company. At night, he straddled and had sex with them until the body decomposed to a point where that was no longer possible. He then buried the body in his backyard or under the floorboards of his flat. Once the smell became too much for those in the flats around him, and the plumbing clogged due to the body parts he flushed down the toilet, the cops came calling. They found ample evidence to convict him in 1983 of six counts of murder (Biography.com Editors, 2023). Sentenced to life in prison, he eventually died of natural causes in 2018. Though Nilsen did not cannibalize his victims, research has noted that many serial killers who engage in necrophilia are also cannibals (Lester et al., 2015).

Cannibalism

Cannibalism is the consumption of another human. The mere idea of this is appalling to most of us. However, some serial killers, spurred by curiosity or sexual desire, have cooked and eaten parts of their victims. Research indicates that serial killers motivated by lust and experiencing delusions are most likely to consume their victims raw, whereas those driven by revenge tend to cook the remains before consumption (Lester et al., 2015). These cannibals had a history of extremely harsh upbringings, psychiatric diagnoses and hospitalization, and fewer instances of sexual sadism (Lester et al., 2015).

Jason Thornburg

Figure 7.16 Jason Thornburg Mugshot, 2001

Jason Thornburg is a recent example of a cannibalistic serial killer. Residing in Fort Worth, Texas, he admitted to killing five people, including a former roommate and his ex-girlfriend, between 2017 and 2021 (Falcon & Vandergriff, 2024). He stated that he killed them because God told him they needed to be sacrificed and provided no information beyond that. One victim was his roommate in a local motel, while the others were acquaintances (Falcon & Vandergriff, 2024). After he killed them, he ate their hearts. Once arrested, authorities discovered a lengthy history of mental illness. Further, he had sex with his girlfriend while there were two bodies in bins under his bed. He admitted that he cut his roommate into pieces and stored the body parts in a large plastic tub (Falcon & Vandergriff, 2024). He was caught when he placed the body parts in a dumpster and set it on fire to remove the evidence. He fled the scene, but cameras placed him at the location. Once arrested, he confessed to the additional murders of his former roommate and ex-girlfriend.

Summary

Modus operandi, or method of operation, has many moving parts. It encompasses the motives behind serial murder, including power and control, money, mental illness, fame, and sexual sadism. It also includes how and why they choose certain victims. Is it personal or was the victim in the wrong place at the wrong time? That often relates to the method by which they kill their victims. Stabbing and strangulation infer anger and hostility, while shooting is more removed, and poison happens to be convenient. Further, how the killer engages with the body post-kill tells you how much they devalue human life. They kill to satisfy their needs and lack regard for anyone else.

Chapter Review Questions

1. How does motive influence the method with which serial killers kill their victims?
2. What are some ways in which serial killers cover their tracks following a murder?
3. How do trophies play a role in the serial killer's life?

Keywords

Cannibalism

Fame

Modus operandi

Money

Necrophilia

Power

References

Alcatraz East Crime Museum. (*n.d.*). *David Berkowitz: Son of sam killer*. Alcatraz East Crime Museum. https://www.alcatrazeast.com/crime-library/serial-killers/david-berkowitz-son-sam-killer/#

BBC News. (2006). Serial killer convicted of murder. http://news.bbc.co.uk/2/hi/uk_news/england/southern_counties/4813234.stm

Belles, H. (2025). *Under the radar: secrets of a Swedish serial killer: Ballad of blood*. Belles.

Biography.com Editors. (2023, October 3). *Dennis Nilsen*. Biography. https://www.biography.com/crime/dennis-nilsen

Bowcott, O. (2006, March 16). *Killer who wanted fame murdered four in random attacks. The Guardian*. https://www.theguardian.com/uk/2006/mar/17/ukcrime.owenbowcott

Centers for Disease Control and Prevention. (2024). Strychnine: Chemical fact sheet. https://www.cdc.gov/chemical-emergencies/chemical-fact-sheets/strychnine.html

Chapman, B., Raymer, C., & Keatley, D. A. (2022). Death and disposal locations of serial homicides: The effect on recovery timeframes. *Homicide Studies, 26*(2), 199–215.

Chopin, J., & Beauregard, E. (2021). Patterns of behaviors in sexual homicide: A criminological perspective. *International Journal of Offender Therapy and Comparative Criminology, 65*(15), 1676–1699.

Culhane, S. E., Walker, S., & Hildebrand, M. M. (2019). Serial homicide perpetrators' self-reported psychopathy and criminal thinking. *Journal of Police and Criminal Psychology, 34*(1), 1–13.

Douglas, J., & Olshaker, M. (2019). *The killer across the table: Unlocking the secrets of serial killers and predators with the FBI's original mindhunter.* HarperCollins.

Dover, K. R. (2023, October 24). *A killer's mind: Kristen H Gilbert.FHE Health Restore*. https://restore-mental-health.com/a-killers-mind-kristen-h-gilbert/

Falcon, J., & Vandergriff, C. (2024, December 8). *Cannibal serial killer Jason Thornburg sentenced to death.* CBS News. https://www.cbsnews.com/texas/news/serial-killer-jason-thornburg-fort-worth-murders/

Frank, C. (2020). Health care serial murder: What can we learn from the Wettlaufer story? *Canadian Family Physician, 66*(10), 719-722.

Gardell, M. (2018). Urban terror: The case of lone wolf Peter Mangs. *Terrorism and Political Violence, 30*(5), 793–811.

Haggerty, K. D. (2009). Modern serial killers. *Crime, Media, Culture, 5*(2), 168–187.

Haritaworn, J. (2019). On these bones: The queer regenerations of the Toronto gay village serial killings. *TOPIA: Canadian Journal of Cultural Studies, 40*, 15–41. https://doi.org/10.3138/topia.2019-0015

Harrison, M. A., Hughes, S. M., & Gott, A. J. (2019). Sex differences in serial killers. *Evolutionary Behavioral Sciences, 13*(4), 295–310.

Healey, J., Beauregard, E., Beech, A., & Vettor, S. (2014). Is the sexual murderer a unique type of offender? A typology of violent sexual offenders using crime scene behaviors. *Sexual Abuse: A Journal of Research and Treatment, 28*(6), 512–33.

Holmes, S. T., Hickey, E., & Holmes, R. M. (1991). Female serial murderesses: Constructing differentiating typologies. *Journal of Contemporary Criminal Justice, 7*(4), 245–256.

Jiwani, Y., & Young, M. L. (2006). Missing and murdered women: Reproducing marginality in news discourse. *Canadian Journal of Communication, 31*, 895–917.

Kumkaria, B., & Tiwari, H. (2024). Understanding serial killers: Motivations, behavioral patterns, and psychological profiling. *African Journal of Biological Sciences, 6*(10), 7009–7023.

Lester, D., White, J., & Giordano, B. (2015). Cannibalism. *Journal of Death and Dying, 70*(4), 428–435.

Levi-Minzi, M., & Shields, M. (2007). Serial sexual murderers and prostitutes as their victims: Difficulty profiling perpetrators and victim vulnerability as illustrated by the Green River case. *Brief Treatment and Crisis Intervention, 7*, 77–89.

Lynes, A., & Wilson, D. (2015). Driven to kill: British serial killers and their occupations. *The Howard Journal, 54*(5), 413–433.

Merriam-Webster. (n.d.). *Modus operandi*. In *Merriam-Webster.com dictionary*. Retrieved April 27, 2025, from https://www.merriam-webster.com/dictionary/modus%20operandi

Morton, R. J., Tillman, J. M., & Gaines, S. J. (2005). *Serial murder: Pathways for investigation*. U. S. Department of Justice. Federal Bureau of Investigation.

Myers, W. C., Husted, D. S., Safarik, M. E., & O'Toole, M. E. (2006). The motivation behind serial sexual homicide: Is it sex, power, and control, or anger? *Journal of Forensic Science, 51*(4), 900–907.

Pettigrew, M. (2022). Staged body disposal sites and homicide: Investigating the multivariate approach of a serial killer. *Journal of Investigative Psychology and Offender Profiling, 19*(3), 221–230. https://doi.org/10.1002/jip.1596

Piccotti, T., & Bertram, C. (2023, December 21). *Green River Killer: A timeline of his murders, arrest, and conviction.* Biography.com. https://www.biography.com/crime/gary-ridgway-green-river-killer-timeline

Poovarasan, P., & Jain, M. (2023). The role of forensic psychology in profiling serial killers. *Medico-Legal Update, 23*(Special Issue), 3468. https://doi.org/10.37506/mlu.v23i5.3468

Raine, A. (2013). *The anatomy of violence: The biological roots of crime.* Pantheon Books.

Ramsland, K. (2006). *Inside the minds of serial killers: Why they kill.* Praeger.

Ressler, R., Burgess, A. W., & Douglas, J. E. (1988). *Sexual homicide: Patterns and Motives.* Free Press.

Ressler, R., & Shachtman, T. (1992). *Whoever fights monsters: My twenty years tracking serial killers for the FBI.* St. Martin's.

Rossouw, Z., & Palys, T. (2024). "Baggage in the business": The investigative challenges of serial homicide. *The Police Journal, 98*(1), 249–268. https://doi.org/10.1177/0032258X241269482

Schechter, H. (2003). *The serial killer files: The who, what, where, how, and why of the world's most terrifying murders.* Ballantine Books.

Synnott, J., Bakker, M., Ioannou, M., Canter, D., & van der Kemp, J. (2018). Crime location choices: A geographical analysis of German serial killers. *Journal of Investigative Psychology and Offender Profiling, 16*(2), 110–123. https://doi.org/10.1002/jip.1521

U. S. Justice Department. (2011). The Equal Credit Opportunity Act. https://www.govinfo.gov/content/pkg/USCODE-2011-title15/html/USCODE-2011-title15-chap41-subchapIV.htm

Wattis, L. (2017). Revising the Yorkshire Ripper murders: Interrogating gender violence, sex work and justice. *Feminist Criminology, 12*(1), 3–21.

Wilson, W., & Hilton, T. (1998). *Modus operandi* of female serial killers. *Psychological Reports, 82*(2), 495–498. https://doi.org/10.2466/pr0.1998.82.2.495

Yardley, E., & Wilson, D. (2016). In search of the 'angels of death': Conceptualising the contemporary nurse healthcare serial killer. *Journal of Investigative Psychology and Offender Profiling, 13*, 39–55.

Image Credits

Fig. 7.1: King County Sheriff's Office, https://commons.wikimedia.org/wiki/File:Gary_Ridgway_Mugshot_11162001.jpg, 2001.

Fig. 7.2: Screenshot from IBTimes UK, "'Racist Sniper' Charged with Malmö Murders," https://www.youtube.com/watch?v=5SSOxfzSR2Q, 2012.

Fig. 7.3: City of London Police, https://commons.wikimedia.org/wiki/File:John_Christie_Mugshot.jpg, 1952.

Fig. 7.4: Copyright © 2014 by Steve Shook (CC BY 2.0) at https://commons.wikimedia.org/wiki/File:Belle_Gunness_and_Children,_1908_(4231878378).jpg.

Fig. 7.5: Copyright © 2014 by Steve Shook (CC BY 2.0) at https://commons.wikimedia.org/wiki/File:Victims,_1908_-_Belle_Gunness_(14598810507).jpg.

Fig. 7.6: Copyright © 2010 by Steve Shook (CC BY 2.0) at https://commons.wikimedia.org/wiki/File:Ruins_of_Gunness_House,_1908_-_Belle_Gunness_(4527624717).jpg.

Fig. 7.7: Vernun Argus, https://commons.wikimedia.org/wiki/File:David_Berkowitz_Arrested_August_10_1977_Mount_Vernon_Argus.jpg, 1977.

Fig. 7.8: Joseph Papin, https://www.loc.gov/item/2017646659/, 1978.

Fig. 7.9: King County Sheriff's Office, https://commons.wikimedia.org/wiki/File:Gary_Ridgway_1982_Mugshot.jpg, 1982.

Fig. 7.10: Screenshot from KATU News, "'Green River Killer' Pleads Guilty – 2003 | KATU In The Archives,"https://www.youtube.com/watch?v=qvZ_FAcSBi4, 2022.

Fig. 7.11: Federal Bureau of Prisons, https://commons.wikimedia.org/wiki/File:Kristen_Gilbert_mug_shot.jpg, 2001.

Fig. 7.12: Copyright © 2008 by Dave Crosby (CC BY-SA 2.0) at https://commons.wikimedia.org/wiki/File:Knife_Blade_III.jpg.

Fig. 7.13: Copyright © 2012 by Augustas Didžgalvis (CC BY-SA 3.0) at https://commons.wikimedia.org/wiki/File:SIG_Pro_by_Augustas_Didzgalvis.jpg.

Fig. 7.14: Copyright © 2007 by ricardo (CC BY 2.0) at https://commons.wikimedia.org/wiki/File:Poison_(543771420).jpg.

Fig. 7.15: Screenshot from The Grim Curriculum, "Rare Interview with Dennis Nilsen Also Known as the British Jeffrey Dahmer," https://www.youtube.com/shorts/clOmSAeXQ1A, 2025.

Fig. 7.16: Texas Department of Criminal Justice, https://www.tdcj.texas.gov/death_row/dr_info/thornburgjasonalan.html. Copyright © 2024 by Texas Department of Criminal Justice.

CHAPTER 8

THE FINAL CUT

The Fall of the Serial Killer

"All I know is I lost control. And I always was very cautious to keep from getting busted. I didn't pick on motherfuckers that would be missed. ... There weren't no women nurses and teachers. That's the reason I didn't get busted a long time ago."

-Samuel Little

How do serial killers live seemingly normal lives, yet continue their hidden perverse behavior? How do serial killers' lives and crimes ultimately come to an end—and what does this reveal about their psychology? To be in the category serial killer, you must get away with murder two to three times, as noted in Chapter 1. This isn't a one and done act. Most serial killers are driven by the thrill of the chase and the sense of power they experience when they evade law enforcement. Their desire is not for capture, but for the satisfaction of controlling and manipulating their environment, while outsmarting police and maintaining anonymity.

Figure 8.1 Samuel Little Mugshot, 2012

Some killers avoid being caught for years, while others are caught within a matter of months. Some manage to evade capture all together. There are several psychological factors involved in their ability to continue to kill and get away with it. Intelligence certainly helps them monitor authorities' next moves and remain undetected. This isn't always an asset, though, as arrogance and brazenness can lead to their identification and **arrest**. However, with advanced DNA technology, forensics, business and residential cameras, and easy access to media, these types of crimes are becoming less common (Mello-Klein, 2023).

When finally captured, some serial killers may experience emotional breakdowns or depression (Ramsland, 2006). This can occur if the killer becomes overwhelmed by the reality of their situation, facing the inevitable consequences of their actions. However, even in these instances, the emotional reactions are often self-centered rather than driven by remorse for the victims. Moreover, others may confess eagerly, providing detailed accounts of their crimes as if they are offering an explanation rather than an admission of guilt (Schechter, 2003). Their confessions may be manipulative, aiming to assert control over how their serial killing narrative unfolds.

Learning Outcomes

After reading this chapter, students will be able to do the following:

1. Describe how serial killers avoid being captured.
2. Understand the various ways in which serial killers are caught.
3. Understand how serial killers react upon and during imprisonment.

Avoiding Capture

Serial killers go to great lengths to avoid detection, using careful planning, camouflage, and disposal techniques to cover their tracks. Over time, many become more confident and brazen, as they gain experience and refine their methods. Indeed, they may alter their modus operandi, which may lead them to take increasing risks, including killing in more public locations, or even leaving behind evidence that could potentially lead to their arrest, but this does not equate to a desire to be caught. Instead, these acts are often indicative of the serial killer's growing sense of invincibility or a need to escalate the violence as part of their psychological drive.

Interstate Highways

One way to avoid capture is to move between law enforcement jurisdictions. Indeed, jurisdictional boundaries and resource limitations can impede the effective coordination necessary for law enforcement to close these complex cases (Rossouw & Palys, 2024). High-speed car chases used to stop when the perpetrator crossed county or state lines. With a growing population and interstate highways, societal and community organization was evolving and serial killers used this to their advantage. Further, police agencies stored their files separately until the Violent Criminal Apprehension Program (ViCAP) was established in 1985 to share information about suspects between police departments (Howlett et al., 1986). ViCAP is a nationwide initiative created by the FBI and designed to assist law enforcement agencies in identifying and apprehending violent criminals, particularly serial offenders (Howlett et al., 1986). ViCAP operates under the FBI's National Center for the Analysis of Violent Crime and is a centralized data system to detect similarities in **unsolved** homicide cases, specifically modus operandi.

Figure 8.2 Samuel Little's Mugshots

Samuel Little

The most notorious case solved with the use of ViCAP is Samuel Little's. The program played a crucial role in linking Samuel Little, one of the most prolific serial killers in U.S. history, as noted in Chapter 1, to a series of unsolved murders across the country (FBI, 2018). Little was arrested in 2012 on drug charges while living at a homeless shelter in Kentucky. He was extradited to California, where DNA evidence tied him to three cold case murders (Stephens, 2023). As he began to confess to more crimes, the FBI used ViCAP to analyze and cross-reference details from his confessions with unsolved cases in their nationwide database. Through this system, analysts were able to identify patterns and connect multiple cases that had gone unsolved for decades. Born in 1940 in Reynolds, Georgia, to a mother who didn't want him, Little was raised by his grandmother (Stephens, 2023). He had few close friends due to moving often, which resulted in him spending time thinking about his fantasies of strangulation. Without resources to buy the things he wanted as a teenager, he stole what he "needed." Additionally, lacking steady employment and housing, he became familiar with the streets in more intimate ways. As such, Little chose his victims specifically due to the likelihood that he could continue to get away with murder; they were sex workers, runaways, and homeless women (FBI, 2019). Preying on disenfranchised members of society while living a transient lifestyle allowed him to murder women in more than 15 states and evade capture for more than 40 years (Stephens, 2023). His modus operandi included rape and strangulation. He confessed to an astounding 93 murders. Police have been able to confirm 50 connected to Little, while several remain unsolved due to the victim's remains being undiscovered or police being unable to match his descriptions of victims to cold cases (FBI, 2019). Little not only bragged about the number of women he killed, he drew pictures of them and recounted an affinity for them (Stephens, 2023). Convicted to four life sentences, Little remained imprisoned until his death in 2020 at age 80. The short amount of time he served was barely justice given the number of lives he took.

His ability to recollect details, including images of the victims, was uncanny. Indeed, authorities have been able to verify the accuracy of several of the drawings. This particular drawing was connected to a missing person case. He was able to portray her likeness along with the location and year she was last seen, in a sense proving he murdered her. Little likely enjoyed drawing these pictures of his victims, as it allowed him to relive the murders. That's what brought him joy in prison.

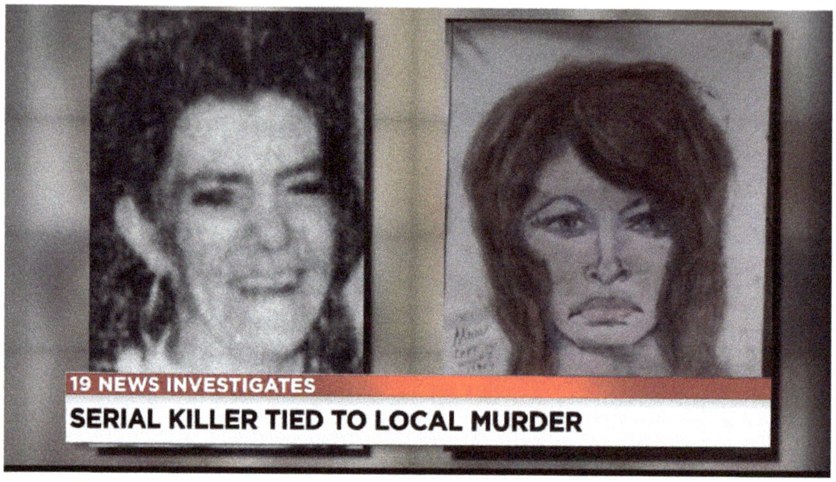

Figure 8.3 A Drawing of One of Samuel Little's Victims

Video of Samuel Little describing one of his murders:

QR Code 8.1

The Mask of Sanity

When serial killers with wives and children are caught, people often wonder how they were able to hide their criminal activity without those closest to them knowing. The ability to live two lives, to compartmentalize their "normal" life from their "serial killing" life, demonstrates these serial killers' ability to manipulate others and wear the mask of sanity. You may wonder which persona was the real person; it's likely both. The ability to lie and act as if they have done nothing wrong is entrenched in their lack of empathy and their psychopathic traits. Once they are caught and the true nature of their lifestyle comes to light, family members are in shock.

How could someone you've known all of your life as your father or husband have done such horrific things to these women? The short answer is that having a family is an ideal cover-up. They love their family to the extent that they can, but the fantasies and urges to engage in abnormal and perverse acts don't subside. Indeed, several serial killers have been married with children, such as Dennis Rader, John Wayne Gacy, and Gary Ridgway, but to reduce redundancy, we will turn to the case of Robert Hansen.

Robert Hansen

Robert Hansen was a serial killer who lured young women to a remote cabin in Alaska, assaulted them, and then set them free in the cold vastness in order to hunt them down (Fouche et al., 2017; Schechter, 2003). All the while his wife and two children went about their lives at home, thinking he was on yet another big game hunting trip. His wife and children often stayed in Arkansas with her family during the summer, leaving Hansen with ample time and freedom to enact his fantasies (Gilmour & Hale, 1991). Born in 1939 in Iowa, he was raised in a staunchly religious household and his authoritarian father expected him to work in the family bakery (Fouche et al., 2017). Due to his father's strict rules, he wasn't allowed to spend much time with friends, leading him to be a shy loner. His speech impediment and severe acne didn't help, either (Gilmour & Hale, 1991). Romantic relationships proved difficult for him, and he eventually sought the company of a sex worker, which would inform his future victims of choice (Fouche et al., 2017).

Figure 8.4 Robert Hansen Posing With a Mountain Goat He Hunted and Killed

Though he eventually married and had children, it never felt natural to him. In fact, he got more of a sexual thrill from stealing than anything else and was arrested several times due to his kleptomania. Another hobby of his was hunting, which became part of his modus operandi as it was an easy excuse to isolate himself from his family so he was able to commit his disturbing crimes. With his urges increasing with manic intensity, Hansen kidnapped an 18-year-old sex worker, raped, and then "freed" her from a remote Alaskan cabin; she was later found with her hands tied and dead from exposure to the harsh Alaskan elements (Fouche et al., 2017). Other times, he would fly the women into the vast wilderness, strip them of their clothing, and let them go so he could hunt them. When one of his victims escaped while he attempted to load her onto his plane and then contacted police, Hansen was finally caught (Gilmour & Hale, 1991). Though he had been convicted of

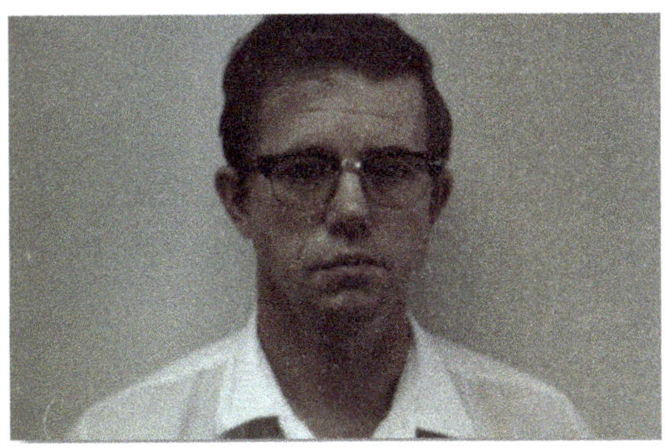

Figure 8.5 Robert Hansen Mugshot, 1983

theft prior to this, his wife stood by him with hopes that he would turn to Christianity and atone for his sins. Once Hansen was convicted of the murders and sentenced to life in prison, she eventually divorced him. He had killed 17 women over 12 years. The sadistic power he relished over these women finally came to a halt. He was sentenced to 461 years in prison and died in 2014 (Fouche et al., 2017).

Discussion question: How are serial killers able to compartmentalize their "normal" life from their "serial killer" persona?

Death Before Capture

Suicide is often viewed as a permanent solution to a temporary problem, unless you're a serial killer. For some serial killers, **death** is a permanent solution to the permanent problem of being incarcerated for the rest of their lives. It also serves as the final means of control. They don't want to lose their autonomy in prison and won't allow anyone else to end their life, so they take matters into their own hands. These are self-destructive tendencies and the collapse of the killer's self-image. Suicide could also be a way to avoid punishment and accountability, which is cowardly. For example, Christopher Wilder shot himself when police tried to arrest him for killing nine women.

They may also be killed by an accomplice, as was the case for Dean Corll. When you devalue those who help you, resentment builds and they lose interest in continuing the partnership. When you take advantage of those around you due to antisocial and narcissistic tendencies, the relationship dissolves and you may end up being the prey. People don't like to be exploited, and these killers precipitate their own personal ruin.

Figure 8.6 Israel Keyes Mugshot, 2012

Israel Keyes

One serial killer who committed suicide prior to being caught was Israel Keyes. Rather than allow law enforcement and society to decide his fate, he took matters into his own hands. Born in 1978 in Utah as one of nine children to Mormon parents, he eventually moved with his large family to Washington state (Rodela, 2022). It was a rural setting and Keyes explored the woods and rivers, looking for small animals to torture. They eventually moved to Maine when he was a teenager. Though his parents were very religious and converted to Christianity, Keyes never believed in a higher power (Rodela, 2022). He moved to Alaska as an adult, where he had a child with his girlfriend. Despite killing people, he seemed to feel some sense of pride as a father, noting he refused kill parents or children. His demise was the result of a traffic stop in 2012, where police found a victim's personal items. After being arrested, he confessed to murder and provided information about the entire incident from beginning to end, including the location of her body, which was cut up and placed in a frozen lake (Rodela, 2022). Killing up to 11 victims, he stashed kill kits (see Figure 8.7) that he could easily access when he chose his next victim. Unable to handle prison life, in 2012 he slit his wrists and strangled himself with his bed sheet, killing himself and leaving many questions unanswered; it was his last stance of defiance (Rodela, 2022). He was a Satanist who likely believed in nonconformity and free will. With no higher power to atone to, killing people, including himself, wasn't a sin in his eyes.

Figure 8.7 Israel Keyes's Kill Kit, Containing a .22-Caliber Gun, Empty Magazines, Ammunition, and a Silencer

The Arrest and Capture

The majority of serial killers have no desire to get caught, as that would end the perverse enjoyment they get from taking lives. Some of the most common ways in which they are caught include diligent police work, a survivor contacting police and providing information about the killer, an accomplice turning them in to reduce the severity of their own sentence, a friend or family member noticing odd behavior, and being apprehended for an unrelated crime (Bonn, 2014; Ramsland, 2006). Once detained, serial killers display little to no emotional response, particularly those with high levels of psychopathy and/or antisocial personality disorder (Bonn, 2014). Some may even attempt to control the investigation by providing misleading information, or confessing to crimes they didn't commit in order to garner attention or maintain a sense of power. This reflects their deep-seated need for control and recognition. These killers often see themselves as intellectually superior and may try to manipulate investigators, viewing the situation as a game or challenge rather than defeat. They don't express remorse or guilt for their crimes, although one or two have (e.g., Robert Spahalski). For some serial killers, being caught provides an opportunity to continue the fantasy of dominance or create a legacy. They may view the media attention, court proceedings, and public trials as a form of validation or even vindication for their actions (Holloway, 2003). This is often apparent in those who feel empowered by the widespread coverage of their crimes. Their reactions to capture can resemble pride in their notoriety rather than fear of punishment.

Mistakes

The research is clear: When serial killers are captured, it usually is the result of the killer's mistakes—for example, being identified by a witness or leaving evidence at a crime scene—rather than an intentional act on their part. Some serial killers, especially those who have killed for long periods of time, might become complacent or overly confident, believing they can continue evading capture indefinitely. In these cases, capture may occur when they miscalculate or underestimate law enforcement's ability to apprehend them.

There are several examples that demonstrate the killer's arrogance, inflated sense of importance and intelligence, and their sick minds. One prime example is Ted Bundy, who was captured three times for traffic violations, only to escape from prison twice (Keppel, 1995). One would think that, after being caught the first time, he would purchase a different vehicle or alter his modus operandi to throw off detectives. Instead, he relied on his charm and confidence, which worked for a while. Another example of sheer narcissism that resulted in capture was Dennis Rader. When his case was revisited by a journalist several years after his last murder, he couldn't stand the thought of not receiving attention for his crimes. He craved recognition. He sent police a floppy disk with information about the murders and thought he'd wiped it clean, but he hadn't. It led authorities to a "Dennis" at "Christ Lutheran Church" in Wichita, Kansas (Schechter, 2003). As the president of the church council, he had access to the church's computer and clearly thought he had removed enough identifying information, but Rader was 100% wrong. He could have gotten away with more murders, but his God complex and risk-taking behavior led to his demise.

Other cases that resulted in capture are less sensational; David Berkowitz got a parking ticket, which led authorities to his house, where he confessed to murder (Tauriello, 2020). Another unfortunate mistake can be trusting the wrong person. People will do whatever it takes to save their own skin. For instance, Aileen Wuornos's girlfriend ratted Wuornos out to police to absolve herself of wrongdoing and reduce her punishment (Arrigo & Griffin, 2004). Additionally, one would think that avoiding the murder location or body disposal site would be an obvious way in which to avoid capture, yet some serial killers, like Ted Bundy, Gary Ridgway, and Arthur Shawcross, just couldn't help themselves. It provides them with gratification for their dirty deeds and, at times, access to their victims to engage in necrophilia. The victims are the ultimate trophy that allow them to relive their kills.

DNA

Deoxyribonucleic acid (DNA) analysis continues to improve with time. Once it began to advance in the 1980s, the number of serial killers who were caught drastically increased, as noted in Chapter 1. Evidence from crime scenes that is used to catch the killer include blood, skin, semen, and bone (Kayser et al., 2023). Though this is widely known, serial killers often get too caught up in the moment, or eventually become sloppy and leave their DNA at the scene. Especially when murders aren't premeditated, killers unknowingly leave trace evidence. Recently, improvements in the sensitivity of DNA analyses used in forensic phenotyping allows us to determine perpetrator characteristics "beyond eye, hair and skin color to additionally comprise other traits such as eyebrow color, freckles, hair structure, hair loss in men, and tall stature" (Kayser et al., 2023, p. 3). This demonstrates technical advancements in DNA analysis techniques. The use of DNA evidence has thankfully resulted in the **imprisonment** of many serial killers. Only one will be discussed here.

Lonnie David Franklin

Lonnie David Franklin, Jr. (the Grim Sleeper) was an active serial killer in Los Angeles, California, from 1984 to 2007. He was finally apprehended in 2010 thanks to creative police work and DNA evidence on the pizza crust he ate for lunch, served to him by an undercover officer (Silverman, 2020). Born in 1952, Franklin served time in the military and seemed to have a fairly normal life, with steady employment and a wife for 32 years (Pelisek & Hanlon, 2022). As with many other serial killers, this mask of normalcy was only concealment for his sexually sadistic fantasies of rape and murder. Franklin chose marginalized and vulnerable targets—young Black women with drug habits who few would be looking for when they went missing (Pelisek & Hanlon, 2022). His level of disrespect for these women was so pronounced that he discarded their bodies in alleys and dumpsters after raping, strangling, and shooting them to death. For unknown reasons, he thankfully stopped killing for several years, resulting in his moniker. What led to Franklin's arrest was familial DNA from his son following his arrest (Pelisek & Hanlon, 2022). Once police had his son's DNA, they were able to connect it to DNA from Franklin's crimes and his pizza crust, leading to his arrest and incarceration. Convicted of murdering nine women and one girl, he was sentenced to death in 2016. While awaiting his fate on death row, he died of apparently natural causes, as no specific cause of death was ever determined (Pelisek & Hanlon, 2022; Silverman, 2020).

Figure 8.8 Lonnie David Franklin Mugshot, 1998

Faulty Police Work/Luck

Serial killers do their best to cover their tracks. When they forget to take evidence with them or clean the scene thoroughly, they are often caught. However, some avoid capture due to human error, such as the mishandling of evidence, improperly analyzing the evidence, and lack of adequate communication between jurisdictions (Kamb, 2023). Additionally, systemic issues such as delays in processing DNA samples can further hinder investigations (Kamb, 2023). A knowledgeable killer may exploit these weaknesses by murdering his victims in different locations, making it problematic for any single agency to detect the pattern. Moreover, sometimes evidence is overlooked or not submitted promptly, slowing the progress of the investigation. Only when modern forensic technologies and more persistent reviews of cold cases are applied do authorities manage to link the cases and identify the perpetrator, ultimately leading to an arrest. This underscores the vital importance of thorough evidence management, timely forensic testing, and interagency cooperation to prevent serial offenders from evading capture for extended periods.

Mistakes made by serial killers can result in their capture; but, more often, faulty police work and luck make it possible for them to evade capture for longer than they should. One disturbing example is Jeffrey Dahmer's case; police were called to the scene and found a man bound and naked running down the street, yet returned the man to Dahmer after he told them they were just playing a gay sex game (Schechter, 2003). Likewise, Paul Bernardo, one half of the Ken and Barbie killer duo in Canada, was questioned by police for the murder of young women on numerous occasions, only to be dismissed as a suspect repeatedly (Butts, 2026). Additionally, Larry Eyler raped and murdered 22 men before being caught and convicted of only one murder. His case was thrown out shortly thereafter due to contamination of evidence, and he was released from prison. This resulted in the death of yet another victim before he was finally incarcerated for good (Kolarik & Klatt, 2012). These are only a few unfortunate examples of killers being dismissed or freed to kill again.

Turning Themselves In

Serial killers turning themselves in is exceedingly rare. In fact, only 2.3% have done so, per one comprehensive research study on this topic (Ramsland, 2023). For example, Ed Kemper called police from a pay phone to tell them he was the serial murderer on the loose that they had been trying to capture for years. Charles Cullen, a nurse, admitted to killing 40 patients at various hospitals when questioned about his role in the death of two patients (Ramsland, 2023). Ángel Reséndiz murdered people who happened to live near railroads, moving between the United States and Mexico to avoid capture, until he saw his face plastered all over the news and decided to turn himself in at the border ("Ángel Reséndiz," 2017). Seemingly, Kemper turned himself in because he was done killing after he killed his mother, while Cullen and Reséndiz likely knew they would be caught soon, so ripped the proverbial Band-Aid off, if you will. None of them showed remorse, so it leaves one wondering why they would turn themselves in if they could continue to live free. Let's focus on Reséndiz's case.

Ángel Reséndiz

Figure 8.9 Ángel Reséndiz Mugshot, 1999

Ángel Reséndiz was born in 1960 in Durango, Mexico (Texas Department of Criminal Justice [TDCJ], n.d.). With a seventh-grade education and on his own at age 12, he worked manual labor jobs and committed crime to support himself. He was in and out of jail most of his life, with one stint for theft and assault lasting 20 years (TDCJ, n.d.). Other incarcerations were for providing false aliases when traveling between the United States and Mexico. However, due to the encouragement of family members, he turned himself in at the El Paso, Texas, border in 1999 ("Ángel Reséndiz," 2017; Lopez, 2025). His crimes were so horrendous that he was placed on the FBI's 10 Most Wanted list. Speculation exists that he only surrendered to save his own neck, as a $125,000 reward was offered for his capture ("Ángel Reséndiz," 2017). He knew he would be ratted out for the reward money sooner than later.

Described as a quiet, small man at 5'6", his unassuming demeanor was a cover for his intense rage, as evidenced by overkill of his victims, all of whom lived near railroad tracks, and thus were convenient targets for this transient killer. Location was his only requirement, as his victims were of all ages, genders, and ethnicities, including a 21-year-old college student, an 87-year-old woman, and a 79-year-old man and his 52-year-old daughter, with an estimated total body count of more than 20 victims ("Ángel Reséndiz," 2017). The safety of his family and his own head is what led to his surrender (Lopez, 2025). It wasn't due to remorse or accountability. In fact, he stated that the people he killed deserved to die (Lopez, 2025). Indeed, this is a common reaction. When caught, many serial killers rationalize their actions, sometimes framing their crimes as a logical or justified response to perceived wrongs (American Psychological Association, 2023). He was only concerned with those he loved and himself, just like a typical psychopath. Reséndiz was put to death by lethal injection in 2006.

Figure 8.10 Ángel Reséndiz Walking Into Court

Imprisonment and Loss of Freedom

A common trait among serial killers is narcissism, as noted in Chapter 3, and when they are caught, they may try to reframe the situation to boost their sense of self-importance. They might boast about their crimes, provide graphic details, or even attempt to portray themselves as antiheroes. Some serial killers, such as Ted Bundy or Dennis Rader (BTK), clearly enjoyed the attention they received during their trials and even attempted to use their media exposure to gain a sense of fame or immortality (APA, 2023). In these cases, they act as if their capture is just another part of the drama they've created, seeing it as part of the larger narrative of their lives. With nothing left to lose, others may attempt to find meaning in prison jobs, making social contacts, and turning to religion for solace (Silva, 2015). Indeed, importation models note that people tend to use skills they attained prior to incarceration to adjust to life in prison (Fowler et al., 2022). Moreover, deprivation models attempt to explain the difficulty experienced upon incarceration with regard to isolation from their previous lifestyle and autonomy; it's a transition to their new shared prison culture (Fowler et al., 2022). They have gone from completely manipulating their environment to having almost no control. These experiences undoubtedly affect a serial killer's mental state.

Table 8.1 Post-Arrest Events

	United States		**International**		**Total**	
Post-arrest event	***N***	**%**	***N***	**%**	***N***	**%**
Confessed to at least one murder	3,177		1,398		4,575	
No	1,148	36.1	419	30.0	1,567	34.3
Yes	2,029	63.9	979	70.0	3,008	65.7
Pleaded NGRI	3,491		1,642		5,133	
No	3,296	94.4	1569	95.6	4,865	94.8
Yes—not successful	157	4.5	44	2.7	201	3.9
Yes—successful for some murders	12	0.3	1	0.1	13	0.3
Yes—successful	26	0.7	28	1.7	54	1.1
Sentence	3,447		1,624		5,071	
Life	1,782	51.7	694	42.7	2,476	48.8
Death	1,059	30.7	494	30.4	1,553	30.6
Prison sentence less than life	276	8.0	232	14.3	508	10.0
Died prior to trial	214	6.2	131	8.1	345	6.8
Not prosecuted	46	1.3	14	0.9	60	1.2

	United States		International		Total	
Post-arrest event	***N***	**%**	***N***	**%**	***N***	**%**
Not guilty by reason of insanity	27	0.8	34	2.1	61	1.2
Acquitted	23	0.7	9	0.6	32	0.6
Forensic hospital prior to trial	6	0.2	3	0.2	9	0.2
Not competent to stand trial	7	0.2	3	0.2	10	0.2
Guilty—sent to forensic hospital	3	0.1	8	0.5	11	0.2
Lynched prior to trial	1	0.0	0	0.0	1	0.0
Guilty but mentally ill	3	0.1	1	0.1	4	0.1
Escaped prior to trial	0	0.0	1	0.1	1	0.0
Executed	3,025		1,494		4,519	
No	2,560	84.6	1162	77.8	3,722	82.4
Yes	465	15.4	332	22.2	797	17.6
Cause of death	1,134		657		1,791	
Legal execution	465	41.0	328	49.9	793	44.3
Natural causes	384	33.9	157	23.9	541	30.2
Suicide	162	14.3	102	15.5	264	14.7

	United States		International		Total	
Post-arrest event	***N***	**%**	***N***	**%**	***N***	**%**
Killed by police prior to arrest	55	4.9	34	5.2	89	5.0
Killed while in prison	29	2.6	14	2.1	43	2.4
Killed by others prior to arrest	19	1.7	10	1.5	29	1.6
Accidental death	10	0.9	5	0.8	15	0.8
Killed by accomplice	4	0.4	6	0.9	10	0.6
Killed by potential victim	4	0.4	0	0.0	4	0.2
Lynched prior to trial	2	0.2	1	0.2	3	0.2

Note. NGRI = not guilty by reason of insanity.

Source: Michael G. Aamodt, Terence Leary, and Senthil Girimurugan, Selection from Radford/FGCU Annual Report on Serial Killer Statistics: 2023, p. 62. Copyright © 2023 by Radford University.

Assisting Police

As a way to feed an unsatiated appetite for murder, even if they are not their own, a few serial killers have aided police in profiling and capturing other serial killers. This makes them feel like experts, feeding into their narcissism. In fact, Ted Bundy contacted police and told them he could help them find the Green River Killer (Gary Ridgway), since he was an expert on the topic of serial killing (Keppel, 1995). This collaboration even resulted in a book about their work together titled *The Riverman: Ted Bundy and I Hunt for the Green River Killer* (Keppel, 1995). After police agreed to talk with Bundy, they received a 22-page letter describing his assessment of the Green River Killer case (Keppel, 1995). In this letter, "Ted revealed that his preferred strategy for catching the Riverman would be to put a newly discovered dump site under surveillance" (Keppel, 1995, p. 73). Knowing that part of the fantasy was to revisit and relive their kills, Bundy understood the Green River Killer's mindset, and he was correct (Malizia, 2017). In interviews, Bundy assisted in the investigation by explaining the rationale for body disposal sites. "Well, first of all, he's trying to dispose of the bodies where they won't be found. This guy doesn't want to get caught. Neither does he want any of his bodies found. I think it's clear that, over time, you can see him trying to improve his dump sites. He's trying to get better at disposing of those bodies" (Keppel, 1995, p. 79). Certainly, Bundy wasn't the altruistic type and had something to gain from these interactions. He enjoyed thinking about murder and reliving his own crimes. With all of the time in the world on his hands, he now had a purpose and was needed. He spent hours assessing the case, writing analyses, and meeting with investigators. It eased his boredom while it fed his narcissistic ego.

Figure 8.11 Ted Bundy in Court, 1979

Finding God

Then there are the serial killers who turn to religion in prison and seek redemption for their deeds. Perhaps it's a façade or a way to garner additional attention, or it might even be authentic, though the latter is the least probable option. David Berkowitz said he found God while in prison. He even changed his moniker from "Son of Sam" to "Son of Hope" (Tauriello,

2020). Diagnosed with paranoid schizophrenia, Berkowitz's view of reality was skewed. He seemed to enjoy the spectacle that ensued once he was arrested, noting the scene was "comical" (Tauriello, 2020). After being sentenced to life in prison and contemplating his purpose in life, he became a born-again Christian, professing his newfound religious faith on television. Berkowitz stated that Satan had a hold on him until he found Christ, who forgave him for his sins. Only he will know if he truly repented.

Figure 8.12 David Berkowitz Reading His Bible

Figure 8.13 David Berkowitz, Son of Sam, Finds Life Change in the Bible

Enjoying Fame

When no one has paid attention to you your entire life, you soak up any attention you can get. We all know serial killers receive fan mail from suitors. I'm sure it helps to pass the time and feed their ego. The need to be adored by fans fills the fantasy that they are special and validates their evil deeds (Griffiths, 2014; Malizia, 2017). It's addictive, which makes them want more attention. The correspondence usually turns sexual in nature, with pictures and explanations of sexual acts. This is no surprise, given the rife sexual sadism amongst serial killers. Numerous serial killers corresponded with fans and some eventually married them. For example, Angelo Buono and Kenneth Bianchi, aka the Hillside Stranglers, both married women while in prison ("The prisoners who got married," n.d.). Richard Ramirez also corresponded with many women, eventually marrying Doreen Lioy ("The prisoners who got married," n.d.). Ted Bundy married and had a child while in prison.

Other serial killers took to art to pass the time and garner more attention. John Wayne Gacy painted pictures of himself as a clown, capitalizing on his previous volunteer work as a clown for hospitalized children (Menz, 2024). He also drew childish pictures of the seven dwarfs. Lawrence Bittaker, one of the Toolbox Killers, also spent time drawing and creating art. However, Son of Sam laws prohibit criminals from monetizing their artwork or books either written by them or about them, and routes any profits to the victims' families (Menz, 2024).

Figure 8.14 John Wayne Gacy Clown Drawing, n.d.

Discussion question: What are the pros and cons of allowing serial killers to sell their art, books, poems, etc.?

Death

Facing death is daunting for many. We may ask ourselves, what lies ahead? Is there life after death? When serial killers are sentenced to death, or life in prison without the possibility of parole, the weight and magnitude of this must be substantial. While people tend to avoid thinking about death, these killers are facing their inevitable end. There are serious emotional and psychological effects of awaiting execution. It's an existential crisis, where one assesses the meaning of their life (Frankl, 1984). Moreover, one seminal work on death and dying, by Kubler-Ross (1969), proposed five stages through which people grieve the loss of their life. The stages are not linear or mutually exclusive, as each person experiences thoughts of their death distinctively. The first stage is denial and isolation, where the individual is in shock and disbelief (Kubler-Ross, 1969). This is a defense mechanism that emotionally removes them from the situation (Tyrrell et al., 2023). The second stage is anger. In this stage, the killer likely is furious with the justice system, their victims, and possibly family members for their perceived role in their impending death. Bargaining is the most common third stage (Kubler-Ross, 1969). This is where the serial killer finds God or attempts to rationalize their behaviors. Then comes depression. This is the pit of despair where nothing matters and there is no reason to go on. In fact, this may be the very stage in which most serial killers commit suicide, if they choose that rather than life in prison or execution. Lastly, acceptance is most often the final stage (Kulber-Ross, 1969), where one comes to grips with the fact that their actions will result in their death.

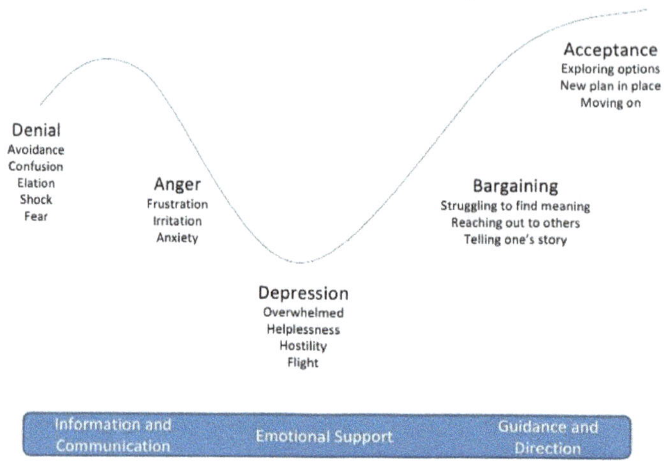

Figure 8.15 Kubler-Ross Grief Cycle

Fred and Rosemary West

Figure 8.16 Police in Fred West's Backyard

Most serial killers who have gotten caught have either been put to death, died of natural causes, or are currently rotting in prison. When none of those options are appealing and they reach the acceptance phase rather quickly, they may commit suicide. This is exactly what Fred West did. He executed himself before the state could, as the ultimate message of control and, likely, guilt. West used his bed sheet to hang himself in his cell, avoiding justice while leaving his wife, Rosemary, to take the brunt of the punishment for their disturbing acts. Born in 1941 in Gloucester, England, West endured and eventually perpetuated incest (Schechter, 2003). His father engaged in sexual relations with Fred's sister, stating that "that's what all dads do with their daughters." Eager to be on his own and out of his house, he stole food and necessities to survive. To be exact, he was a thief with a disturbing sexual appetite for minors. Upon marrying a young girl who was already pregnant, West quickly impregnated her again shortly after she gave birth and they had their own child together. They divorced due to West's perversions and he married again almost immediately (Schechter, 2003). Unfortunately, when things went sour, he murdered his second wife. Not only was she not a burden anymore, but he was finally able to live out his sadistic fantasies.

Then he met Rosemary, his next wife and eventual accomplice. They molested his previous children in addition to the children they had together, murdering anyone who complained or might have ratted them out, like his ex-wife (Schechter, 2003). The couple lured, sexually assaulted, and murdered ten girls and women, with the last one being their own daughter, until they were finally arrested due to neighbors contacting the police about the child abuse.

Finally, in 1994, case workers went to their home and found sex toys lying around, in addition to the children telling the case workers that their parents kept them quiet by threatening to "bury them in the backyard like Heather," who had been their own kin (Ramsland, 2006). The children were promptly removed and the investigation began. Police located several bodies in the backyard, including Heather's, and arrested Fred and Rosemary. After West committed suicide, Rosemary was convicted of their crimes and sentenced to life in prison (Schechter, 2003). She didn't take the easy way out by committing suicide, and likely went through all of the stages of grief repeatedly until she eventually accepted her fate of life inside of a tiny cell.

The Unsolved and Vanished

There are many unknowns when it comes to serial killers who were never caught. Did they stop due to age and physical decline, no longer able to overpower their victims? Was the advent of DNA evidence a deterrent? There are more cameras around buildings and homes nowadays, so hiding has become virtually impossible. Perhaps they started a family and spent their time raising children; maybe this resulted in their first feelings of empathy. Maybe they passed away from illness or were imprisoned on other charges. Hypotheses about the decline in serial killers recently also note the teaching of social emotional learning in primary schools as a preventative measure (Mello-Klein, 2023). This helps children learn important coping skills, thus reducing their levels of anger. It allows them to heal from trauma, rather than project it onto others or never develop adequate empathy.

Figure 8.17 Police Sketch of the Zodiac Killer

Zodiac Killer

The Zodiac killer is one of the most infamous unsolved serial killer cases. The killer ended the lives of five people between 1968 and 1969 (Briese & Comiter, 2025). He taunted police with letters, yet was never caught due to a lack of DNA technology, and that's still the case since most of the evidence has reached a level of degradation where forensics teams are no longer able to extract it. Moreover, several suspects have been interrogated, including Arthur Leigh Allen, who had a criminal record, but the evidence against them wasn't strong enough to solidify an arrest and conviction (Briese & Comiter, 2025). On August 1, 1969, three newspapers (*San Francisco Examiner*, *San Francisco Chronicle*, and *Vallejo Times-Herald*) were sent a cryptic letter claiming that the writer was the killer of two victims, giving details of the crimes, and threatening to kill more people if the letters were not on the first page of the papers (Piccotti, 2024). These letters also included a part of a cipher that contained his identity. They were all enclosed with a symbol of a circle with a cross through it, the symbol of the Zodiac killer. Another letter arrived at the *San Francisco Examiner*, taunting police with more details of the murder. Three days after the murder of Paul Stine (the final Zodiac victim), the *San Francisco Chronicle* received a letter detailing the murder as well as a piece of clothing from the victim. Moreover, on July 5, 1969, within an hour of the shooting of Darlene Ferrin and Mike Mageau, a phone call was made to the police, claiming responsibility and providing the location of the victims. Further, on September 27, 1969, the Zodiac left a message on the car door of his victims for the police to find and made a phone call taking accountability for the killings (Piccotti, 2024). Letters to the newspapers stopped in 1974 with no confirmation of his identity. While the case still haunts us, the mystery of it will remain forever.

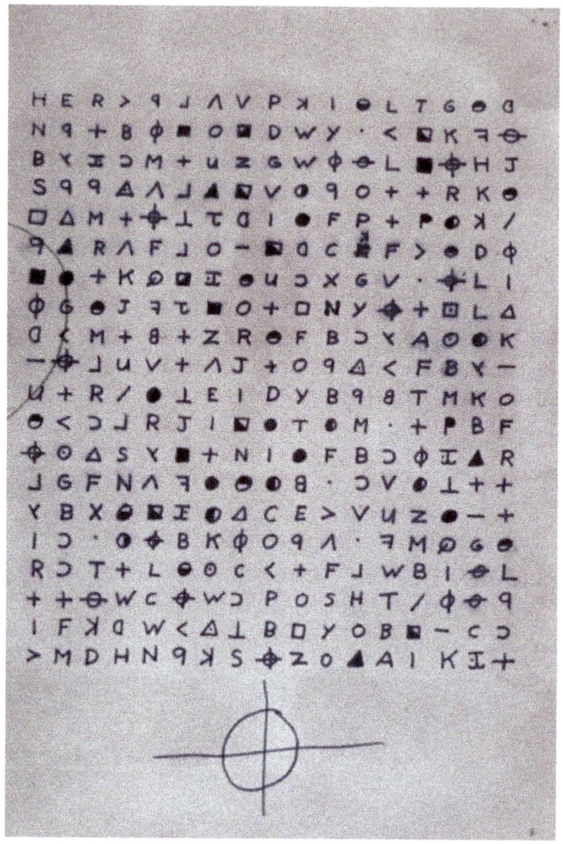

Figure 8.18 A Cryptogram the Zodiac Killer Submitted to the San Francisco Chronicle in 1969

I-70 Killer

One of the most notorious unsolved cases is the I-70 serial killer, who terrorized women along the I-70 corridor during the 1990s. Though much is obviously unknown about this person, he is believed to be an older white male. Further, his modus operandi is unusual for a serial killer in that this person shot and killed victims from afar (Kettler, 2024). Most serial killers prefer to be up close and personal with their victims, and their crimes often include a sexual component, as explained previously in this book. Sometimes the motive for serial killers is financial gain, but the I-70 killer did not take money or valuables from victims (Kettler, 2024). Another way in which the I-70 serial killer was atypical is that they traveled great distances (700 miles) between each murder (Kettler, 2024); ballistics provided evidence that the same gun was used in each case. Serial killers tend to stick to a specific area with which they are familiar and feel comfortable, so this behavior was an aberration and possibly the very reason that the case remains unsolved (Canter et al., 2000). Perhaps that is why they chose these particular methods, or maybe the I-70 killer experienced episodes of psychosis that led to each of the murders. One can only speculate.

Figure 8.19 The I-70 Killer's Crime Scene

Video of the search for the I-70 serial killer:

QR Code 8.2

Pedro Lopez

Figure 8.20 Pedro Lopez

This is one of the few cases in which we know who the serial killer is, but he has been caught and released numerous times and, currently, his whereabouts are unknown. Lopez, known as the Monster of the Andes, was born and raised in Colombia. He never knew his father, as his father cheated on his wife with a prostitute and that encounter resulted in Lopez being born on October 8, 1949 (Biography.com Editors, 2023). As a young boy, he was caught touching his sister's breasts, which led his mother to kick him out of the home at age eight; his mother was reported to be abusive as well (Biography.com Editors, 2023; Schechter, 2003). After being caught and convicted of stealing to survive, he reported being gang-raped in prison; he murdered his attackers. Lopez served only two years in prison for killing his assailants and he was released. While this seems like a short sentence for such a crime, keep in mind the time in history that this occurred; this is also a reminder that there are stark differences in judicial systems across countries. Lopez's rage and hatred for others intensified. Between 1978 and 1980, he stalked and killed more than 300 young girls (Lewis, 2009; Schechter, 2003). When he was caught while trying to abduct a 12-year-old girl, law enforcement placed a priest disguised as an inmate in the prison to solicit information from Lopez about his crimes, which is why we have the information about his case. He was given a 16-year sentence and was released in 1999 after serving his time (Schechter, 2003). He has not been seen since.

The Highway Serial Killers

The person(s) behind another spate of long-standing and recent unsolved serial killer cases has been named the Highway Serial Killer(s). The perpetrators in this case are long-haul truck drivers who travel around the country and murder under the guise of frequenting truck stops and other locations solely for work purposes (McClellan, 2008). Utilizing this type of cover is only as new as interstates in the United States. One of the first reported examples of this was the Big Rig Killer back in the 1970s and 1980s, yet the concern continues today. While a few of these highway serial killers have been caught (Dellmus Colvin, Bruce Mendenhall), many are still at large, leading the FBI to create a Highway Serial Killings Initiative (Buckler, 2024; McClellan, 2008). Many of these serial killing truckers drive along highway I-40, which runs from Barstow, California, to Wilmington, North Carolina. Indeed, there are so-called "hot spots" along the route where numerous serial killings have taken place, including Nashville, Little Rock, Albuquerque, and Flagstaff (Buckler, 2024). These serial killers may choose this profession specifically due to its vagabond lifestyle, where disenfranchised sex workers are readily available at truck stops. It also allows them to place distance between them and the victims' bodies, as the long stretches of highway provide ample options for body disposal (McClellan, 2008).

Figure 8.21 Interstate 40

Summary

Though the desire and motivation may still be strong, they have aged and their bodies are no longer capable of overpowering others. Some serial killers may have gotten caught for other crimes or died, resulting in the end of their victimization of others. One thing we do know is that they don't quit willingly, and our ability to capture them is the only way to make them stop. While interstate highways and double lives aid in their ability to remain undetected, improvements in collaboration between law enforcement jurisdictions has allowed us to locate them faster. Some beat us to it, and commit suicide prior to incarceration. This may be due to the need for control and avoidance of responsibility. For others, arrogance and overconfidence may lead to their demise when they are accustomed to getting away with murder, then make a mistake or leave DNA evidence that connects them to the crimes. Their narcissistic tendencies get the better of them. In other cases, the mistakes are made by authorities and evidence isn't collected properly or departments don't communicate adequately.

Some serial killers simply confess when caught for the murders or other crimes. They realize the end is imminent and then shift to creating excitement by bragging or embellishing the "truth." Media attention can be a strong motivator. With little else to do, assisting police in other serial killer cases, finding God, and soaking up the attention are ways to pass the time and continue to feed their ego. Once their death is near, existential crisis may set in. Was it worth it? Was it really their fault, or is society to blame?

Chapter Review Questions

1. What leads to mistakes made by serial killers that results in their arrest?
2. What are some of the ways serial killers continue to garner attention in prison?
3. Which serial killer cases are unsolved and how to you think the killer got away with it?

Keywords

Arrest

Death

Deoxyribonucleic acid (DNA)

Imprisonment

Suicide

Unsolved

References

Ángel Maturino Reséndiz: The "Railroad Killer". (2017, September 2). *CBS News*. https://www.cbsnews.com/pictures/angel-maturino-resendiz-the-railroad-killer/

Arrigo, B. A., & Griffin, A. (2004). Serial murder and the case of Aileen Wuornos: Attachment theory, psychopathy, and predatory aggression. *Behavioral Sciences and the Law, 22*, 375–393.

Biography.com Editors. (2023, October 3). Pedro Alonso Lopez. *Biography*. https://www.biography.com/crime/pedro-alonso-lopez

Bonn, S. A. (2014, September 8). Serial killer myth #4: They want to get caught. *Psychology Today*. https://www.psychologytoday.com/us/blog/wicked-deeds/201409/serial-killer-myth-4-they-want-to-get-caught

Briese, N., & Comiter, J. (2025). *Who did the Zodiac Killer murder? What to know about the notorious serial killer's victims. People. https://people.com/what-to-know-about-zodiac-killer-victims-11873535*

Buckler, L. (2024, June 12). FBI targets 500 truckers suspected of serial killings across US highways. *Irish Star*. https://www.irishstar.com/news/us-news/fbi-serial-killer-truckers-hunt-33014163

Butts, E. (2026). *Paul Bernardo and Karla Homolka case. The Canadian Encyclopedia*. https://www.thecanadianencyclopedia.ca/en/article/paul-bernardo-and-karla-homolka-case

Canter, D., Coffey, T., Huntley, M., & Missen, C. (2000). Predicting serial killers' home base using a decision support system. *Journal of Quantitative Criminology, 16*(4), 457-478.

Federal Bureau of Investigation. (2018, November 27). Convicted killer linked to 90 murders. https://www.fbi.gov/news/stories/vicap-links-murders-to-prolific-serial-killer-112718

Federal Bureau of Investigation. (2019, October 6). FBI seeking assistance connecting victims to Samuel Little's confessions. https://www.fbi.gov/news/stories/samuel-little-most-prolific-serial-killer-in-us-history-100619

Fouche, P., Rogers, C., & Naidoo, P. (2017, September 18-21). *A psychobiography of Robert Hansen: The 'butcher baker'* [Paper presentation]. Pan-African Psychology Congress Conference, Durban, South Africa. https://www.researchgate.net/publication/313161952_A_psychobiography_of_Robert_Hansen_The_Butcher-_Baker

Fowler, S. K., Blackburn, A. G., Smith, W. T., & Mullings, J. L. (2022). Prison culture as rape supportive: Applying importation and deprivation models to examine inmate beliefs. *Journal of Interpersonal Violence, 37*(11–12), NP8793-NP8817.

Frankl, V. E. (1984). *Man's search for meaning*. Pocket Books.

Gilmour, W., & Hale, L. E. (1991). *Butcher, baker: A true account of a serial murder*. Onyx.

Griffiths, M. D. (2014, March 24). *Why we seek the high of stardom. Psychology Today*. https://www.psychologytoday.com/us/blog/in-excess/201403/why-we-seek-the-high-stardom

Holloway, J. D. (2003, January). The perils of profiling for the media. *Monitor on Psychology, 34*(1). https://www.apa.org/monitor/jan03/perils

Howlett, J. B., Hanfland, K. A., & Ressler, R. K. (1986). The Violent Criminal Apprehension Program: ViCAP—a progress report. *FBI Law Enforcement Bulletin, 55*(12), 14–22.

Kamb, L. (2023, May 15). How *missed evidence helped a serial killer evade capture for nearly two decades. Yahoo News*. https://www.yahoo.com/news/missed-evidence-helped-serial-killer-150042097.html

Kayser, M., Branicki, W., Parson, W., & Phillips, C. (2023). Recent advances in Forensic DNA Phenotyping of appearance, ancestry and age. *Forensic Science International: Genetics, 65*, 1–24.

Keppel, R. D. (1995). *The riverman: Ted Bundy and I hunt for the Green River killer*. Pocket Books.

Kettler, S. (2024, February 26). The ongoing search for the I-70 killer of the 1990s. *A&E*. https://www.aetv.com/articles/i-70-killer-search

Kolarik, G., & Klatt, W. (2012). *Freed to kill: The true story of serial murderer Larry Eyler*. Garrett County Press.

Kubler-Ross, E. (1969). *On death & dying: What the dying has to teach doctors, nurses, clergy & their own families*. Scribner.

Lopez, R. (2025, February 14). *'He has to be stopped': Officials reflect on the manhunt for the 'Railroad Killer' who murdered 20-plus people decades ago. ABC 8 News*. https://www.wfaa.com/article/news/crime/crime-reporters-notebook/officials-reflect-on-railroad-killer-who-murdered-20-plus-people-decades-ago/287-3b0ca55f-6b76-4837-a357-10af67b1affe

Malizia, N. (2017). Serial murder: The mechanisms from imagination to the murder phases. *Sociology Mind, 7*, 44–59.

McClellan, J. (2008). Delivery drivers and long-haul truckers: Traveling serial murderers. *Journal of Applied Security Research, 3*(2), 171-190.

Mello-Klein, C. (2023, April 26). *Why are there fewer serial killers now than there used to be? Northeastern Global News*. https://news.northeastern.edu/2023/04/26/serial-killer-decline/

Menz, G. (2024, October 11). Making the monster pay: Can victim funds help us reconcile great art created by bad people? *The Columbia Journal of Law and the Arts*. https://journals.library.columbia.edu/index.php/lawandarts/announcement/view/723

Mills, K. I. (2023, October 4). Understanding the mind of a serial killer, with Louis Schlesinger, PhD (No. 281) [Audio podcast episode]. *Speaking of Psychology*. American Psychological Association. https://www.apa.org/news/podcasts/speaking-of-psychology/serial-killer-mind

Pelisek, C., & Hanlon, G. (2022, October 15). The 'Grim Sleeper' serial killer: 7 things to know after Lonnie Franklin's death. *People*. https://people.com/crime/grim-sleeper-serial-killer-death-7-things-to-know/

Piccotti, T. (2024, October 22). Zodiac killer. *Biography*. https://www.biography.com/crime/zodiac-killer

Ramsland, K. (2006). *Inside the minds of serial killers: Why they kill*. Praeger.

Ramsland, K. (2023, June 19). *Can serial killers feel remorse? A recent case raises the question of why some serial killers turn themselves in. Psychology Today*. https://www.psychologytoday.com/us/blog/shadow-boxing/202306/can-serial-killers-feel-remorse

Rodela, B. (2022, June 28). How to catch a criminal: From the other side of the tracks. *Officer. https://editions.mydigitalpublication.com/article/How+to+Catch+a+Criminal%3A+From+the+Other+Side+of+the+Tracks/4301789/752016/article.html*.

Rossouw, Z., & Palys, T. (2024). "Baggage in the business": The investigative challenges of serial homicide. *The Police Journal, 98*(1), 249–268. https://doi.org/10.1177/0032258X241269482

Schechter, H. (2003). *The serial killer files: The who, what, where, how, and why of the world's most terrifying murders*. Ballantine Books.

Silva, S. M. (2015). One the meaning of life: A qualitative interpretive meta synthesis of the lived experience of life without parole. *Journal of Social Work, 15*(5), 498-515.

Silverman, H. (2020, March 30). Convicted serial killer known as the 'Grim Sleeper' found dead in prison cell. *CNN*. https://www.cnn.com/2020/03/30/us/grim-sleeper-dies-death-row

Stephens, H. M. (2023). Samuel Little: A brief summary and analysis of America's most prolific serial killer. *The Mid-Southern Journal of Criminal Justice, 22*(4), 1–15.

Tauriello, R. (2020). *From Son of Sam to son of hope: The amazing story of David Berkowitz*. Christian Faith.

Texas Department of Criminal Justice. (n.d.). *Death row information*. https://www.tdcj.texas.gov/death_row/dr_info/resendizangel.html

The prisoners who got married behind bars. (n.d.). *Crime and Investigation UK*. https://www.crimeandinvestigation.co.uk/articles/prisoners-who-got-married-behind-bars

Tyrrell, P., Harberger, S., Schoo, C., & Siddiqui, W. (2023). *Kubler-Ross stages of dying and subsequent models of grief.* Stat Pearls Publishing. https://www.ncbi.nlm.nih.gov/books/NBK507885/

Image Credits

Fig. 8.1: Los Angeles Police Department, https://commons.wikimedia.org/wiki/File:Samuel_Little.webp, 2012.

Fig. 8.2: Federal Bureau of Investigation, https://commons.wikimedia.org/wiki/File:Samuel_Little_Mugshot_Collection.png, 2019.

Fig. 8.3: Screenshot from Sara Goldenberg and Misty Stiver, "Serial Killer Tied to Local Murder," https://www.cleveland19.com/2019/10/11/akron-mother-murdered-was-victim-serial-killer-samuel-little/, 2019.

Fig. 8.4: Anchorage Times, https://commons.wikimedia.org/wiki/File:Robert_C._Hansen,_1971.jpg, 1971.

Fig. 8.5: Alaska State Troopers, https://commons.wikimedia.org/wiki/File:Robert_Hansen%27s_1983_mugshot_in_Alaska.png, 1983.

Fig. 8.6: Federal Bureau of Investigation, https://commons.wikimedia.org/wiki/File:Israel_Keyes_FBI_mugshot.jpg, 2012.

Fig. 8.7: Federal Bureau of Investigation, https://commons.wikimedia.org/wiki/File:Israel_Keyes_New_York_kill_kit.jpg, 2012.

Fig. 8.8: Los Angeles Police Department, https://commons.wikimedia.org/wiki/File:Lonnie_David_Franklin_(Grim_Sleeper).png, 1998.

Fig. 8.9: Federal Bureau of Investigation, https://commons.wikimedia.org/wiki/File:%C3%81ngel_Res%C3%A9ndiz.jpg, 1999.

Fig. 8.10: Screenshot from KPRC-TV, "Arrest of Angel Maturino Reséndiz (1999) – KPRC-TV Collection," https://texasarchive.org/2022_00796. Copyright © 1999 by NBCNews.com.

Fig. 8.11: Donn Dughi, https://commons.wikimedia.org/wiki/File:Ted_Bundy_in_court.jpg, 1979.

Fig. 8.12: Screenshot from Inside Edition, "A Look Back: 'Son of Sam' Reads His Favorite Bible Passage in 1999 Interview," https://www.youtube.com/watch?v=WTh85197LJ8. Copyright © 2017 by CBS Broadcasting Inc.

Fig. 8.13: Screenshot from American Bible Society, "David Berkowitz, Son of Sam, Finds Life-Change in the Bible," https://www.youtube.com/watch?v=Qdv78w6MN04, 2011.

Fig. 8.14: Adapted from Copyright © 2007 by The Orchid Club (CC BY 2.0) at https://commons.wikimedia.org/wiki/File:John_Wayne_Gacy_art.jpg.

Fig. 8.15: Copyright © 2019 by U3173699 (CC BY-SA 4.0) at https://commons.wikimedia.org/wiki/File:Kubler-ross-grief-cycle-1-728.jpg.

Fig. 8.16: Screenshot from The Mirror, "The Fred West Tapes: How the Killer Confessed," https://www.youtube.com/watch?v=0-S89oXRGCc, 2025.

Fig. 8.17: San Francisco Police Department, https://commons.wikimedia.org/wiki/File:Zodiac-Killer.jpg, 1969.

Fig. 8.18: Zodiac Killer, https://commons.wikimedia.org/wiki/File:4abc_-_San_Francisco_Chronicle_Dripping_Pen_Card_November_8_1969_340_Cipher_COLOR.jpg, 1969.

Fig. 8.19: Screenshot from Pandox, "The I-70 Serial Killer," https://www.youtube.com/watch?v=gjwfo5DWIGO, 2021.

Fig. 8.20: Screenshot from A&E Biography, "Pedro Lopez," https://www.youtube.com/watch?v=YcxlxA0LazM, 2021.

Fig. 8.21: Nick Nolte, https://commons.wikimedia.org/wiki/File:Interstate_40_map.png, 2006.

CHAPTER 9

THE FUTURE OF SERIAL KILLING

Emerging Trends and Challenges

"As our society grows more mobile ... the ability of the antisocial personality to realize his rapacious and murderous fantasies grows apace."

-Robert Ressler

We know about the history and current state of serial killing, but what does the future hold? Catching a serial killer will always be a complex process. Police must balance transparency, manage the spread of inaccurate information, and solicit the public's assistance when needed (Tila, 2026). Resources like social media can be useful for generating tips, but can also influence witnesses, since serial killing is a media event, yet statistically one of the rarest forms of crime. This is detrimental to society, as information about serial killing from the media provides a template for potential killers to follow, along with reinforcing the fact that serial killers receive ample attention. This can provide fuel to people with dark desires. It may foster a culture of serial killing, as it glorifies serial killers by providing them with fame (Haggerty & Ellerbrok, 2016). Thankfully, advances in **digital forensics** and neurocriminology may combat that. Additionally, surveillance has increased at businesses and homes, providing evidence for the jury and judge.

Figure 9.1 Robert Ressler, FBI, 1986

The popularity of and fascination with serial murder has been driven by the media, and this is nothing new. This increased knowledge of serial murder cases may assist in the understanding of these individuals; families and friends may notice red flags or warning signs and suggest **mental health** help prior to an increase in violent behavior. Further, the assistance of artificial intelligence (AI) may aid in locating and capturing these killers, ideally resulting in fewer serial killers overall. Also, with the world becoming more aware of global issues due to media coverage, international collaboration could reduce incidence rates.

Learning Outcomes

After reading this chapter, students will be able to do the following:

1. Understand some of the ways in which serial killing will change in the future.
2. Assess how advances in technology and forensics will assist in capturing serial killers.
3. Consider how media and societal changes influence serial murder.

Technological Advances

Technology continues to improve by leaps and bounds, and that will influence the way serial killers operate from here on out. **Social media** is changing, with new apps and ways to connect with others. Moreover, use of AI is broadening and increasing. This may change the way serial killers use technology to lure victims, and is currently being used to assist in catching these murderers. Additionally, neurocriminology is helping us understand more about how the brains of serial killers function differently than others. Those changes, coupled with increased societal surveillance, may be a deterrent for serial killers, resulting in lower prevalence rates as time goes on.

Social Media

Figure 9.2 Social Media Collection, 2020s

The advent of social media began with Myspace back in 2004 (Ortiz-Ospina, 2019). It rapidly expanded to larger and more widely used sites, including Craigslist, Facebook, and YouTube. When Facebook was formed, it changed the cultural landscape of social media. It opened the door for additional social sites, including Twitter, Reddit, Instagram, Snapchat, and TikTok. Social media is used by a majority of people, especially in developed countries, with roughly 3.5 billion people accessing social media sites regularly in 2019 (Ortiz-Ospina, 2019). This has increased to 5.24 billion people in 2025 (Tila, 2026). While the intention of these platforms was to facilitate social connection amongst users, serial killers have used these apps as avenues for luring innocent victims with promises of jobs or goods. With the accessibility of victims growing, we will likely see social media used for criminal activity at higher prevalence rates in the future.

Stephen John Port

Figure 9.3 Stephen John Port in Interrogation Room

One example of a serial killer who used social media to lure his victims was Stephen John Port, aka the Grindr Killer (De Simone, 2016). Using the online platforms Grindr, Hornet, Gaydar, and Slaveboys, to name a few, he lured young, gay men by presenting himself as a kind and trustworthy man (Simmons, 2016). As a chef in London, he purported to live a life of normalcy. However, this was all a façade. His profiles advertised a man who attended Oxford University and served in the Royal Navy (Simmons, 2016). In reality, Port, who was born in London, England, in 1975, had grown up as a shy, tall boy who kept to himself (Basu, 2016). This resulted in the inadequate development of social skills, which made it difficult for him to initiate friendships and foster relationships (Basu, 2016). As an adult, his lack of interpersonal skills, in part, led him to develop psychopathic and sexually sadistic traits, which resulted in his use of the date rape drug gamma-hydroxybutyric (GHB) to render his four victims unconscious before he had his way with them (De Simone, 2016). He lured them to his flat and then offered them a drink spiked with this drug, resulting in an overdose.

Figure 9.4 St. Margaret's Church

Social media provided an outlet he felt ease and comfort with to initiate contact with his victims. Hiding behind the computer afforded him anonymity and the ability to present himself as someone much more desirable than he really was. In essence, he catfished these men. Further, bringing them back to his flat or having them meet him there reduced the likelihood that the young men would get up and leave; they were in his home after all, and he could lock doors or find other ways to keep them contained. After he raped and murdered them, he dumped their bodies close to his flat in a church graveyard. Once police connected the dots, which apparently took longer than it should have due to Port being gay and police lacking the urgency needed to close the case due to that fact, he was finally interrogated, arrested, and sentenced to life in prison for all four murders in 2015 (Basu, 2016).

Digital Forensics

The most recent development in digital forensics is the use of **artificial intelligence**. Generative Artificial Intelligence (AI) is capable of combing through large files of information and creating offender profiles (Maschke, 2024) It would be ideal if these killers utilized AI to indulge in their fantasies, creating virtual victims that fit their imagination. Perhaps that occurs and results in fewer lives being destroyed by serial killers, but those are activities that aren't brought to authorities' attention, so we may never know. Since there are no confirmed cases of serial killers using AI to lure and murder victims, I will focus on law enforcement's use of AI in catching them.

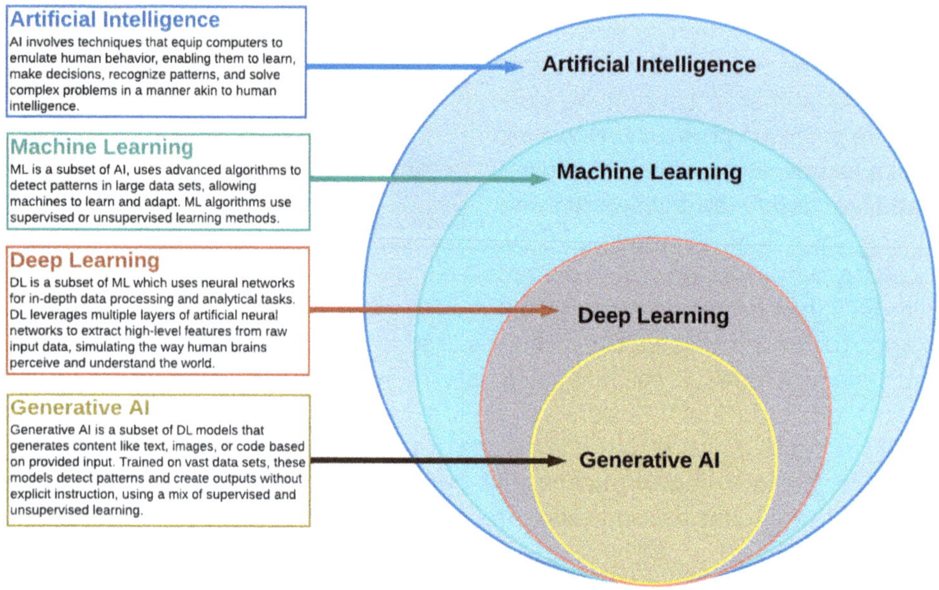

Figure 9.5 Unraveling AI Complexity—a Comparative View of AI, Machine Learning, Deep Learning, and Generative AI

AI is in its infancy as a tool to bolster investigations. In fact, research has found an increasing reliance on digital evidence to solve cases (Klasén et al., 2024). In serial murder cases, digital evidence can include data from smartphones, surveillance cameras, social media, cloud storage, and even smart home devices. In fact, AI algorithms can rapidly scan and analyze digital evidence such as communications, location data, images, and metadata, which may reveal a suspect's movements, motives, or connections to a crime scene (Maschke, 2024). However, these traces are often scattered, encrypted, or fragmented, requiring advanced digital forensics to detect, recover, analyze, and interpret them (Klasén et al., 2024). As AI technology continues to improve and become more sophisticated, it may be used to profile cases, assisting in the conceptualization of the killer's typology and modus operandi to create a more complete picture of the perpetrator.

Furthermore, a subcategory of AI that may proffer assistance in catching serial killers is called machine learning (ML). In a sense, the machine has the ability to take available information and discern patterns, mimicking human learning (Dunsin et al., 2024). AI and ML offer solutions to expediting the investigation by automating the processing and analysis of vast, complex datasets, allowing investigators to uncover critical digital evidence more efficiently and accurately (Dunsin et al., 2024). Indeed, subtle patterns in digital behavior may point to premeditation, attempts to cover up a murder, or links between multiple murder cases. Moreover, there is an increasing use of AI in reconstructing crime timelines and detecting anomalies in large datasets, correlating digital events (such as deleted messages or altered files) with physical evidence to build a more complete picture of what happened before, during, and after a homicide (Dunsin et al., 2024). AI can also help to reconstruct timelines, and even predict criminal trends by analyzing ongoing cases and intelligence reports. In murder investigations, such capabilities can be crucial for linking suspects to crime scenes, reconstructing events, and providing reliable evidence for prosecution. These skills are especially useful in cases where digital evidence is fragmented, encrypted, or deliberately obfuscated by perpetrators. However, within any new technology lies limitations, such as privacy and interpretability, and it should not replace traditional investigative methods, but instead should supplement them.

Neurocriminology

Neurocriminology is an emerging subfield of criminology that combines neuroscience with criminology to study the brain-based underpinnings of deviant and felonious behavior (Coppola, 2018; Focquaert, 2019; Zico Junius et al., 2023). We continue to learn more about the brain and how it affects our behavior, as explained in Chapter 4. Neurocriminology is taking this a step further by utilizing this information to assist in criminal investigations (Raine, 2013). Indeed, we have learned more about structural and functional brain abnormalities, especially in regions involved in emotion regulation, impulse control, and moral reasoning, and how that can predispose individuals to violence, aggression, and a lack of empathy (Coppola, 2018). Raine (1997), a prominent researcher in this field, even posited a clinical diagnosis for criminal behavior given his knowledge and understanding of its roots in the brain.

In terms of prediction and prevention, this subfield focuses on identifying neurobiological risk factors, such as reduced amygdala volume, poor frontal lobe functioning, low heart rate, and hormonal imbalances, that correlate with antisocial and violent behavior (Focquaert, 2019). As these detection capabilities improve, the ability to predict antisocial behavior using neural markers (so-called "neuroprediction") may change how law enforcement and legal systems identify individuals at risk of committing serial murder (Focquaert, 2019; Zico Junius et al., 2023). For example, reduced activity in the anterior cingulate cortex and abnormalities in the amygdala and prefrontal cortex have been linked to violent recidivism, psychopathy, and impaired empathy (Focquaert, 2019). Furthermore, these markers may one day be used to flag individuals at higher risk for committing violent crimes like serial killings, potentially allowing for earlier interventions. As technology progresses, neurocriminology could influence how serial killers are monitored or intercepted before they act. For instance, brain imaging or physiological assessments might be incorporated into forensic profiling, identifying those who exhibit traits linked to impulsivity, emotional detachment, or aggression (Coppola, 2018). While this might humanize certain offenders, it also raises concerns about determinism and the ethics of judging people by their biology (Zico Junius et al., 2023). This would likely alter how serial killers operate in the future. For example, social behaviors may be adapted to mask neurological red flags, and new methods of targeting victims (e.g., through anonymous or encrypted platforms) may evolve to avoid detection.

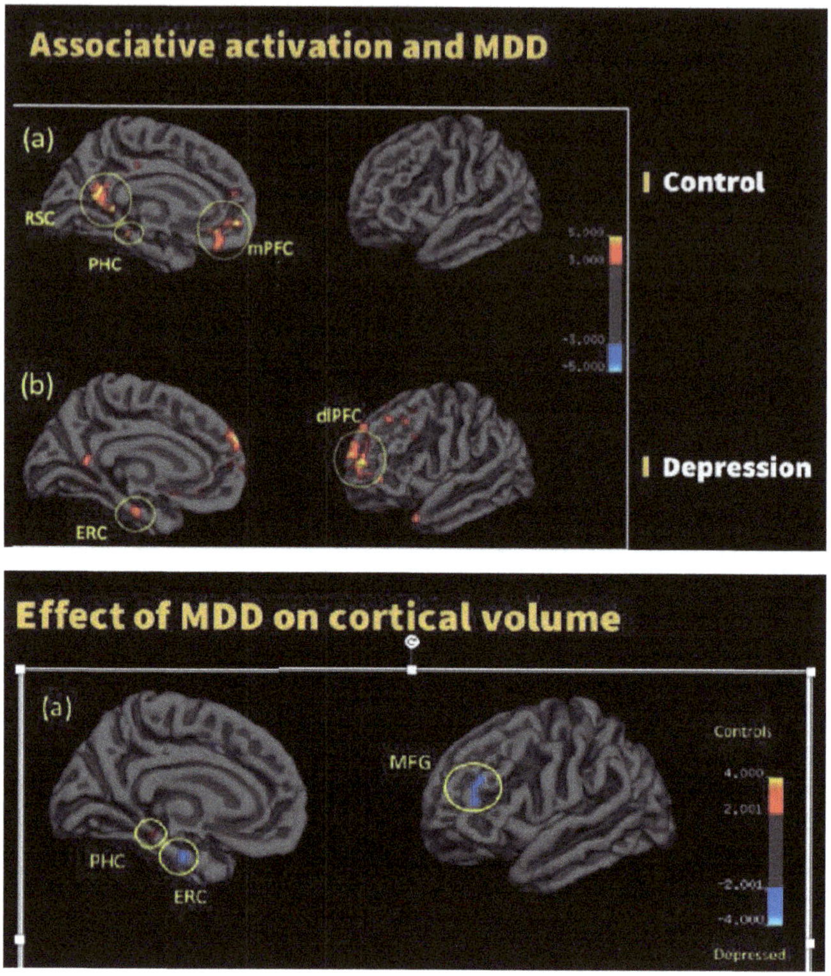

Figure 9.6 Associative Activation With MDD and Effect of MDD on Cortical Volume

Ultimately, neurocriminology could lead to a justice system that integrates biological, psychological, and social dimensions in both sentencing and rehabilitation. For serial killers, this means that future legal outcomes may be influenced not only by what they did, but by the neurobiological context of why they did it (Raine, 2013). In fact, courts have already started considering neuroimaging data to argue for diminished responsibility or to mitigate sentencing, particularly in cases involving brain abnormalities or trauma (Zico Junius et al., 2023). Rehabilitation programs could include non-invasive neuro-interventions aimed at improving impulse control or emotional regulation. However, the success of these programs will depend on ethical oversight, informed consent, and a balanced understanding of the complex interplay between biology and behavior.

Discussion question: Do you think it is ethical to use neurocriminology in serial murder cases?

Surveillance

Image 9.1

CCTV cameras are attached to almost every business building. Ring cameras line front doors in suburbia. We use our phone's global positioning system to find our way through the streets of a new city, or to locate the nearest gas station, with cellular towers pinging our location to ensure accuracy of our destination. While these **surveillance** devices were created to make our lives easier and safer, they have also been used to tie killers' locations to those of the victims. It has impeded serial killers' ability to commit their crimes, as their movements are caught on camera, connecting them to the proximity of the victim, or showing them attacking the victim, and/or placing the body in a vehicle for disposal to another more secluded location. In fact, these technologies allow for precise spatial and temporal analysis of crime scenes, helping to identify patterns, predict offender behavior, and even locate the likely base of operations for serial killers. The use of layered geographic information systems and software like Dragnet is cited as having directly led to the identification and capture of offenders (Somma, 2023). Serial killers will likely need to be more intelligent and creative to "get away with it" three or more times.

Levi Bellfield

Figure 9.7 Levi Bellfield in an Interrogation Room

In London, England, in 2011, cameras caught Bellfield following women as they got off a public bus on their way home. Surveillance assisted in providing pictures of him at bus stops trolling for these women before their death. All of his victims were young women, one of whom was only 13 years old (BBC, 2016). Bellfield was born in 1968 and his father passed away when he was only 10 years old. This left him with no male role model and resulted in an enmeshed relationship with his mother (BBC, 2016). He was unable to form and maintain normal relationships. While in custody, he shifted from charming to violent rapidly and without warning. This was how he initially charmed women. They saw his true side once they were under his control. If not for the presence of cameras in the community, outside shops and homes, he might still be at large. Instead, he is serving life for the murder of three women. One could surmise that the presence of cameras would be a deterrent for these killers, though that notion would almost be too rational; they are driven by emotion.

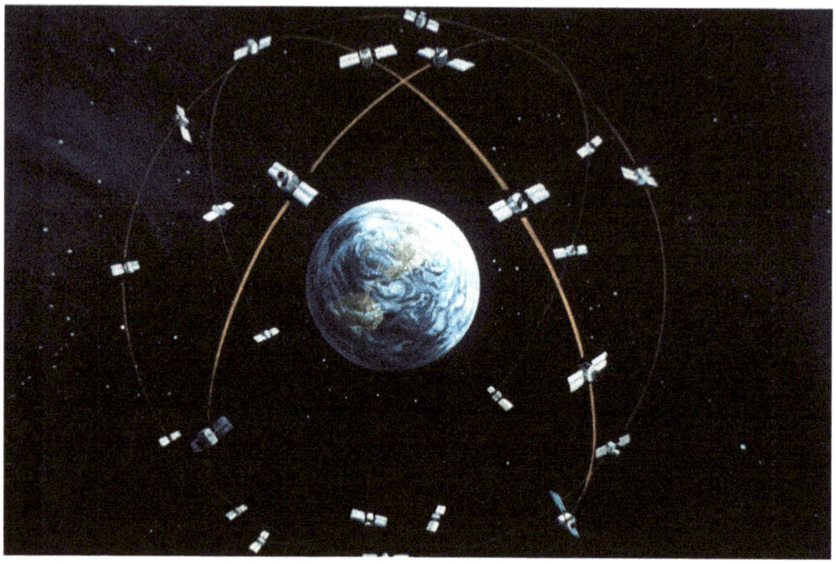

Image 9.2

Sociocultural Implications

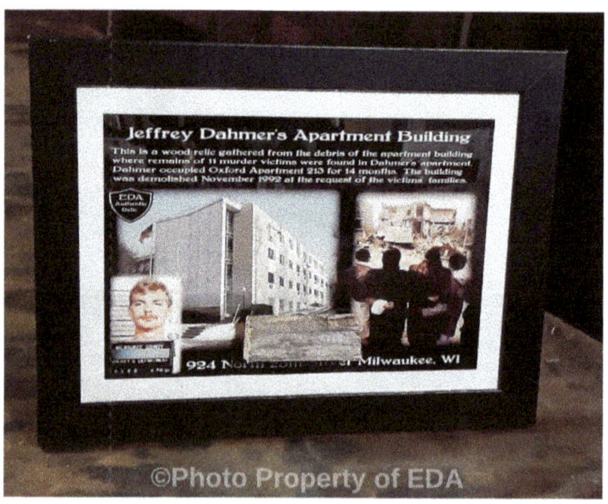

Figure 9.8 Relic From Jeffrey Dahmer's Apartment Building for Sale

Serial killing is not merely a product of individual psychopathology, but is deeply embedded in the broader social and cultural norms of modernity (Haggerty & Ellerbrok, 2016). These sociocultural implications are evident in our transition to a digital lifestyle; we have moved as a society toward an online culture. This has influenced how the media has portrayed serial killers and our easy access to their books and artwork. Further, societal norms for women especially have shifted, making them more likely to be investigated for serial murder. While women still tend to kill family members and utilize poison or other drugs to end the lives of their victims, their ability to remain undetected is lessening over time. Profiling may point to a larger range of demographic killers due to increased sociocultural knowledge of gender, cognitive, socioeconomic, and ethnic variations. Indeed, our understanding and acceptance of mental health issues has increased and we continue to understand more about how early childhood experiences shape our cognitions and behavior as adults. Though mental illness is viewed differently around the globe, homicide is still condemned in most parts of the world, allowing for common ground in collaboration on these cases.

Media Portrayal

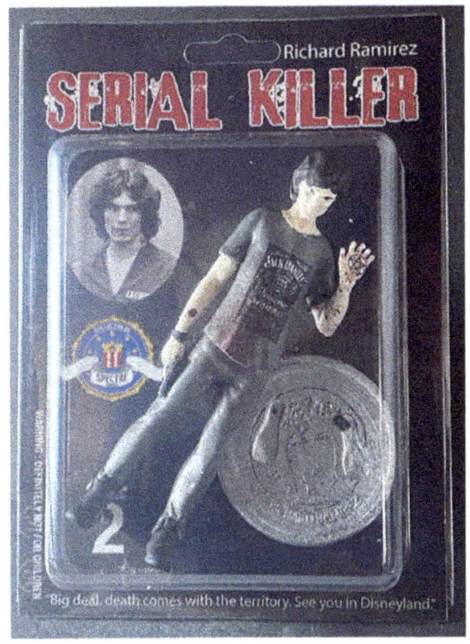

Figure 9.9 Richard Ramirez Collector's Doll

The serial killer industry has become a growing part of global culture. This business includes the selling of action figures based off of serial killers, personal items belonging to serial killers, and even paintings and drawings made by serial killers in prison (Schmid, 2004). As depicted in Figure 9.8, someone is attempting to sell a piece of Jeffrey Dahmer's apartment after it was demolished. The authenticity of the piece of wood/apartment building siding may never be known, but this demonstrates people's interest in murderabilia. Media has propagated this fascination. Indeed, the Richard Ramirez collector's doll is one of many options; you can also buy dolls that depict other serial killers and even famous musicians who have since passed away.

There are strong opinions that murderabilia should be banned, as it takes the focus away from the victims and the severity of the crimes. Yet, the money made by selling murderabilia can be a source of income for the victim's families (Schmid, 2004). Indeed, news media sensationalizes serial killers by painting them as celebrity monsters that have extraordinary powers. Serial killers are being glorified by media outlets instead of just highlighted as predators that have committed unspeakable acts (Foong-Reichert et al., 2021; Haggerty & Ellerbrok, 2016). This phenomenon reflects a modern obsession with visibility and recognition, fueled by media, which may incentivize future killers seeking notoriety. The irony of this interest can be seen in the serial killer shot glasses shown in Figure 9.10. The shot glasses glorify these murderers and even connect them to alcohol use, further solidifying the drug addictions that many serial killers endure, in addition to society's potential "addiction" to the abnormal and macabre.

Changing Societal Norms

Figure 9.10 Serial Killer Shot Glasses

The cultural conceptualization of a serial killer has changed throughout the years. Serial killers used to be predominantly viewed as belonging to society's underbelly—white men with dirty clothes and a mean scowl. Women certainly weren't capable of murder, let alone serial murder. However, these identities are socially constructed based on the cultural norms of the time, and because serial killers consciously borrow them, any evolution in public attitudes toward sexuality, gender, violence, or mental health will reshape the narratives available to future killers (Bartels & Parsons, 2009). For instance, if emerging norms stigmatize sexualized violence more stringently or offer alternative frameworks (e.g., trauma-informed discourse, neurodiversity), tomorrow's serial killers may adopt novel rhetorical strategies, perhaps casting themselves as distressed radicals, uncontrollable addicts, or misunderstood neuro-outliers instead of lust-driven predators (Bartels & Parsons, 2009). Certainly, the only reason for this would be to mitigate responsibility.

Profiling

Law enforcement is becoming more sophisticated at understanding the psychological and behavioral patterns of serial killers. Behavioral analysis and psychological profiling could help predict and prevent crimes before they escalate (Haggerty & Ellerbrok, 2016). Psychological techniques, particularly those rooted in investigative and environmental psychology, are vital to serial killer case investigations (Lampley, 2020). Understanding the mental maps, cyclical emotional phases (such as periods of "emotional cooling"), and personality disorders of serial killers allows profilers to anticipate future behaviors and refine search areas. The study of organized versus disorganized offenders, for instance, informs investigators about the likely planning and predictability of an offender's actions. Research has pointed to the fact that understanding these typologies can aid forensic psychologists and law enforcement in identifying, profiling, and potentially intervening before another murder is committed. The framework offers important practical applications in criminal investigations and behavioral analysis, highlighting the value of psychological insight in addressing serial murder (Lampley, 2020). Further, the application of these psychological insights, combined with spatial data, enables a more targeted and effective investigative process.

OFFENDER PROFILE

"BTK" – Bind Torture Kill

- Single, White male – late 20s to early 30s
- Resides close to victims' residences
- Owns a house, not living in an apartment
- Tall – at least 6'0", neat appearance
- Keeps to himself, conservative
- Psychopathic traits
- Owns a dark vehicle
- Feels at ease with those younger than he is

Figure 9.11 Profile for Dennis Rader

Increased Awareness of Mental Health

The stigma surrounding mental illness is slowly decreasing, which may lead to improved identification and treatment of individuals who might otherwise become violent criminals. However, stigma reduction could also make it more difficult to distinguish between those who are dangerous and those who aren't. Research has noted that focusing on traits such as sociopathy or childhood trauma in relation to the underpinnings of serial murder discounts the impact of sociocultural influences, such as increased urbanization and the continued marginalization of certain populations (Haggerty & Ellerbrok, 2016). Improved focus on early warning signs and intervention, particularly in the context of children or young adults with behavioral issues, could help stop potential serial killers before they act. This could be a future focus in many countries. In contrast to even 50 and certainly 100 or more years ago, tightly knit societies are no longer the norm. Most of us currently live among countless strangers, eroding traditional community ties. This anonymity allows serial killers to operate in environments where victims are unknown, encounters are fleeting, and accountability is diminished (Haggerty & Ellerbrok, 2016). Modern cities offer ideal conditions for predatory behavior to flourish without immediate detection.

Image 9.3

International Collaboration

Scholars have also noted the value of international and multidisciplinary collaboration, stating that sharing forensic intelligence across borders and involving diverse experts enhances the ability to combat crimes that span multiple regions (Lopez et al., 2020). Examples from Switzerland demonstrate that implementing forensic intelligence strategies has led to more linked cases, quicker suspect identification, and higher conviction rates. As noted in Chapter 6, it is important to be aware of and understand varying definitions and inconsistent documentation standards amongst countries (Lopez et al., 2020).

Summary

These insights suggest that future serial killers might one day be flagged by predictive models based on neurobiological data, possibly even before they commit crimes, allowing for early intervention strategies, monitoring, or treatment. Other possibilities regarding the changing landscape of serial killing could include killers using natural disasters, blackouts, or civil unrest as cover. The killer could cyberstalk victims prior to attacking them. The list goes on, but if we can increase mental health awareness and use technology to catch these killers before they harm more people, we will be on the right path as a society. Ultimately, only time will tell what the future of serial killing becomes.

Famous Last Words

John Gacy—"Kiss my ass."

Aileen Wuornos—"I'd just like to say I'm sailing with the Rock, and I'll be back like Independence Day, with Jesus, June 6th. Like the movie, big mother ship and all. I'll be back."

Peter Kürten—"Tell me. After my head has been chopped off, will I still be able to hear, at least for a moment, the sound of my own blood gushing from the stump of my neck? That would be a pleasure to end all pleasures."

George Bernard Harris—"Somebody needs to kill my trial attorney."

Robert Alton Harris—"You can be a king or a street sweeper, but everyone dances with the Grim Reaper."

Jeffrey Dahmer—"I don't care if I live or die. Go ahead and kill me."

Albert Fish—"I don't even know why I'm here."

Keywords

Artificial intelligence

Digital forensics

Mental health

Neurocriminology

Social media

Surveillance

Chapter Review Questions

1. How might increased acceptance of mental illness assist in preventing serial killing?
2. In what ways could AI assist in investigations?
3. What is neurocriminology's role in the future of serial murder?

References

Bartels, R., & Parsons, C. (2009). The social construction of a serial killer. *Feminism & Psychology, 19*(2), 267–280. https://doi.org/10.1177/0959353509102224

Basu, I. (2016, July 24). 'Grindr Killer' Stephen Port hid in plain sight for years. *A&E*. https://www.aetv.com/real-crime/stephen-port-serial-killer

BBC News. (2016, February 10). *Levi Bellfield: Profile of 'heinous' serial killer*. https://www.bbc.com/news/uk-england-35541060

Coppola, F. (2018). Mapping the brain to predict antisocial behaviour: New frontiers in neurocriminology, 'new' challenges for criminal justice. *Journal of Law and Jurisprudence, 1*(1), 103–126. http://dx.doi.org/10.14324/111.444.2052-1871.008

De Simone, D. (2016, November 25). *The killer the police missed. BBC News*. https://www.bbc.com/news/resources/idt-d32c5bc9-aa42-49b8-b77c-b258ea2a9205

Dunsin, D., Ghanem, M. C., Ouazzane, K., & Vassilev, V. (2024). A comprehensive analysis of the role of artificial intelligence and machine learning in modern digital forensics and incident response. *Forensic Science International: Digital Investigation, 48*, 1–22. https://doi.org/10.1016/j.fsidi.2023.301675

Focquaert, F. (2019). Neurobiology and crime: A neuro-ethical perspective. *Journal of Criminal Justice, 65*, 1–9. https://doi.org/10.1016/j.jcrimjus.2018.01.001

Foong-Reichert, A., Grindrod, K. A., & Houle, S. K. D. (2021). Exploring health professional criminality and competence using the case of Canadian health care serial killer Elizabeth Wettlaufer. *Journal of Medical Regulation, 107*(3), 19–27.

Haggerty, K., & Ellerbrok, A. (2016). The social study of serial killers. *Criminal Justice Matters, 86*, 6–7. https://www.crimeandjustice.org.uk/publications/cjm/article/social-study-serial-killers

Klasén, L., Fock, N., & Forchheimer, R. (2024). The invisible evidence: Digital forensics as key to solving crimes in the digital age. *Forensic Science International, 362*, 1–7. https://doi.org/10.1016/j.forsciint.2024.112133

Lampley, S. (2020, August 25). The psychological phases of serial killers. *Psychology Today*. https://www.psychologytoday.com/us/blog/captivating-crimes/202008/the-psychological-phases-serial-killers

Lopez, B. E., McGrath, J. G., & Taylor, V. G. (2020, October 21). Using forensic intelligence to combat serial and organized violent crimes. *National Institute of Justice Journal, Department of Justice*. https://nij.ojp.gov/topics/articles/using-forensic-intelligence-combat-serial-and-organized-violent-crimes

Maschke, M. (2024). The impending impact of artificial intelligence on digital forensics. *The Judges' Journal, 63*(2), 35-37.

Ortiz-Ospina, E. (2019). *The rise of social media.Our World in Data*. https://ourworldindata.org/rise-of-social-media

Tila, C. (2026, April 28). *Number of internet users worldwide from 2005 to 2025*. Statista. https://www.statista.com/statistics/273018/number-of-internet-users-worldwide/?srsltid=AfmBOopX9x_x90IollaMqAquOm67I2eHB9RVcN8P493FEnlmjOkPXR3M

Raine, A. (1997). *The psychopathology of crime: Criminal behavior as a clinical disorder.* Academic Press.

Raine, A. (2013). *The anatomy of violence: The biological roots of crime.* Vintage.

Schmid, D. (2004). Murderabilia: Consuming fame. *M/C Journal, 7*(5). https://doi.org/10.5204/mcj.2430

Simmons, S. (2016, December 2). *How a serial killer used social media to attract his victims—and why we should all take note. The Independent*. https://www.the-independent.com/tech/how-a-serial-killer-used-social-media-to-attract-his-victims-and-why-we-should-all-take-note-a7449216.html

Somma, R. (2023). The space and time dimensions in the criminal behaviour of lust murderers. *AAPP Physical, Mathematical & Natural Sciences, 101*(S1), 1–36. https://cab.unime.it/journals/index.php/AAPP/article/view/AAPP.101S1A19/AAPP101S1A19

Zico Junius, F., Rosmanila, Laily, R., Achmad, C., & Bhanu Prakash, N. (2023). The role of neuroprediction and artificial intelligence in the future of criminal procedure support science: A new era in neuroscience and criminal justice. *Yuridika, 38*(3), 593–620. https://doi.org/10.20473/ydk.v38i3.46104

Image Credits

Fig. 9.1: Federal Bureau of Investigation, https://commons.wikimedia.org/wiki/File:Robert_Ressler_2.png, 1986.

Fig. 9.2: Copyright © 2024 by Ibrahim.ID (CC BY 4.0) at https://commons.wikimedia.org/wiki/File:Social_media_collection_2020s.png.

Fig. 9.3: Screenshot from Metropolitan Police/International Newz, "Metropolitan Police Releases Interviews with Man Who was Found Guilty of Murder," https://www.youtube.com/watch?v=3l19Zk9htSc, 2016.

Fig. 9.4: Copyright © 2008 by Adrian Cable (CC BY-SA 2.0) at https://commons.wikimedia.org/wiki/File:St.Margaret%27s_Church,Barking_-_geograph.org.uk_-_998305.jpg.

Fig. 9.5: Copyright © 2023 by PopovaZhuhadar (CC BY-SA 4.0) at https://commons.wikimedia.org/wiki/File:Unraveling_AI_Complexity_-_A_Comparative_View_of_AI,_Machine_Learning,_Deep_Learning,_and_Generative_AI.jpg.

Fig. 9.6: Eiran Vadim Harel et al., https://commons.wikimedia.org/wiki/File:Associative_activation_with_MDD_and_Effect_of_MDD_on_cortical_volume.jpg, 2016.

IMG 9.1: Copyright © 2022 by EFF (CC BY 3.0) at https://commons.wikimedia.org/wiki/File:A_close-up_of_the_cameras_and_sensors_of_a_Remote_Video_Surveillance_System_(RVSS)_in_Nogales,_AZ_(2).jpg.

Fig. 9.7: Screenshot from Surrey Police/The Telegraph, "Police Interview Levi Bellfield in 2005," https://www.youtube.com/watch?v=bvq7sOVyMtI, 2005.

IMG 9.2: American Forces Information Service, Defense Visual Information Center, https://commons.wikimedia.org/wiki/File:Artist%27s_global_concept_of_the_NAVSTAR_Global_Positioning_System_Satellite_-_DPLA_-_e1743941362296beee266682f3b33ed0.jpeg, U.S. Department of Defense, 1981.

Fig. 9.8: EDA/SpookyCuriosities, https://www.etsy.com/listing/1735710460/jeffrey-dahmer-apartment-wood-relic. Copyright © 2024 by EDA.

Fig. 9.9: SpectreToys, https://www.etsy.com/listing/1170819681/richard-ramirez-the-night-stalker-action. Copyright © 2022 by SpectreToys.

Fig. 9.10: GlitterBonesCo, https://www.etsy.com/listing/1398906206/serial-killer-shot-glass-true-crime. Copyright © 2023 by GlitterBonesCo.

Fig. 9.11: Adapted from TruTV, https://www.psychologytoday.com/ie/blog/wicked-deeds/201712/criminal-profiling-the-original-mind-hunter. Copyright © 2017 by Turner Broadcasting System, Inc.

Fig. 9.11a: Screenshot from A&E, "Exposing a Serial Killer's Double Life (S1, E1) | BTK: Confession Of A Serial Killer | Full Ep," https://www.youtube.com/watch?v=wX5gb48oMLM. Copyright © 2025 by A&E Television Networks, LLC.

Fig. 9.11b: Copyright © Freepik Company S.L.U./freepik.

IMG 9.3: Copyright © 2018 Depositphotos/arloo.

INDEX

H

I

J

K

L

M

N

O

P

R

S

T

V

W

Z

www.ingramcontent.com/pod-product-compliance
Ingram Content Group UK Ltd.
Pitfield, Milton Keynes, MK11 3LW, UK
UKHW052008041026
15590UKWH00008B/2223

9 798823 369343